WORD-READER, LIGHT-BRINGER

———

VIGNETTES FROM THE BIBLE
FOR SHINING GOD'S LIGHT

ADELYNN SPIECKER

Includes discussion questions for personal or small group study

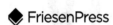 FriesenPress

One Printers Way
Altona, MB R0G 0B0
Canada

www.friesenpress.com

ISBN
978-1-03-911458-6 (Hardcover)
978-1-03-911459-3 (Paperback)
978-1-03-911460-9 (eBook)

Religion, Christian Life, Women's Issues

Distributed to the trade by The Ingram Book Company

TABLE OF CONTENTS

TABLE OF CONTENT

ENDORSEMENTS

From the first words of the book to the last, it is clear that Adelynn is a woman after God's own heart who is deeply steeped in Scripture and desires you to be too. She relentlessly pursues to bring the reader out of the darkness and into the light of Christ by communicating a Biblical view of Who God is and who we are called to be, God's chosen dwelling place. Adelynn uses God's stories, given in His Word, to illuminate God's greatness and His restorative work in us. If you desire to be ignited by God's Word to pursue Christ, *Word-Reader, Light-Bringer* is a good place to start.

Karin Stetina, PhD, associate professor of
Biblical and Theological Studies
Talbot School of Theology, Biola University, La Mirada, CA

Adelynn's passion for God's Word is contagious! It's apparent on every page of *Word-Reader, Light-Bringer*, a lovely and engaging reminder of the power of Scripture to change us and ignite in us a zealous love for our great Father and His people. She effectively debunks the lie that the Bible is, at best, a self-help book for those moments when we "need something" or, at worst, a tired, irrelevant piece of ancient literature. *Word-Reader, Light-Bringer* is a gift to the church, and I'm so thankful for it!

Martha Harding, director of women's ministries, Grace Baptist Church,
Saugus, CA

John Newton, the hymn writer of "Amazing Grace," once wrote in a letter to a struggling friend: "You will get more solid comfort by looking to Jesus and admiring *Him*." *Word-Reader, Light-Bringer* trains the Bible reader to look carefully at Him in order to stand firm in His salvation—herein is great comfort in the midst of a broken world.

Lisa LaGeorge PhD, director, Children's Hunger Fund Academy,
Sylmar, CA

Word-Reader, Light-Bringer is a beautiful book written by our friend Adelynn, who faithfully lives out its truths. Each chapter focuses on retelling God's stories in a fresh way with the intention of re-examining Biblical truths and falling more in love with Jesus. Adelynn inspires women to be diligent Word-readers with the goal of becoming daily light-bringers—those who seek to encourage others through Spirit-infused living. Women in the church will benefit from Adelynn's passion and zeal for God's Word.

Tim & Donna Borruel, founders of Legacy Christian Academy,
Valencia, CA

WOW! Creative—refreshing—challenging and winsome! As a serious Word reader for over fifty years, I found Adelynn's delightfully fresh and novel approach to timeless Biblical truths SO invigorating. This gifted wordsmith invites women of all ages to "drink from the firehose" of God's Word and go "spiritual spelunking" in the Scriptures. I am now motivated even more than ever to "stop, drop, and shine" for Jesus!"

Sandy Dunbar, Bible teacher and speaker, Nashville, TN

Adelynn is a firehose of truth for the reader. Her passion for Jesus is evident as she invites you on a journey through the Bible. You will be challenged to see Biblical narratives come alive as you dig deeply into the Word and learn to be a light-bringer to the watching world.

Michelle Spansel, Bible teacher, speaker, pastor's wife
Crossroads Community Church, Valencia, CA

DEDICATION

This book is dedicated to:
Jesus,
my mom and dad,
my husband and children,
and the local church.

ACKNOWLEDGMENTS

This project could not have been birthed, launched, and completed without the help of my prayer-warriors, cheerleaders, proofreaders: the Holy Spirit, Eric Spiecker, Ann Lauterbach (and her prayer-army), Karin Stetina, Stephanie Beals, Larry Thrailkill, Hans and Jonie Spiecker, Christina Marcaccini, John and Judy Maly, Tim and Donna Borruel, and many friends, contacts, and acquaintances (you know who you are) who gave me direction, support, and prayer in uncharted territory.

A special thanks goes to Karin Stetina who first encouraged me to publish and mentored me throughout the process. Also, I am eternally grateful to Ann Lauterbach, my mom, for proofreading this manuscript as a Scriptural and literary whisperer, to Stephanie Beals for going through this manuscript with a Spirit-led theological fine-toothed comb, and to Larry Thrailkill for reading this manuscript through his Biblically, Gospel-minded lens. This project would be incomplete without their partnership with me in faming God's great name.

Thank you to Desiree Keoshian for her artistic gift of photography for the back cover, as well as to the brilliant staff at Friesen Press (especially Kerri my editor and Carly my publishing specialist) for helping me navigate through uncharted publishing waters and endless footnotes. Also, I'm thankful for the best husband in the universe who helped me with my daily technology issues. God knew what He was doing when He hand-picked my mate. I love you, Eric. Last, I thank my best friend, Jesus, for speaking to me through His Holy Spirit, written Word, fellow believers, and the church. To God be the glory.

AUTHOR BIOGRAPHY

Adelynn Spiecker loves God and is passionate about His Word. When she's not reading-studying-teaching the Bible and writing about the living Jesus, she's a wife, mother, daughter, private trainer, and friend. She loves spending time outdoors with her husband, three children, and dog. Adelynn approaches everything in her life motivated by this guiding question: "Can it be hung on the walls of heaven?" Though Adelynn loves the Bible as a whole, she especially enjoys the Old Testament. She attended Hillsdale College, married Eric in 1996, and then graduated from Covenant College with a BA in English Literature. Though fitness training has been her professional career for over twenty years, being a wife, mother, and Christ-follower are her life's calling. Adelynn's end game is Revelation 21:3:

Behold, the dwelling place of God is with man.
He will dwell with them, and they will be His people,
and God Himself will be with them as their God.

FOREWORD

There are so many things today that grab our attention: work calls, social media, entertainment, streaming at our fingertips, sporting events, children's activities, online shopping. Our lives are full—even full of good things. But these things can easily distract us from the Main Thing; they can cause us to lose focus of God. This book is a call to recognize God for Whom He is, to remember the status He really holds: He is the Creator and Sustainer of the universe. "In Him we live and move and have our being," as we read in Acts 17:28. And one of the easiest ways to put God in the forefront of our minds is to read His Word every day.

If you believe that God is your Creator and that His Son is your Redeemer, then you believe a very good thing! Now ask yourself: is this what others know about you? Do your co-workers recognize you as a Christian? How about the other parents of your child's soccer team? Are your neighbors aware of your faith in Jesus Christ? If you're committed to being Word-readers every day—even for just fifteen to thirty minutes a day—it would fundamentally change your relationships above. It would enable you to be light-bringers. "For out of the abundance of the heart [the] mouth speaks," Jesus said in Luke 6:45.

In what you are about to read, Adelynn will not only encourage you to see God in His rightful place, but she will exhort you to put down the book because you will want to read about Him in the Bible instead. Then when you pick up this book again, you will feel the urge to share the light of Christ with others: with co-workers and parents of your child's soccer team and neighbors. And pretty soon, all the things that grab your attention today will be shaped by what you read in the Bible. As you become Word-readers, you won't be able to help but to be light-bringers.

Colleen J. McFadden
Bachelors in Business Administration, Master of Divinity
Director of Women's Ministries, Trinity Community Church, Abington, PA
Director of Women's Workshops, The Charles Simeon Trust

INTRODUCTION

In the beginning was the Word, and the Word was with God,
and the Word was God. He was in the beginning with God.
All things were made through Him,
and without Him was not anything made that was made.
In Him was life, and the life was the light of men.
The light shines in the darkness,
and the darkness has not overcome it.

John 1:1–5

A GOOD PLACE TO START

In the beginning was the Word. We can start and end right here. It's strange, I know. How is a single word a *Him*? And to top it off, what does it mean that this living Word was the biggest light the world has ever seen?[1] And grab a helmet, because this will blow your mind— this Word-light-Him is God![2] His name is Jesus. I'm totally fine if you put this book down and go read about this Word-light-God in the Bible. You can read about how He is *God with us* and brings His light to the world[3]—to you, to me, to us. Grab your Bible. Start with John 1, and read the whole book. Then go to the very beginning: Genesis. It's a good place to start. Genesis 1 opens with, "In the

---

1   John 8:12; 1 John 1:5, 7.
2   John 1:1.
3   John 8:12; 2 Corinthians 4:6; 1 John 1:5.

beginning God…." That sums up everything I'm going to share with you in this book. It starts with Him. It continues into eternity with Him. This is an Alpha and Omega God.[4] He is a to-the-end-of-the-ages God.[5] He doesn't need us to believe this for it to be true. He is unchanged by our opinions. Isn't that how it should be, at least if He is God? If any human changes whom he or she is based on another human's opinion, don't we see that as being controlled by others, inauthentic, and flat out untrue? Please do not miss this: God is controlled by no one. He authenticates Himself. His name is True.[6] He wants utter access to our souls to be with, to dwell in, and to pitch His tent within.[7] We'll be discussing all the exciting manifestations He has planned for us as we give Him the deed to our hearts.

OUCH! GIVING OVER OUR TERRITORY

One day my little son was talking about God living inside his heart. He said, "But Mommy, that might hurt. A big God coming to live inside me won't fit. It'll hurt too much." My son is right, you know—it'll cost us; it'll stretch us; it'll be uncomfortable; it'll hurt. When God nails down the pegs of His tent to tabernacle within us that means giving over our territory. Death to self will hurt.[8]

When God nails down the pegs of His tent to tabernacle within us that means giving over our territory. Death to self will hurt.

---

4   *Alpha and Omega*, being the first and last letters of the Greek alphabet, are synonymous with *beginning and end*. Revelation 1:8, 21:6, 22:13; Ecclesiastes 3:11; Isaiah 44:6; Hebrews 7:3.
5   Matthew 28:20.
6   Revelation 19:11.
7   Revelation 21:3.
8   Romans 6:6; Galatians 2:20.

Let me ask you this question: *Aren't you hurting anyway?* Be honest. The Chief Cornerstone[9] is not interested in renovation or restoration. He has grander plans. You're condemned like an old building that is dangerous to itself and others. You need a foundation-up rebuild. You're past the point of being a fixer-upper. Tear down the old; raise up the new. And *His* silos are definitely who you want to be— storehouses overflowing with His light and greatness that many will visit.[10] The Master Builder made perfect blueprints of you before the beginning of time, before you *missed the mark* (in archery, missing the mark is called sinning). He'll want to go back to those divinely drawn-up plans. He'll incorporate all the wonderful you-ness, which is the image of Himself in you—the humor, the joy, the idiosyncrasies, the strength, the empathy, the tidbits of world-changing capacity that are distinctively inside all of us.

We cannot come to a saving knowledge *of* God until we come face-to-face *with* God. Lovers fall into an intimate relationship by intently getting to know each other. I think it's safe to say that the God Who created us knows us. Only with the help of the Holy Spirit's drawing of us and awakening faith inside us can we reach out our fearful, trembling, not-able[11] hands and grab hold of the gift that He is always holding out to us while we're alive on this earth:[12] a loving, safe, holy, eternal relationship with Him.

---

*We cannot come to a saving knowledge **of** God*
*until we come face-to-face **with** God.*

---

9   Psalm 118:22; Isaiah 8:11–15, 28:16; Matthew 21:42; Luke 20:17–18; Acts 4:11; 1 Peter 2:6–8.
10   To be clear, there are those who will never want to be near Christ or us, His little lights. See John 1:9–10.
11   Augustine named the second stage of the Christian's post-fall life *non posse non peccare*, that is, *not able not to sin*. Augustine. *Saint Augustine's Enchiridion of Manual to Laurentius Concerning Faith, Hope & Charity* S.P.C.K., 1953.
12   Isaiah 55:6.

CAPITALIZATION, CONTEXT, & SCRIPTURE SPELUNKING

God is so mighty and worthy of all honor that you'll notice I capitalize words that are conventionally lower case, like His names and pronouns. I do this as well with differing words for Bible/Scripture/Word/Gospel and when referring to the person of God and His utterances. Conversely, in my writing I won't give satan any territory at all, even down to using a lower case letter for his name. I do this because of holy fear and a deep-heart belief that Jesus is the name that is above every name, literally.[13] With this holy fear comes holy pauses as we take in the very words and truths of God. You'll see I insert the word "selah" (a pause-and-reflect word commonly found in the Psalms) at specific times. I do this in hopes that you'll pause and reflect on what you've just read about God. In addition to capitalization, we must address context.

In reading all of Scripture (which I encourage each of us to do over and over in our lives), it appears we've intercepted someone else's mail. Let's not forget this fact every single time we read God's Word. In crafting the Bible, God handpicked specific writers in specific times to specific recipients in specific locations. There should be little room for "how does this make you feel?" For example, assume that I work for an international company in their public relations department. Let's say I'm asked to review a situation, including the emails attached to it, to shed light on a current and similar situation with the goal of not repeating a past mistake or of improving how a current issue is handled. What good comes from reading over past emails and documentation and then asking myself and my staff, "How does this make me feel?" We should be chuckling to ourselves right about now. From a professional, teachable, responsible angle, the goal would be to get to the bottom of the original situation, including the people involved, cultural framework, and hard facts. Then we'd ask the question, "Why was this email written to them then, and how can we apply what we learn from their reality to us now?"

Imagine how your boss would respond if you parachuted into someone else's email with your presuppositions, agendas, and biases. Your boss

---

13   Philippians 2:9.

doesn't want you to revise the facts to fit your purposes, so neither should we revise history (i.e., by interpreting passages in Scripture to our liking). In reading and studying the Bible, we must get to the bottom of the original situation, original people involved, original cultural framework, and original hard facts. We must be Scripture spelunkers.

In reading and studying the Bible, we must get to the bottom of the original situation, original people involved, original cultural framework, and original hard facts. We must be Scripture spelunkers.

This objective analysis is called *context*. According to the Merriam-Webster Dictionary, context is defined as "the parts of a discourse that surround a word or passage and can throw light on its meaning; the interrelated conditions in which something exists or occurs: environment, setting." There are three types of context to consider when reading and studying the Bible:

- *Literary* **context**—of the book as a whole and the surrounding paragraphs/passages of the primary text.
- *Historical* **context**—related to the circumstances of the original author and audience.
- *Biblical* **context**—citations, allusions, or connections to sections apart from the primary text as well as to other books in the Bible that the author makes.

We all know that taking anything out of context puts the topic or content being discussed into a subjective realm that questions our understanding of the subject's meaning and validity. Just watch any modern-day news channel or media network to see this in action. Knowing the context of anything you read, especially the Bible, directly informs the meaning.

Once we've applied what we learn from *them/then* to *us/now*,[14] we'll know and feel what the writer knew and felt and what the writer's audience knew and felt. *Then* we will best be able to apply it to our own lives today.

I LOVE TO TELL THE STORY

God's stories are so much better than everyone else's stories, my own included. That's why I'm retelling *His* stories to you. They never get old, just familiar, like a favorite movie we watch over and over. And they're not all "happily ever after." God's stories are tools—hammers, nails, shovels, levels, saws, glue, etc. God doesn't give us His Word as a tool to dig gouges into us but rather as a tool to dig out of us all the gems He personally placed there from the beginning of time, primarily His image.

---

*God's stories are tools—hammers, nails,
shovels, levels, saws, glue, etc.
God doesn't give us His Word as a tool to dig gouges into us
but rather as a tool to dig out of us all the gems He personally
placed there from the beginning of time, primarily His image.*

God's stories display His greatness as He recovers us, His useful vessels and His purified metals. The dross and the rubbish fall aside and become nothing.[15] "It is God Who works in you, both to will and to work for His good pleasure," according to Philippians 2:13. This sounds so pretty, but it was a bloody work that got us to this point. Jesus worked *in heaven and on*

---

14   *Them/then* and *us/now* is a concept taught by The Charles Simeon Trust Organization. Simply put, when reading the Bible, we must study through the lens of what the original author was conveying to the original audience back then, which informs us now today. www.simeontrust.org, see "Small Group Preparation Guide."

15   Isaiah 1:25; Philippians 3:8–9.

eurth und under the earth[16] for us. The shine to which we get access is death-defying—literally. Once we gaze upon Jesus personally, we will automatically stop, drop, and shine—which is the goal of this book. Bringing Christ's light to the world around us is the automatic result of the wedding between the Holy Spirit in us and our meditation upon God's very words. I hope you are already acquainted with this mighty from-the-beginning Lover-God.[17] You might be a reader-of-the-Word, bringer-of-the-light yourself. Or at the very least, you're curious. Let's define the terms.

WORD-READER, LIGHT-BRINGER:

- **Word-Reader**: reads the Bible in light of the original author and audience.
- **Light-Bringer**: after reading the Bible, brings light to his or her audience today.

- **Word-Reader**: focuses on contextual interpretation of the Word.
- **Light-Bringer**: focuses on current application of the Word.

- **Word-Reader**: sees the thread of the living Word, Jesus, throughout all of Scripture.
- **Light-Bringer**: manifests what is learned in a transformative,[18] illuminating way.

---

16   Philippians 2:10.
17   John 3:16; Romans 5:5; 1 John 4:9–11.
18   Roman 12:2.

OUR AIM:
READING ABOUT THE LIVING WORD (JESUS)
SHINING THE LIGHT OF JESUS (US)

Our relationship *with* Jesus draws us to a knowledge *of* Jesus which then informs our life *for* Jesus. These two threads of our aim, *the living Word—* Jesus—and the *lights that shine*—us—pop off the pages in all of Scripture. My hope for us in this book is that we become readers of the Bible as it was originally written in its own context, so we can be bringers of the light of Christ to our daily lives. In the first section of this book, we'll study "Who God Is" as we see Him in Scripture as the Redeemer, Provider, and Knower. Second, we'll look at "What God Does"—enlighten, indwell, and unveil. Third, we'll address "Who To Be" in our mental, spiritual, and prayerful spheres. Last, we'll identify "What to Do" as we reflect upon what leveled-up lifestyles look like (our response), what God's presence promotes (our worship), and what God does through us for others (out-loving rather than self-loving).

---

*Our relationship **with** Jesus draws us to a knowledge **of** Jesus which then informs our life **for** Jesus.*

In most stories, we'll get our feet wet as we walk alongside relatable, real, messed-up, divinely-used humans, just like each of us, God's children. In some stories, we'll get to see what we don't want to look like. I saved the best for last as we'll cheer for the image of God in those around us as well as invite new guests to our spiritual feast. Are you ready to get fire-hosed? Because that's my exact desire for you as you read *Word-Reader, Light-Bringer*: that you will come away with an innate passion to fire-hose yourselves with God's Word. And once His living water is in you and all over you—washing your heart, mind, and soul—the watching world will see you shining like a star in the universe as you hold out the Word of life to the glory of God the Father.[19]

---

19 Philippians 2:15–16, 11.

WHO GOD IS:
REDEEMER/KNOWER/PROVIDER

CHAPTER 1
BEAUTY FROM AVALANCHES

Philippians 2:5-18; Luke 23:26-24:12

Years ago, my son and I were skiing at a local ski resort. We came to one of our favorite ski spots and stopped at the top to take in the beauty. The reality was that just a week prior, in the exact spot we were standing, an avalanche had occurred. It almost killed people, but thankfully did not. But last week's avalanche turned out to be this week's best run. I can't help but reflect on the figurative avalanches in my life that have fallen down upon me and almost crushed me. But as the years go on, I stand on top of those avalanches and see the beauty and God's sovereign plan that came out of them. Of course, my own state of sin was the worst avalanche in the bunch for me personally! And the beauty of God's saving came from it. Deadly avalanches happen to good and bad people alike. Further, sin has no favorites; it is an equal opportunity offender. The cross happened to Jesus, Who knew no sin.[1] And from where we stand today, this is the best place for us to be—on His resurrected holy ground. He is our Redeemer, our Savior from the avalanche of eternal darkness.

---

1   2 Corinthians 5:21.

The cross happened to Jesus, Who knew no sin. And from where we stand today, this is the best place for us to be— on His resurrected holy ground.

To all of you readers of the Word, bringers of the light, including those aspiring to gain this eternal title (those who don't know God): keep gazing at the Word, Jesus. Keep stepping into His light in such a way that you yourselves shine like lights, or stars, in your current, daily world.[2] In Philippians 2:5–18, we find one of the clearest pictures of what the living Word, Jesus, did to be light in this fallen world, followed by an exhortation of how to bring His light to the world around us. Let's read this passage together to see Word-reading and light-bringing redemptively fleshed-out.

> Have this mind among yourselves, which is yours in Christ Jesus, Who, though He was in the form of God, did not count equality with God a thing to be grasped, but emptied Himself, by taking the form of a servant, being born in the likeness of men. And being found in human form, He humbled Himself by becoming obedient to the point of death, even death on a cross. Therefore God has highly exalted Him and bestowed on Him the name that is above every name, so that at the name of Jesus every knee should bow, in heaven and on earth and under the earth, and every tongue confess that Jesus Christ is Lord, to the glory of God the Father.
>
> Therefore, my beloved, as you have always obeyed, so now, not only as in my presence but much more in my absence, work out your own salvation with fear and trembling, for it is God Who works in you, both to will and to work for His good pleasure. Do all things without grumbling or disputing, that you may be blameless and

---

2   Philippians 2:15.

innocent, children of God without blemish in the midst of a crooked and twisted generation, among whom you shine as lights in the world, holding fast to the Word of Life, so that in the day of Christ I may be proud that I did not run in vain or labor in vain. Even if I am to be poured out as a drink offering upon the sacrificial offering of your faith, I am glad and rejoice with you all. Likewise you also should be glad and rejoice with me.

Philippians 2:5–18

THE DEADLY AVALANCHE

This passage is not all smiles and roses. In the middle of this beautiful scenic route depicting Christ, Paul (the author of Philippians) drives us through this text only for an avalanche to occur right in the middle of it. That avalanche was Christ's death on a cross, found in verse eight. Death on a cross was indeed a disaster, a catastrophe. A bad thing happened to a good person. Or did it? What if the most treasured reality of all time comes from this avalanche? What if beauty really comes from ashes?[3] What if a bruised reed doesn't break and a smoldering wick is not quenched?[4] What if a bad thing happening to a good person turns into a good thing? What if crucifixion turns out to be our eternal salvation? And this is indeed the case.

What if a bad thing happening to a good person turns into a good thing? What if crucifixion turns out to be our eternal salvation? And this is indeed the case. ... The script gets flipped. The good news comes to the bad guys. "While we were still sinners, Christ died for us" (Romans 5:8).

---

3   Isaiah 61:3.
4   Isaiah 42:3; Matthew 12:20.

Redemption, power, and God's glory are the outcomes of this historically unjust, deadly avalanche. This was no ordinary crucifixion—the Son of God, Who was God Himself, was killed. And nope, it did not surprise an all-knowing, all-powerful, all-present God. Neither did our sin. He's outside of linear time, and He redeems souls through all the sorts of ugly in this world and the sin it throws at us. Let's not deceive ourselves and think we escape the need for this salvific avalanche to hit us too.[5] We've already been hit, long ago in a garden, by one bite of forbidden fruit.[6] This is where the script gets flipped. The good news comes to the bad guys. "While we were still sinners, Christ died for us" (Romans 5:8). Death did not stop Him, which is why it no longer has the power to stop us.[7] Jesus bore the wrath-avalanche of all time for us, and His resurrection proved this victory about which 1 Corinthians 15:54–57 speaks. This historical fact is indeed a hill to die on, as it leads us to a Savior through Whom we live.

A LETTER OF ENCOURAGEMENT

Before we go any further, let's do our due-diligence by asking for whom this passage was written. Paul wrote this epistle, which is a fancy name for a letter, to the church in Philippi,[8] a city that was not his home. He had traveled there previously and was writing a letter to his dear church friends in his absence.[9] He wrote the above words to formerly unchurched people who were proud of their Roman citizenship. The Philippian church responded to Paul's message about God's vast pursuit of them as Gentiles and His mighty workings. Christ now extended the Jews' covenantal destiny to non-Jews. Like all believers from all races, the Philippian church received the Old Testament law-abolishing upgrade of the indwelling of the Holy Spirit. Now they needed instruction and encouragement in their new-found faith. In the first half of his letter, Paul paints a beautiful

---

5   Romans 3:23.
6   Genesis 3.
7   Hosea 13:14; 1 Corinthians 15:54–57.
8   Philippians 1:1.
9   Philippians 1:27, 2:12.

relatable canvas that his Philippian friends were sure to understand. They were Romans. They understood equality and citizenship. They understood cultural servanthood. They understood high-ranking people being given the highest place. They understood bowing a knee and submitting to a superior. They understood what being in chains in a Roman prison looked like. So Paul, a Roman citizen in prison, verbally sculpts a masterpiece of Jesus in Philippians 2:5–11 that his readers understood. This Christological passage is like Michelangelo's *David*, but even better; it was about a real man, not a sculpted one. So when Paul tells them—and us—that they should have the mind of Christ as he had, they—and we—should listen![10] We must stand in line and take in the goods that are about to follow.

A PORTRAIT OF JESUS

In Philippians 2:5–11, we find a timeless description of *Whom* Jesus was, *what* Jesus did, and *why* He did it. In gazing upon Him, we see not only Whom He was but also that we are not He, that is, gods to be self-worshiped, stroked, idolized—which is our natural tendency.[11] Christ alone is to be worshiped and adored. He is divine and always will be. Yet here His attitude was everything but self.[12] He willingly set aside His God-attributes and His appearance as God (though He never ceased to be God). He chose not to use all that He had access to as God, even attributes that would make us recognize, or "grasp," His God-equality.[13] Doesn't that challenge today's politically correct jargon? He made Himself nothing; that is, He emptied Himself of all His privileges as God, His divine road signs and universal reputation, to the point of not being recognized.[14] He took on the

---

10 Philippians 2:5.
11 Philippians 2:3; James 3:16.
12 Philippians 2:7a.
13 Philippians 2:6.
14 Philippians 2:7–8a.

nature of a servant, "human form"[15]—He *doulos-ed*[16] to show us the way. Today He asks us to willingly submit to His authority. He did the same thing by willingly submitting to the Father's authority.[17]

Submission gets such a misunderstood reputation, but here we see Christ, not leveling-up as He deserves, but leveling-down to serve. This is God we're talking about. This is a big deal. And then He, God, became human.[18] He temporarily traded His eternality[19] for limited space, time, and frame. As I think about my Lord and how big I know Him to be, I get a sort of divine claustrophobia thinking about this. God contained in man. How was this possible? And you think you're in a bind. Let that sink in. Jesus' incarnation[20] becomes our restoration. His very bondage of flesh is the gateway for our salvation. His human enclosure is our eternal escape hatch.[21] This is the kind of Word-light-God-man I want as my Boss. Look what the Boss does next.

Submission gets such a misunderstood reputation,
but here we see Christ, not leveling-up as He deserves,
but leveling-down to serve.

---

15   Philippians 2:7.
16   *Doulos* is Greek for a bond-slave—one who belongs to another without any ownership rights of their own. In the N.T., *doulos* is used with high dignity and it describes believers who willingly live under Christ's authority as His devoted followers. *Bible Hub,* https://biblehub.com/greek/1401.htm. Accessed April 27, 2021.
17   John 12:49–50.
18   Luke 1:31–32; John 1:14; Philippians 2:7c–8a.
19   Deuteronomy 33:27; Psalm 90:2; Isaiah 40:28; 1 Timothy 1:17.
20   *Incarnation* is Christ taking on our humanity, in its entirety, while at the same time still being God. This hypostatic union between Jesus' humanity and deity is independent, equal, and constant. *Bible Hub,* https://biblehub.com/topical/i/incarnation.htm. Accessed April 29, 2021.
21   Galatians 3:13–14, 5:1.

SAVIOR RELIANCE

Jesus humbled Himself.[22] He dismissed relying on Himself (we see this throughout the Gospels in His prayer life and submission to the Father). In a culture of self-reliance, Jesus is calling us to Savior-reliance.[23] Culture will argue the whole way down to hell that this reliance isn't necessary, and if we try hard enough, if we love ourselves well enough, if we daily manifest our destiny, we don't need a Savior. We don't have to manifest our destiny because Christ already manifested our eternity.[24] His reputation, Lordship, and glory are now ours because we belong to Him, our Word-light-God. From now on, we get to say, "We're with Him"—co-heirs,[25] royalty! That's us. If "glory of God" in Philippians 2:11b doesn't thoroughly invoke the brightest, shiniest image of Shekinah[26] light in your mind, then I don't know what does. This is good news! This is our best news! I encourage you to stop a minute—right here and now—and read the account of Jesus' crucifixion and resurrection in Luke 23:26–24:12 to remind yourself of the exact story so that you can get a better grasp on Paul's thoughts and feelings as he writes to the church in Philippi. I encourage you as you're reading to enter your name and first person pronouns into the text: for example, "There Adelynn crucified Him…and Jesus said, 'Father, forgive Adelynn, for she knows not what she does.'"

In a culture of self-reliance, Jesus is calling us to Savior-reliance.

---

22   Philippians 2:8b.
23   Matthew 11:28–30.
24   John 3:36, 17:2; Romans 5:21; Titus 3:7; 1 John 2:25, 5:11.
25   Romans 8:17, Titus 3:7.
26   *Shekinah glory* is an extra-biblical concept used by the Hebrews. It is the visible majesty of God's presence. *Bible Hub,* https://biblehub.com/topical/s/shekinah.htm. Accessed May 7, 2021. Webster's Revised Unabridged Dictionary defines *Shekinah* as "that which dwells."

THE CRUCIFIXION

And as they led Him away, they seized one Simon of Cyrene, who was coming in from the country, and laid on him the cross, to carry it behind Jesus. And there followed Him a great multitude of the people and of women who were mourning and lamenting for Him. But turning to them Jesus said, "Daughters of Jerusalem, do not weep for me, but weep for yourselves and for your children. For behold, the days are coming when they will say, 'Blessed are the barren and the wombs that never bore and the breasts that never nursed!' Then they will begin to say to the mountains, 'Fall on us,' and to the hills, 'Cover us.' For if they do these things when the wood is green, what will happen when it is dry?" Two others, who were criminals, were led away to be put to death with Him. And when they came to the place that is called The Skull, there they crucified Him, and the criminals, one on His right and one on His left. And Jesus said, "Father, forgive them, for they know not what they do." And they cast lots to divide His garments. And the people stood by, watching, but the rulers scoffed at Him, saying, "He saved others; let Him save Himself, if He is the Christ of God, His Chosen One!" The soldiers also mocked Him, coming up and offering Him sour wine and saying, "If You are the King of the Jews, save Yourself!" There was also an inscription over Him, "This is the King of the Jews." One of the criminals who were hanged railed at Him, saying, "Are You not the Christ? Save Yourself and us!" But the other rebuked Him, saying, "Do you not fear God, since you are under the same sentence of condemnation? And we indeed justly, for we are receiving the due reward of our deeds; but this Man has done nothing wrong." And he said, "Jesus, remember me when You come into Your kingdom." And

He said to him, "Truly, I say to you, today you will be with Me in paradise."

THE DEATH OF JESUS

It was now about the sixth hour, and there was darkness over the whole land until the ninth hour, while the sun's light failed. And the curtain of the temple was torn in two. Then Jesus, calling out with a loud voice, said, "Father, into Your hands I commit My spirit!" And having said this He breathed His last. Now when the centurion saw what had taken place, he praised God, saying, "Certainly this man was innocent!" And all the crowds that had assembled for this spectacle, when they saw what had taken place, returned home beating their breasts. And all His acquaintances and the women who had followed Him from Galilee stood at a distance watching these things.

THE BURIAL OF JESUS

Now there was a man named Joseph, from the Jewish town of Arimathea. He was a member of the council, a good and righteous man, who had not consented to their decision and action; and he was looking for the kingdom of God. This man went to Pilate and asked for the body of Jesus. Then he took it down and wrapped it in a linen shroud and laid Him in a tomb cut in stone, where no one had ever yet been laid. It was the day of Preparation, and the Sabbath was beginning. The women who had come with Him from Galilee followed and saw the tomb and how His body was laid. Then they returned and prepared spices and ointments. On the Sabbath they rested according to the commandment.

THE RESURRECTION

But on the first day of the week, at early dawn, they went to the tomb, taking the spices they had prepared. And they found the stone rolled away from the tomb, but when they went in they did not find the body of the Lord Jesus. While they were perplexed about this, behold, two men stood by them in dazzling apparel. And as they were frightened and bowed their faces to the ground, the men said to them, "Why do you seek the living among the dead? He is not here, but has risen. Remember how He told you, while He was still in Galilee, that the Son of Man must be delivered into the hands of sinful men and be crucified and on the third day rise." And they remembered His words, and returning from the tomb they told all these things to the eleven and to all the rest. Now it was Mary Magdalene and Joanna and Mary the mother of James and the other women with them who told these things to the apostles, but these words seemed to them an idle tale, and they did not believe them. But Peter rose and ran to the tomb; stooping and looking in, he saw the linen cloths by themselves; and he went home marveling at what had happened.

Luke 23:26-24:12

WORKING ON OUR SHINE GAME

From the story of Christ's death and resurrection, we see that our redemption is a side-bleeding one—literally.[27] Our redemption power is blood-bought. According to Paul in Philippians 2, our shine comes from obedience, sacrifice, and service motivated by Christ's love and fellowship of the

---

27   Isaiah 53:5; John 19:34.

Spirit.[28] And if anyone ever left a shine-trail behind him, it was Paul. As a result of his shining like a light or star and holding out the Word of life, many new churches emerged. But Paul knew the Philippians' tendencies and weaknesses (which are also like ours); he suffered from the same self-full sickness. He knew what happened when Dad wasn't home. If we're honest, we're like the Philippians. We grumble and complain. We dispute and argue. We give in to the crowd around us. We give up. We stop sacrificing. We stop serving. We have pride in ourselves. This is why in the second portion of this passage, he gave them (and us) very practical ways to take the focus off themselves and to live out the mind of Christ.

We see from the context of Philippians 2:12–18 that this new church needed hope and exhortation. Paul verbally encouraged and spiritually equipped them to do all of the following: have the mind of Christ, obey (especially since he was no longer with them), work hard in their faith, stop grumbling and disputing, be pure and stand strong against the culture around them, shine like stars sharing about Jesus, boast in their God, be sacrificial and serving, and rejoice. That seems like a whole lot of stuff. I can't even get through a day without complaining and arguing, let alone accomplish all these other things. Working-out our salvation is not an easy assignment. This side of heaven, we will sin.

Instead of focusing on all we have to *do*, we must focus on who we *are* in Christ. We have unlimited Scriptures to do this. Here's a practical way I personalize the Bible to meditate on truth in such a way that it changes my mindset and soul-scape, which then changes my actions. I choose Isaiah 42:1–4 for my example because it complements Philippians 2:5–18 and Luke 23:26–24:12 as it speaks about Christ. Note, it is not my purpose to break down the context of this Isaiah passage but to compare it to the two key texts.

---

*Instead of focusing on all we have to **do**,*
*we must focus on who we **are** in Christ.*

---

28 Philippians 2:1.

SCROLL THIS. POST THIS. PRAY THIS.

> Behold My servant, whom I uphold, My chosen, in whom
> My soul delights; I have put my Spirit upon Him; He will
> bring forth justice to the nations. He will not cry aloud or
> lift up His voice, or make it heard in the street; a bruised
> reed He will not break, and a faintly burning wick He will
> not quench; He will faithfully bring forth justice. He will
> not grow faint or be discouraged till He has established
> justice in the earth; and the coastlands wait for His law.
>
> Isaiah 42:1–4

This is just one of the many passages we can apply as we scribble them down on sticky notes. We are to post Word-nuggets about Christ in our souls *and* on our bathroom mirrors. This is the start of working-out our salvation with fear and trembling; this is the willing of His good pleasure in us.[29] From this passage, we can reword all of the truths about Christ to which we must hold fast.[30] We can personalize them like this:[31]

- God upholds Jesus. God upholds me through Jesus.
- God chose Jesus to save and to reign. Jesus' salvation and reign ensure I'm His forever.
- God delights in Jesus. God delights in me, as I'm covered by Jesus' work on the cross.
- God's Spirit is in Jesus. God's Spirit is in me, because Jesus fulfilled the promise (in this verse and others) for which He was sent.
- God redeems all that is broken. God redeems and fashions me for His glory.
- God keeps smoldering wicks from going out. God is my Sustainer.

---

29   Philippians 2:12.
30   Philippians 2:16; Deuteronomy 10:20; Romans 12:9; 1 Thessalonians 5:21; Hebrews 3:6, 3:14, 4:14; Revelation 3:11.
31   For deeper application, study Isaiah as a whole in order to best comprehend the text's meaning to its original audience, as you would do for any passage.

- God faithfully rights all wrongs. God is my Defender.
- God never gets tired. God is my Strength.
- God is never discouraged. God is my Encourager to show me that His justice will be established.

---

*We are to post Word-nuggets about Christ in our souls **and** on our bathroom mirrors.*

Romans 8:12–17 calls us *co-heirs* with Christ. So we get what He gets! We suffer with Him to be glorified with Him. As children of God, the Spirit leads us, adopts us, and calls us to every promise of our Abba Father. God's promises are our portion as we make God our portion.[32] Study them. Meditate on them. Hang them on the walls of your heart. Trade your social media posts for these types of posts, and your shine game will change from the inside out. And pray "at all times in the Spirit"[33] like a mad woman … like Hannah, whom we'll study in chapter nine. Pray for the Spirit of God to rise up in you and do His thing—illuminate. That's the job right in His sweet spot. We cannot talk about being light-bringers apart from the essential work of the Holy Spirit to illuminate.

Illumination is "the act of illuminating or supplying with light … that which … gives light … especially intellectual light or knowledge; the special communication of knowledge to the mind by God."[34] The situation may not change, your to-do list will most-likely increase, and failures are certain along the way. But let's take advantage of the endless moments and opportunities to be in God's presence and exercise all the Spirit-infused conquering He says is already ours.[35] Our Redeemer never forgets that He's redeemed us, but many times our own lips audibly need to remind our own ears about the saving of our very souls that came from the hypothetical

---

32   Lamentations 3:24.
33   Ephesians 6:18.
34   *Bible Hub,* https://biblehub.com/topical/i/illumination.htm. Accessed May 7, 2021.
35   Romans 8:37.

avalanche of the cross. Trust the Boss. We've got this because He's got this. He walks with us. He talks with us. He tells us we are His own. The joy we share as we tarry there, none other has ever known.[36]

HUMAN STARS

Let's go back to Philippians 2:5–18. Do you see how the context of this letter helps us to know what Paul's recipients knew (that they ought to live lives worthy of the Gospel, aka shine like stars),[37] and to feel what they felt (struggling to be united and to rejoice in suffering)?[38] Already the application overflows to us. In this passage, we know and feel:

- Eternal perspective when the rat race of life tries to steal our MOJO (mind-of-Jesus-outlook).
- Encouragement in Christ that we can handle what this old world throws at us, like job loss, illness, relationship damage, cultural temptation, injustice, and overall hardship.
- Exhortation to obey, work out our faith, shine like stars as we share the Gospel, and rejoice.

I love that Paul, through the guidance of the Holy Spirit, tells us today to shine like lights, or stars, in the universe. I don't know about you, but when I'm away from the city in the mountains in my happy place (Hume Lake, California), looking up at the celestial heavenlies, I'm a wide-eyed, mouth-gaping, neck-craning, breath-holding taker-inner of all that is above and around me. This is the response Paul says the watching world should have when they see us being like Jesus: "Being of the same mind, having the same love, being in full accord and of one mind" (Philippians 2:2).

Do you have this effect on those around you? Do they have to stop and pause a moment to take a second look? You're *living* the Gospel much

---

36   C. Austin Miles, "In the Garden," *Hymnary.org*. https://hymnary.org/text/i_come_to_the_garden_alone.

37   Philippians 1:27.

38   Philippians 1:27, 29, 2:2.

more than preaching it, which is what Christ commanded.[39] And some people for the first time ever will taste and see that the Lord is good[40] by looking at you, you shining star! Sure, some people will think you're a Jesus freak. I literally look those people in the eye and say, "Everyone needs a token Jesus-freak in their life. Let me be that person." They'll smile, laugh, and walk away. I promise, if your shine is the real deal, they'll still feel it, whether they admit it or not. Don't forget that the Bible says we will be the aroma of either life or death to others.[41] By the Lord's grace, I've had people ask me point blank if I'm the real deal. I tell them absolutely not—it's all Jesus.

We have the privilege of showing others that Jesus is the real deal. And if they outright tell you that your Jesus isn't for them, let them know that no matter what they think, believe, or feel, you love them anyway. None of us wears the nametag "God." Let Him do His job and save people. We must stop word-vomiting our Christianese all over people. They can feel us label them and haughtily presume their eternal destination. Stop already. Seriously. Let God do His part—draw and save. And we do ours—shine and love. The only way to "shine and love" is to share the Gospel, that all might know Jesus. Read Matthew, Mark, Luke, and John if you've missed this divine memo.

We have the privilege of showing others that Jesus is the real deal.

FREE PIZZA VERSUS THE BREAD OF LIFE

The best way to shine like lights in the world is winsomely. According to dictionary.com, *winsome* means "attractive or appealing in appearance

---

39   "*Observing* all that I have commanded you" (Matthew 28:20).
40   Psalm 34:8.
41   2 Corinthians 2:14-17.

or character." Synonyms include "engaging, charming, winning, attractive, pretty, sweet, cute, endearing, darling, dear, lovable, adorable, lovely, delightful, enchanting, captivating, and fetching." I see Paul in some of these words. He doesn't have to offer free pizza to captivate us. We can feel his affinity for and adoration of his church family and his God. Do we convey this fondness for people and God when we share our faith story? Do others feel our joy when we, through God's might, *work out* our personal great commission?[42] If not, they can feel a cheap-sell. They can smell all that is not real. And let's be honest, they're not coming for free pizza. They want the Bread of Life.[43] The image of God in them makes them genetically crave truth, while their sinful state blocks their knowledge of it. Which is why they need the light of special revelation.[44] And we, through the Holy Spirit, are the blessed ones to bring it! Rather than chucking hard, stale rolls at them, perhaps try biting into the Bread of Life right where you are. Just sit down, put out the hypothetical picnic blanket, and start chewing truth morsels on your own. The walkers-by will notice. And those who are hungry will stop, sit down, and join us in this Bread-of-Life picnic. This is at the heart of authentic, real-deal evangelism/soul-winning/Romans-roading.[45] At the end of the day, call it what we will, but don't forget—it is God Who saves, Who enters into our avalanches, every time divinely purposing them for His great glory and our beautiful, redemptive good.

It is God Who saves, Who enters into our avalanches, every time divinely purposing them for His great glory and our beautiful, redemptive good.

---

42   Philippians 2:13; Matthew 28:16–20.

43   John 6:33, 35, 48, 51.

44   "People reject the natural knowledge they have of God. ... The sin of mankind is in refusing to *acknowledge* the *knowledge* they have. ... The believer who acquiesces in special revelation is now in a posture to respond properly to general revelation." R.C. Sproul, *What Is Reformed Theology?* (Ada, MI: Baker Books, 2016) 19. Romans 1:18–21.

45   The *Romans Road* is a systematic way of explaining the Gospel from the book of Romans (Romans 3:23, 6:23, 5:8, 10:9–10, 10:13).

I can tell you without a doubt that the avalanche of my father dying of a heart attack in my arms when I was seventeen was crushing. I'd be lying if I didn't tell you that I got half buried by the avalanche of the diagnosis of my daughter's genetic medical condition when she was born. These avalanches drive me to say this: God brings beauty from avalanches. He did it at Calvary. He's doing it now, in your life and in mine. The Bible stories that contain this saving thread are countless—Noah, Joseph, Rahab, Ruth, Esther, and Paul, just to name a few. Trust the Redeemer. He's more than an Avalanche-Whisperer; He's a Soul-Saver, Sin-Destroyer, Life-Changer, Shine-Maker, and Glory-Showcaser.

PRAYER

Jesus,
Worker for my salvation and Will-er of Your good pleasure,
shine Your saving Light into every moment of my day.
Give me a Jesus-mindset, even when I'm buried by life's avalanches.
Help me to hold fast to You, my Word of Light.
Help me to be like You, to make myself nothing,
as I humbly bow my knee to You
and boldly confess with my tongue
that You are my greatest good,
that You are the greatest good the world has ever known.

Lord, Your name is above every name.
Because of Your humility, obedience, and forgiveness
I can be with You in paradise forever.
Thank You for this secure relationship.
Father, teach me and enable me to commit my daily life into Your hands,
just like Jesus did, even when it's hard.
May I marvel because of Who You are and what You do
in my daily happenings.
Be my daily happening, my moment-by-moment life-breath.
Amen.

DISCUSSION QUESTIONS

1. According to the text (Philippians 2:5ff), how do we "mind ourselves" in Christ (have the mind of Christ)?

2. If humble is how we are supposed to look (Philippians 2:3–4, 6–8, 12–18), how do we grow this from the inside-out, starting with having the mind of Christ and dribbling-out into living the life of Christ? How might the body of believers, especially the church, fit into this humility equation?

3. Worship Activity: "Jesus, the name that is above every name" (Philippians 3:9). Expound upon this concept by writing out the attributes of Jesus from Philippians 2:1–11 *as names*. For example, Philippians 2:1 contains "Encourager." Don't forget to capitalize His names! Pray through this list.

4. Why do you think Paul contrasts humility and complaining when describing Jesus, the Light of the world, and us, His mini-light-bringers? Could pride and lack of gratitude be some of the greatest detriments to light-bringing? Read Luke 23:35, 37-39 to see the contrast of divine humility in the presence of human pride.

CHAPTER 2
WORSHIP OF THE WHY

Lamentations 3

I have a confession to make: I worship the why. I discovered this mental shrine that I've neatly built in the simple normal scenarios of my daily life. For example, this worship emerged in my foolish response to my little girl as she had a meltdown before school over her shoes (that she'd picked out). I also got a glimpse of my graven image in my immature reaction to my son, who lost his cool on the tennis court. Again, it emerged in biting words towards my husband when he missed a perfect parking spot and someone else grabbed it. After the great shoe fiasco, tennis court drama, and parking lot loss unfolded, I was surprised by the amount of mental energy I spent trying to figure out *why* these things occurred, and potentially to fix them or avoid having them happen again. In this private one-person think tank, I really do feel like I discovered something about myself: *I worship the why.* Let me explain.

I have this internal drive to know why things happen. There's nothing innately wrong with the mental pursuit of wanting to know why things happen ... until I realize I value knowing *why* at the expense of trusting the One Who knows all the *whys*. I like to know:

- Why I got sick
- Why I didn't sleep
- Why my child had a hissy fit over shoes
- Why I have a migraine
- Why I got angry over nothing
- Why my friend has cancer
- Why my husband disagrees with me

The *why* list is endless.

IT MUST GO

I mentally ruminate on the why. Rumination is what cows do. It's how they eat. They open their mouths, chew their food, swallow it, regurgitate it into their mouths, and then re-swallow it. Rumination in and of itself is no enemy. It's actually good to get to the bottom of things most of the time. But somewhere amidst the mental chewing and swallowing and chewing it over again, I can feel my worship of the why. When we worship something or someone, we spend energy, attention, and time on it or them. My worship of the why focuses my attention on the symptoms, possible causes, and consequences of life around me, as opposed to the solutions, or more importantly, *the Solution*, Who in reality is a Person, God. Sure, I could justify my zealous pursuit of the why. After all, this inner landscape can come across as care, empathy, intelligence, spiritual maturity, depth, and discernment. But it's worship. I know it, and God knows it. And it must go. What we chew on should be God's Word.

What if instead of trying to figure out the why, I call my mind over and over again to *Who* God is? You know ... steadfast, unceasing, abundant Lover, eternally merciful, faithful, my portion, object of hope, good, Savior, compassionate, Most High, All-Seer, All-Hearer, Come-Nearer, cause Taker-Upper, Redeemer, Judge.[1] These are all words and phrases straight out of Jeremiah's mouth in the book of Lamentations. Jeremiah knew the All-Knower. He ruminated on the All-Knower. We can sense it in his words, in what he calls to his mind, in the heartbeat of his writing, in what he tells himself over and over again. Open your Bible and read Lamentations 3 out loud in one sitting. I've included selected verses below for deeper study.

> But this I call to mind, and therefore I have hope: The steadfast love of the Lord never ceases; His mercies never come to an end; they are new every morning; great is Your faithfulness. "The Lord is my portion," says my soul, "therefore I will hope in Him." The Lord is good to those who wait for Him, to the soul who seeks Him. It is good that one should wait quietly for the salvation of the Lord.
>
> … For the Lord will not cast off forever, but, though He cause grief, He will have compassion according to the abundance of His steadfast love; for He does not afflict from His heart or grieve the children of men. To crush under foot all the prisoners of the earth, to deny a man justice in the presence of the Most High.
>
> … My eyes will flow without ceasing, without respite, until the Lord from heaven looks down and sees.
>
> … I called on Your name, O Lord, from the depths of the pit; You heard my plea, "Do not close Your ear to my cry for help!" You came near when I called on You; You said, "Do not fear!" You have taken up my cause, O Lord; You have redeemed my life. You have seen the wrong done to me, O Lord; Judge my cause.
>
> Lamentations 3:21–26, 31–35, 49–50, 55–59

---

1   Lamentations 3.

In Lamentations 3, we see God as the All-Knower through Jeremiah's story in a siege, and we receive hope as we counsel ourselves about these qualities of God:

1. Steadfast, Unceasing, Abundant Love.
2. Unending New-Morning Mercies.
3. Great Faithfulness.
4. Our Portion.
5. Object of Our Hope.
6. Good.
7. Savior.
8. Compassionate.
9. Most High.
10. All-Seer.
11. All-Hearer.
12. Come-Nearer.
13. Cause Taker-Upper.
14. Redeemer.
15. Judge.

Just reading this list gives us hope! Let's do more than read it. Let's dissect what these attributes of God mean and how essential they were to Jeremiah and how essential they are to us. Let's chew on this over and over again. Jeremiah's raw, unedited, real daily life shows us how to be light-bringers into a dark world, and also into the dark moments of our afflicted hearts. Do you know his story? Do you know what a siege is? Have you read Lamentations and Jeremiah? Before we study the main text, Lamentations 3, we need to look at this great prophet's backstory.

JEREMIAH'S BACKSTORY

Jeremiah's calling sheds light on this Godly man's mindset, mental choices, and relationship with God. The Bible introduces him in Jeremiah 1.

Now the word of the Lord came to me, saying, "Before I formed you in the womb I knew you, and before you were born I consecrated you; I appointed you a prophet to the nations." Then I said, "Ah, Lord God! Behold, I do not know how to speak, for I am only a youth." But the Lord said to me, "Do not say, 'I am only a youth;' for to all to whom I send you, you shall go, and whatever I command you, you shall speak. Do not be afraid of them, for I am with you to deliver you," declares the Lord.

Jeremiah 1:4–8

Jeremiah was called by God as a youth. In this passage, Jeremiah himself questioned God regarding the *why* of his age. God replied not to worry about the *why* but instead to focus on *Who* was sending him, *Who* was giving him words, and *Who* was with him. In his seventy-year life, Jeremiah saw a lot of hardship. From an early age, he was living amidst a people for whom he was divinely called to hold out God's truth. This is the very definition of a prophet. It appears from the text that Jeremiah felt ill-equipped for this calling based on his youth and inability to speak. But his response to obey God was astounding and inspiring. His knowledge of God trumped his fears and feelings of inadequacy. Oh to be like this great prophet!

Youth and inexperience did not disqualify Jeremiah from being called by God; neither do they disqualify us when God calls us. Whom God calls, God qualifies. To Jeremiah, God said,

But you, dress yourself for work; arise, and say to them everything that I command you. Do not be dismayed by them, lest I dismay you before them. And I, behold, I make you this day a fortified city, an iron pillar, and bronze walls, against the whole land, against the kings of Judah, its officials, its priests, and the people of the land. They will fight against you, but they shall not prevail against you, for I am with you, declares the Lord, to deliver you.

Jeremiah 1:17–19

Youth and inexperience did not disqualify Jeremiah from being called by God; neither do they disqualify us when God calls us.

What if God says this about us? He does. We are fortified cities! We are iron pillars ... as we obey His calling. I know, I know, Jeremiah was a prophet of God with a specific message to a specific people. Of course, we're not literal cities, nor are we the cities to which Jeremiah referred. We aren't literal pillars. But we *do* face hardship, calling, and tough prophetic words (from God's Word itself), just like the people in Jeremiah's day. Obeying the Great Commission can be challenging. And we certainly do turn our backs on God and worship other gods, like Jeremiah's hearers did. Can we learn from his message to them? Yes! What are we waiting for? Let's get spiritually dressed[2] and do everything God commands us. It's all mapped-out in His infallible Word. Let us not for a moment forget Who is with us. Jeremiah didn't, so neither should we.

NOT FEELING IT

Raise your hand if you've ever felt inadequate, inexperienced, fearful, and/or disqualified? Jeremiah did; Moses certainly did.[3] I know I've felt this way many times, especially in writing this book. Flash forward in Jeremiah's story to see how he felt. Lamentations 3:1–20 carries an astounding emotional burden. It is heavy. Read this passage and underline all the words, phrases, and concepts having to do with hardship, trial, or misfortune of any kind.

> I am the man who has seen affliction under the rod of
> His wrath; He has driven and brought me into darkness
> without any light; surely against me He turns His hand

---

2   Ephesians 6:10–17.
3   Exodus 4:1–17.

again and again the whole day long. He has made my flesh
and my skin waste away; He has broken my bones; He has
besieged and enveloped me with bitterness and tribulation; He has made me dwell in darkness like the dead of
long ago. He has walled me about so that I cannot escape;
He has made my chains heavy; though I call and cry for
help, He shuts out my prayer; He has blocked my ways
with blocks of stones; He has made my paths crooked. He
is a bear lying in wait for me, a lion in hiding; He turned
aside my steps and tore me to pieces; He has made me
desolate; He bent His bow and set me as a target for His
arrow. He drove into my kidneys the arrows of His quiver;
I have become the laughingstock of all people, the object
of their taunts all day long. He has filled me with bitterness; He has sated me with wormwood. He has made my
teeth grind on gravel, and made me cower in ashes; my
soul is bereft of peace; I have forgotten what happiness
is; so I say, "My endurance has perished; so has my hope
from the Lord." Remember my affliction and my wander-
ings, the wormwood and the gall! My soul continually
remembers it and is bowed down within me.

Lamentations 3:1-20

Clearly, Jeremiah was not "feeling it," for obvious reasons. He was in the
middle of an ancient siege, getting punished for Judah's sins as he obediently spoke God's words to them. In 589 BC, the southern kingdom of
Israel, called Judah, was attacked by King Nebuchadnezzar, the biggest
world power at that time. (The northern kingdom, Israel, had already been
conquered, or rather cursed, for disobedience, and Judah was about to
follow suit.)[4] He had previously conquered the city in 607 and 597 BC.
To completely defeat Judah, this time this Babylonian king laid siege[5]
on Jerusalem, utterly destroyed the city, and burned the temple to the

---

4 Leviticus 26:14–39; Deuteronomy 28:15–68.
5 Jeremiah 39:1.

ground.[6] After an eighteen-month siege, Jerusalem fell in 586 BC.[7] A siege is AWFUL. Let me describe it.

UNDER SIEGE

When a city was under siege, it was cut off from everything that sustained life. First, the enemy surrounded the city and cut off all water and travel. Without water, food, goods, and medicine, the people within the city walls began to starve, get sick, and die. Immediately, the weakest died—the elderly, the infants,[8] and the ill. From all of history, we know that people, when they were diseased and starving to death, resorted to doing things they would never do otherwise. People searched refuse piles for morsels of food.[9] They ate bird refuse and even sold it.[10] Mothers ate their own children.[11] Jeremiah says, "Happier were the victims of the sword than the victims of hunger."[12]

We see in the first part of Lamentations 3 that Jeremiah's skin was wasting away and his bones were breaking, he was surrounded by bitterness and tribulation, he was walled in without escape and his chains were heavy, his prayers were shut out, his ways were blocked, he was devastated, he was a laughingstock among and taunted by his own people, his teeth were ground down and he was humbled, he was as far away from peace as he could be and happiness was dead to him,[13] endurance was no longer an option for him and his hope was destroyed, his soul was bowed down within him. Also, Jeremiah was thrown into the pit, or imprisoned, not once but twice in his life.[14] When dehydration and vitamin and mineral

---

6   2 Chronicles 36:19.

7   *Bible Hub*, https://www.bible-history.com/map_fall_of_judah/fallofjudah_overview.html. Accessed May 8, 2021.

8   Lamentations 2:11–12.

9   Lamentations 4:5.

10   2 Kings 6:25.

11   Lamentations 2:20, 4:10.

12   Lamentations 4:9.

13   Lamentations 3:17.

14   Jeremiah 37:15, 38:6; Lamentations 3:53, 55.

deficiencies set in, skin dries up and wastes away, and bones become brittle. As a nutritionist, sometimes I can tell a person is dehydrated and nutrient-deficient by his or her skin and hair.

Further, Jeremiah, as a man called by God to be a prophet to his own people, was mocked by them. Jeremiah was the voice of God to these people, and they laughed at him, which was pretty much the same as laughing at God. And they were laughing through toothless smiles for this reason: there was no food, so people resorted to gathering dirt, dust, and small stones and eating them. Their teeth actually ground down from eating rocks. Obedient Jeremiah was suffering with disobedient Judah. Have you ever suffered as the result of those around you making poor choices? Again and again, Jeremiah conveyed God's message for God's people to return to Him. They just would not listen. In Lamentations 3, Jeremiah all but gave up and was downcast and depressed. Can you blame him? Then *this* happened in the text.

Have you ever suffered as the result of those around you making poor choices?

SELF-COUNSEL

The first half of Lamentations 3 is horrific. But there in the middle of the starvation, darkness, and death, this Godly man—I think he's crazy, but he's on to something—started talking to himself inside his head. Then he just outright started talking to himself out loud, as recorded in Lamentations 3:22ff. What did he say to himself? Rather than staying downcast or trying to figure out why hardship was happening to him, Jeremiah advised himself to focus on the One Who knew all the answers to all the whys. He focused on God and His character. Jeremiah counseled himself with these words:

> But this I call to mind, and therefore I have hope: The
> steadfast love of the Lord never ceases; His mercies never

come to an end; they are new every morning; great is Your faithfulness. "The Lord is my portion," says my soul, "therefore I will hope in Him." The Lord is good to those who wait for Him, to the soul who seeks Him. It is good that one should wait quietly for the salvation of the Lord.

... For the Lord will not cast off forever, but, though He cause grief, He will have compassion according to the abundance of His steadfast love; for He does not afflict from His heart or grieve the children of men, to crush under foot all the prisoners of the earth, to deny a man justice in the presence of the Most High.

... My eyes will flow without ceasing, without respite, until the Lord from heaven looks down and sees.

... I called on Your name, O Lord, from the depths of the pit; You heard my plea, "Do not close Your ear to my cry for help!" You came near when I called on You; You said, "Do not fear!" You have taken up my cause, O Lord; You have redeemed my life. You have seen the wrong done to me, O Lord; Judge my cause.

Lamentations 3:21–26, 31–35, 49–50, 55–59

Rather than staying downcast or trying to figure out why hardship was happening to him, Jeremiah advised himself to focus on the One Who knew all the answers to all the whys. He focused on God and His character.

Do you see the omniscient God in this man's seemingly last breath? Do you see the Object of his hope? Do you see all the qualities of Yahweh coming after Jeremiah's heart, mind, and soul, including breath itself? He has indeed put all of his eggs in the right basket, the only basket, the saving basket. Jeremiah could've easily said, "It's not my fault." He could've easily pointed fingers. And he'd be justified in doing so. But instead, *he calls his mind to this and therefore he has hope.*[16] I arrange his self-counsel into the following chart as a means of visually organizing familiar Scripture next to its meaning from the original Hebrew.

JEREMIAH'S SELF-COUNSELING MANUAL FROM LAMENTATIONS 3

(Definitions of the Scripture words below come from the
Strong's Concordance)

Descriptions of God	Definitions
Steadfast, unceasing abundant love (3:22, 32)	Covenant loyalty; favor; "God's loving kindness descending to the needs of His creatures."
Unending new morning mercies (3:22–23)	Never failing, never finished, never spent-up; daily, daybreak; tender love, mercy, like the womb.
Great faithfulness (3:23)	Abundance; steadfastness, fidelity, stability.
Portion (3:24)	Tract, territory, inheritance, legacy, share.
Object of hope/wait (3:21, 24, 29)	Wait expectantly, waste time, tarry, trust, ground of hope, "thing that I long for."
Good (3:25)	Beautiful, pleasant, agreeable, best, precious.
Savior (3:26)	Deliverer, Helper, Victor usually said of God through human agency from oppression; also a spiritual Savior.

---

15   Lamentations 3:21.

Descriptions of God	Definitions
Compassionate (3:32)	To love, have mercy, have pity.
Most High (3:35)	A name of God, upper, most, exalted above, elevation, lofty, the supreme.
All-Seer (3:50, 59, 60)	One who has absolute access, is aware, considers, examines, gives attention to, keeps on looking, perceives, supervises, understands.
All-Hearer (3:56, 61)	Complete Comprehender, ultimate Discerner, attentive Listener, Understander, intelligent Hearer; to obey.
Come-Nearer (3:57)	Approacher, Assister, Draw-Nearer, Joiner; all these in absolute space and time.
Cause Taker-Upper (3:58)	Striver, Contender, Arguer, Disputer, Judge, vigorous Pleader, Debater; can involve bodily struggle.
Redeemer (3:58)	Kinsman, Avenger, close relative, Rescuer, Deliverer, Purchaser ... of all that has been lost.
Judge (3:59)	Governor, Arguer of our case, Decider, Defender, Ruler, Vindicator, Contender, Punisher.

God was the Object of the counsel Jeremiah gave himself. Instead of continuing to talk to himself about his despair, he talked to himself about the Knower of his despair. The Almighty Omniscient Most High God was the center of Jeremiah's hope and wait. In the very hour when his people's land was taken by the enemy, Jeremiah called God his Portion, or his inheritance. He even went so far as to buy a field[16] in faith from prison[17] during a siege. Who does that? One whose internal bearing is fixed on the Most High God. God should always be the Object of what we counsel our own minds and hearts. He should always be the epi-center of our hope, even when we don't feel like it. Jeremiah admitted where he was at, but he didn't stay there! This man struggled. This man hurt in every way possible. He let us see his pain and anguish, and then he pointed to Whom was with him ... and is with us. We're allowed to admit to God where we're at. Exhale deeply. Isn't that a relief? But we are not to stay our minds upon our anguish, bitterness, and devastation. We are not to trouble our troubles. Rather than talking to God about our hardships, we must talk to our hardships about our God.

The Almighty Omniscient Most High God was the center of Jeremiah's hope and wait. ...God should always be the Object of what we counsel our own minds and hearts. He should always be the epi-center of our hope, even when we don't feel like it.

We must wait for the morning, for daybreak, like Jeremiah did. Day breaks the night. The primary sense of the five senses that comes to us at daybreak is sight. Morning brings light and, with it, sight. God brings light and, with it, He brings sight. One could do an entire Biblical study on "daybreak/dawn" and the prosperity, hope, and victory that it brings, both physically and spiritually. Daybreak reveals the character of God triumphing over darkness, night, and the blind choices one makes when walking

---

16 Jeremiah 32:1–15.
17 Jeremiah 32:2.

apart from God's righteous guiding light. Jeremiah's response leads the way for us. He stayed his mind upon the Lord. As we can see, it's not an easy way, but it's the only way. Are we more like Jeremiah or the people of Judah? I hate to admit it, but I, like Judah, can be stubborn, idolatrous, and prideful. Many times, I have placed myself in a self-inflicted spiritual siege. I bet you have too.

SELF-INFLICTED SPIRITUAL SIEGE

Jeremiah was surrounded by idolatrous people. They bought into the culture around them, the fear within them, and the imminent annihilation so near to them. Disobedience has a price. I can't blame them, as I too face the cultural pressures of my times pressing in around me and trying to sell me fear. Could Judah's physical siege have been directly related to what was going on in their hearts? Had they cut themselves off from the very One who supplied them with life? Yes, they had. They rebelled against Him and His Word.[18] They listened to false prophets.[19] The number of times that God, through His chosen prophets, gave His children extra chances were many. Yet they continually committed two sins: "They have forsaken Me, the spring of living water, and have dug their own cisterns, broken cisterns that cannot hold water."[20] The bottom line is that physically and spiritually, what they needed most was living water. Their physical need explicitly highlighted their spiritual need. For us Christ-followers today, I think *many* of our responses to physical sieges (fatigue, low patience, physical pain, self-absorption, anger, bitterness, lack of empathy, critical minds, slanderous mouths, unstable hearts, worship of self, and all the many other real and present daily ailments) *can be* directly related to our self-inflicted spiritual sieges.

---

18   Lamentations 1:8, 18.
19   Deuteronomy 18:20; Ezekiel 13:9; Jeremiah 14:14, 23:16.
20   Jeremiah 2:13.

Our responses to physical sieges (fatigue, low patience, physical pain, self-absorption, anger, bitterness, lack of empathy, critical minds, slanderous mouths, unstable hearts, worship of self, and all the many other real and present daily ailments) can be directly related to our self-inflicted spiritual sieges.

Note I say "many of these sieges" and "can be related;" of course there are physical and spiritual ailments that are outside of our control. These circumstances can help us give up the wells we've dug with our own hands—the trials that are part of all humanity. My daughter's seizures are trials brought about in my story by my all-knowing God; they are opportunities to stay close to Him and steer clear of discouraging self-inflicted spiritual sieges that tempt me daily.

EARTHQUAKE KITS

I live in southern California. We have earthquakes, which is why we keep earthquake kits in our garages. If a substantial one ever hits (God forbid), we have water and supplies to help us until relief comes. What if a large earthquake hits, and I block access, both for myself and my loved ones, to the earthquake kit? That would be insane. But this is exactly what Judah did. Have you been guilty of this? Have you cut yourself off from your Life Source and necessary supplies of friends, prayer, the Word, the Holy Spirit, church, honesty with yourself, and repentance? And you wonder why you're encountering an internal siege?

Have you cut yourself off from your Life Source and necessary supplies of friends, prayer, the Word, the Holy Spirit, church, honesty with yourself, and repentance?

There are many ways I have been guilty of cutting myself off from the Living Water. They include but aren't limited to busyness, fear of missing out, laziness, pride, outright sin, poor choices, wasting time (on my phone), lack of preparation, comparison, idolatry, wanting what I want, lying to myself, lying to others, lack of submission to God's voice, etc. I'm sure at times we've all cut ourselves off from the Lord and felt alone and experienced the real effects of the absence of His power in our lives. It's not because He moved; we did. We dug cisterns with our own hands by trusting in our own abilities and provisions. We didn't go out into the garage and grab the divine earthquake kits that our loving God prepared for us. We sat in terror in the rubble, eating rocks rather than the Bread of Life.

IT WASN'T I

Maybe it wasn't your fault. Maybe you're surrounded by beloved fools … no, really. Just like Jeremiah, he "went down with the ship" when he obeyed the Lord. He delivered God's message to God's beloved (disobedient) children, and from a human perspective, he got what he didn't deserve. It wasn't fair. Perhaps you're like Jeremiah—you're in the trenches, you've confessed your own sin, you've stood strong for the Gospel message, and you see no relief in sight. You're under siege (your home, your family, your marriage, your children's hearts, your church, your closest friendship, your job, your health, and your finances). Jeremiah could've easily said, "It's not my fault! It wasn't I!" He could've easily pointed fingers. But we see he *never* did that. What we *do* see is compassion. He spoke to God's people of the Lord's compassion![21]

Do we show the same compassion to others when they're in the middle of a self-inflicted spiritual siege? Do we show compassion to coworkers when they lack integrity, and the whole department suffers? Do we show compassion when a spouse crosses sinful and behavioral lines and continues to walk away from the Lord? As Word-readers, we will not hoard God's new morning compassions to ourselves. As light-bringers we will spread

---

21 Lamentations 3:32.

the compassionate goods to those who need them, including those who are bringing us down. Please don't confuse compassion with the folly of remaining in an unsafe environment and compromising God's protective directives for His children as clearly laid out in His Word.

As Word-readers, we will not hoard God's new morning compassions to ourselves. As light-bringers we will spread the compassionate goods to those who need them, including those who are bringing us down.

WWJD

What would *Jeremiah* do? He cried out to God. Do we pray-pray-pray for God to remain true to His promises and true to His nature? I have a praying stool. I place it at the foot of my family members' beds and sit down and pray for them. Many times, I'm paralyzed when I begin to enter God's presence. I mean—people are hard. Family is hard. Parenting is hard. Co-workers are hard. Friends are hard. Neighbors are hard. Many times I leave my prayer stool and nothing has changed, or so it seems. But I've waited on God. I've repped faith. I've obeyed. And even if it seems He doesn't answer, my hope is in Him alone. My prayer stool is a testament to Him that I believe He is God, that He will rescue me. And it is a testament to myself that I will wait for Him as I worship the Who.

WORSHIP OF THE WHO

Thinking about God, Who knows all the whys, and rethinking on Him, His character, and what He does—over and over again—now becomes *not* idolatrous worship of the why but rather spiritual worship of the Who. This is where life-changing faith grows legs. We've traded our idolatry of the unknown for our worship of the All-Knower. Remember in the

"Not Feeling It Section" where we circled all the words in Lamentations 3:1–20 that had to do with hardship, trial, and misfortune? The words we circled are the mess out of which Lamentations 3:21–66 emerge. Jeremiah's response to all the tumult that life threw at him is our application. Jeremiah worshipped the Who:

- the God Who "advises minds" and "gives hope."[22]
- the God Who "unceasingly loves with surety and abundance."[23]
- the God Who shows "endless compassion."[24]
- the God Who doles out "new morning mercies."[25]
- the God Who is "great in faithfulness."[26]
- the God Who is "our portion, our inheritance."[27]
- the God Who is "good" and worth "waiting for."[28]
- the God Who "saves."[29]
- the God Who is "just" and "Most High."[30]
- the God Who "speaks all things into being."[31]
- the God Who is ever-waiting for "our return and praise."[32]
- the God Who "looks down and sees," especially the wrong done to us.[33]
- the God Whose "name is to be called upon," anywhere, anytime.[34]
- the God Who "hears."[35]
- the God Who "comes near."[36]

---

22   Lamentations 3:21, 24b, 29b.
23   Lamentations 3:22, 32b.
24   Lamentations 3:22, 32a.
25   Lamentations 3:23.
26   Ibid.
27   Lamentations 3:24.
28   Lamentations 3:25–26.
29   Lamentations 3:26b.
30   Lamentations 3:35, 38a.
31   Lamentations 3:37–38.
32   Lamentations 3:40–41.
33   Lamentations 3:50, 59–60.
34   Lamentations 3:55.
35   Lamentations 3:56, 61.
36   Lamentations 3:57.

- the God Who says, "Do not fear."[37]
- the God Who "takes up causes" and "redeems lives."[38]
- the God Who "judges our cause."[39]
- the God Who "repays" and "destroys enemies."[40]
- the God Who "owns the heavens."[41]

---

*Thinking about God, Who knows all the whys, and rethinking on Him, His character, and what He does—over and over again— now becomes **not** idolatrous worship of the why but rather spiritual worship of the Who.*

You should've heard me reading this list aloud to my daughter as we dealt with the disappointment of cancelling hoped-for plans because of my calf injury (which took away driving for six weeks). My girl was kind and compassionate but also angry that my injury interrupted her fun. We discussed that God, from His All-Knowing position, is worth our worship, even when disappointment occurs. Choosing to worship God in day-to-day life is our practice for worship of God in our millennium-to-millennium eternity. My daughter better accepted her disappointing reality as she focused on the fact that God knew her plans would change and that He had ordained them all along. Who God was enabled her to be resilient, Godly, and compassionate in the midst of real disappointment. It is this same worship of the Most High God we must take with us into deeper waters than mere disappointment. We must preach Who God is to injustice and hardship.

---

37 Lamentations 3:57b.
38 Lamentations 3:58.
39 Lamentations 3:59.
40 Lamentations 3:64, 66.
41 Lamentations 3:66b.

---

*God, from His All-Knowing position, is worth our worship,
even when disappointment occurs. Choosing to worship God
in day-to-day life is our practice for worship of God
in our millennium-to-millennium eternity.*

VERTICAL REMEMBRANCE

I see phrases on social media, T-shirts, and greeting cards that say something like this: "She remembered who she was, and the game changed." There's a partial truth here, but there's also idolatry of self if we're not careful. To take what Jeremiah teaches us and plug it into current society, let's break down this phrase through a Biblical lens. The Scriptures instruct us to remember things over and over again. It's a divine command. But never do the Scriptures instruct us to remember ourselves outside of the vertical plane that connects us to the One Who makes us who we are, gives us worth, calls us His own, and gives us His divine power to change any and all games, namely the sinful one at the core of all our beings. So please, when we quote and post these truth nuggets, let's point others to who they are in Christ and how their knowledge of that fact and their relationship to Him is the mac-daddy game changer. Anything else outside this lens is a dangerous lie. Remember who we are; remember Whose we are; remember the cornerstone First Cause[42] of all things, including our very ability to remember anything at all. Christ alone causes and frames our reality.[43]

---

42 Aquinas' original document, *Summa Theologicae*, is written in Latin; therefore, I quote a website written in English. Aquinas' *First Cause Argument*, theorized by Plato and Aristotle before him, extra-biblically and logically lays out proof for God being the First Cause of all things. "Aquinas—the cosmological argument for the exisetence of God," *Grademiners*, grademiners.com/free-papers/religion-theology/aquinas-the-cosmological-argument-for-the-existance-of-god. Accessed April 30, 2021.

43 Christ alone frames our theology. Rev. Dr. Mark Birkholz, "Solus Christus." *Lutheran Reformation.org*, 28 Sept. 2016, lutheranreformation.org/theology/solus-christus/. Accessed April 30, 2021.

Christ alone causes and frames our reality.

CALLING CARD

Do you see what the prophet Jeremiah did when he was afflicted, besieged, enveloped … when his soul was bowed down within him?[44] He called specific attributes of God to mind; therefore, this man living in a tumultuous time had hope. In Lamentations 3, we experience God as the All-Knower through Jeremiah's story in a historical siege; and we receive hope as we advise ourselves about God's steadfast, unceasing, abundant love, His unending new-morning mercies, His great faithfulness, Him being our Portion, Him being the Object of our hope, His goodness, Him being Savior, His compassion, Him being the Most High, Him being the All-Seer, Him being the All-Hearer, Him being the Come-Nearer, Him being the Cause Taker-Upper, Him being the Redeemer, and Him being the Judge. Jeremiah is my people. He's real. He struggles. He can be a hot mess. And God uses him.[45] Here's his calling card …

Mentally strong.
Emotionally depressed.
Physically protected.
Socially mocked.
Personally alone.
Spiritually hopeful.
Divinely called human.

What's on our calling cards? What can be said about us after we've called on (visited) someone, dropped by, lived through a trial, bled in our souls? Do we put Jeremiah's fight song from Lamentations 3 on repeat?

---

44 Lamentations 3:20.
45 Lamentations 3:21.

Do we write 2 Corinthians 4:7–9[46] on our hearts and minds? Through our imperfect humanity do we point to an all-knowing, loving, merciful, faithful, good, saving, all-seeing, all-hearing, intimate, redeeming, defending, just God?

Through our imperfect humanity do we point to an all-knowing, loving, merciful, faithful, good, saving, all-seeing, all-hearing, intimate, redeeming, defending, just God?

JOIN THE ROCKS AND CRY OUT

Like Jeremiah, every believer is an ambassador in his and her imminent circles. Like Jeremiah, we are living amidst a people for whom we are divinely called to hold out God's truth.

- If you're a woman, you're divinely called to hold out God's truth to your own soul.
- If you're an older woman, you're divinely called to hold out God's truth to younger women.
- If you're a younger woman, you're divinely called to hold out God's truth to your peers and the little eyes watching you.
- If you're a wife, you're divinely called to hold out God's truth to your husband.
- If you're single, you're divinely called to hold out God's truth to your friends.
- If you're a mother, you're divinely called to hold out God's truth to your children.

---

46   "But we have this treasure in jars of clay, to show that the surpassing power belongs to God and not to us. We are afflicted in every way, but not crushed; perplexed, but not driven to despair; persecuted, but not forsaken; struck down, but not destroyed."

- If you're employed, you're divinely called to hold out God's truth to those above you, next to you, and below you in the workplace.
- If you're an employer, you're divinely called to hold out God's truth to your employees.
- If you're a human, you're divinely called to hold out God's truth to all other humans.
- If you're breathing, you're divinely called to hold out God's truth to the universe.[47]

Because if you don't, even the rocks will cry out and testify to Jesus' all-knowing mighty reign, in the world and in our lives.[48] Let's join all of creation and worship the Who—the redeeming, all-knowing Lord. Selah.

---

47   Philippians 2:15.
48   Isaiah 55:12; Habakkuk 2:11; Luke 18:40.

PRAYER

Great God,
You've got my heart with Your steadfast covenant loyalty.
You surround me with Your new morning mercies.
You are the most faithful Friend I could ever have.
I have hope because You are my inheritance.
In You, I have won the greatest prize.
I will wait, tarry, and invest time in Your presence.
I petition You, as the faithful God, to see me and hear me.
Look down from Your heavens that You spoke into being and come near.
Be my Advocate, my Cause-Taker-Upper, my Redeemer.
Judge my cause as the Most High God.
I call my mind to You.
And when it wanders away, I return it back to You time and time again.
I talk to my soul about You. I counsel my heart about Who You are.
I actively and expectantly wait for You.
Restore me; return me face-to-face to Yourself; renew me.
You, O Lord, reign forever.
Amen.

DISCUSSION QUESTIONS

1. Go through Lamentations 3 and highlight in your Bible every instance confirming that God knows, that He sees, that He's aware of *everything*.

2. Take what you just highlighted and personalize as much of it as possible into your current life, not losing sight that, "Is it not from the mouth of the Most High that good and bad come" (Lamentations 3:38)?

3. Settle into the "sweet spot" of this passage, Lamentations 3:22–24. Rewrite it as if you were explaining it to a ten year old. Oftentimes, this style of rewriting helps me simplify complex topics.

4. The Lord's steadfast love and new morning mercies come alongside us and cover us in our laments, whether they are few or daily. Read Psalm 136 and highlight in each verse what the repetitive phrase "for His steadfast love endures forever" explains.

CHAPTER 3
LESSONS FROM A JUICE BOX

Exodus 16; Numbers 21:4-9

The juice box conundrum looks like this: "I didn't get one. He's got one. Everyone else is getting one. Why don't I ever get one? Why do you always say no to one? She took mine. I want that one. I don't like this one. Hers is better. I want yours. I spilled mine. Mine doesn't taste good. Yours looks better than mine. Mine smells funny. My box is bent. I don't have a straw."

Our responses to the hypothetical juice boxes that come our way reveal two facts:
- Our view of the juice box Distributor.
- Who we really are.

"Our circumstances don't make us what we are. They merely reveal what we are."[1] Do you seriously think the God Who spoke the world into being,[2] Who thought you up prior to the beginning of time,[3] Who promises to

---

1 Nancy DeMoss Wolgemuth, *Lies Women Believe: and the Truth That Sets Them Free.* Chicago, IL: Moody Publishers, 2001) 219.
2 Genesis 1–2.
3 Psalm 139:16.

give you everything pertaining to life and Godliness[4] would give you the wrong juice box? Would the Lord of love not also hold back any and all the juice boxes that He knows are toxic and bad for your soul? How are you responding to the hypothetical juice boxes that come your way? How does your response reveal who you really are? How does your response unveil your view of God?

Our responses don't change who God is; they merely reveal our understanding of His infinite provision as well as show the blind spots blocking our accurate view of Whom He is as the Provider. God is relentlessly holy; He is wholly relentless. He can't not ignore the bane of our hearts while at the same time never stop pursuing our brokenness in utter love. This is because He is the omniscient Provider. He knows our needs ... all of them ... the *Tall* ones, the *Grande* ones, the *Venti* ones, the faux ones, the unknown ones, the ones that are actually just wants. He sees us. He provides for us. Stock that in your spiritual cupboard.

Our responses don't change who God is; they merely reveal our understanding of His infinite provision as well as show the blind spots blocking our accurate view of Who He is as the Provider.

In this chapter, we must start on the common ground that God is the All-Provider. It's not my purpose to prove this fact to you but rather to read together about His provisional character and see it as the basis for our contentment. Do we *live* like God provides? What does that kind of life look like? A life of contentment. We're going to read Exodus 16 and watch God's people wandering in the wilderness. We'll study their not-so-wise response to hardship and hunger, which is revealing of their belief that God was not their Provider but that they seemed to think He had neglected them. His "manna and quail-flavored juice boxes" to His beloved people were not received so well. They grumbled prior to receiving sustenance. They griped afterwards. Poor Moses! He was God's appointed leader of God's children.

---

4   2 Peter 1:3.

He wrote Exodus. I can't imagine having his job of managing these whiny people. Let's read Moses' *juicy, meaty* accounts of God's people in the wilderness. Humbly, we might see a lot of ourselves in them—I know I sure do. By looking at the Israelites in the story of the manna and the quail, these three facts emerge: who the Israelites were, how the Israelites viewed God, and what we need to think and do based upon knowing that God is our Provider.

I'M HUNGRY!

First, the Israelites complained. Bottom line: the word *grumble* is used eight times in Exodus 16 between verses two and eleven. Second, the Israelites did not believe that God provided for them. Last, their story encourages us that God is *our* Provider. It's from this belief that we become authentically *content* light-bringers. Let's look at all the goods God distributed in Exodus 16. Of course, the provisional stage was already set in the fact that God powerfully provided for them prior to this story; we see this in God's blessing them with Egyptian plunder,[5] visibly guiding them day and night,[6] eliminating their enemies,[7] and causing their enemies to fear them.[8] Pause and take a breath. Let's pray for God's Spirit to teach us as we read the following passage aloud in one sitting.

EXODUS 16

> They set out from Elim, and all the congregation of the people of Israel came to the wilderness of Sin, which is between Elim and Sinai, on the fifteenth day of the second month after they had departed from the land of Egypt. And the whole congregation of the people of Israel

---

5 Exodus 12:36.
6 Exodus 13:21–22.
7 Exodus 14:13–14, 19–20, 21–31.
8 Exodus 15:14–16.

grumbled against Moses and Aaron in the wilderness, and the people of Israel said to them, "Would that we had died by the hand of the Lord in the land of Egypt, when we sat by the meat pots and ate bread to the full, for you have brought us out into this wilderness to kill this whole assembly with hunger."

Then the Lord said to Moses, "Behold, I am about to rain bread from heaven for you, and the people shall go out and gather a day's portion every day, that I may test them, whether they will walk in My law or not. On the sixth day, when they prepare what they bring in, it will be twice as much as they gather daily." So Moses and Aaron said to all the people of Israel, "At evening you shall know that it was the Lord who brought you out of the land of Egypt, and in the morning you shall see the glory of the Lord, because He has heard your grumbling against the Lord. For what are we, that you grumble against us?" And Moses said, "When the Lord gives you in the evening meat to eat and in the morning bread to the full, because the Lord has heard your grumbling that you grumble against Him—what are we? Your grumbling is not against us but against the Lord."

Then Moses said to Aaron, "Say to the whole congregation of the people of Israel, 'Come near before the Lord, for He has heard your grumbling.'" And as soon as Aaron spoke to the whole congregation of the people of Israel, they looked toward the wilderness, and behold, the glory of the Lord appeared in the cloud. And the Lord said to Moses, "I have heard the grumbling of the people of Israel. Say to them, 'At twilight you shall eat meat, and in the morning you shall be filled with bread. Then you shall know that I am the Lord your God.'"

In the evening quail came up and covered the camp, and in the morning dew lay around the camp. And when the dew had gone up, there was on the face of the wilderness a fine, flake-like thing, fine as frost on the ground. When the people of Israel saw it, they said to one another, "What is it?" For they did not know what it was. And Moses said to them, "It is the bread that the Lord has given you to eat. This is what the Lord has commanded: 'Gather of it, each one of you, as much as he can eat. You shall each take an omer, according to the number of the persons that each of you has in his tent.'" And the people of Israel did so. They gathered, some more, some less. But when they measured it with an omer, whoever gathered much had nothing left over, and whoever gathered little had no lack. Each of them gathered as much as he could eat. And Moses said to them, "Let no one leave any of it over till the morning." But they did not listen to Moses. Some left part of it till the morning, and it bred worms and stank. And Moses was angry with them. Morning by morning they gathered it, each as much as he could eat; but when the sun grew hot, it melted.

On the sixth day they gathered twice as much bread, two omers each. And when all the leaders of the congregation came and told Moses, he said to them, "This is what the Lord has commanded: 'Tomorrow is a day of solemn rest, a holy Sabbath to the Lord; bake what you will bake and boil what you will boil, and all that is left over lay aside to be kept till the morning.'" So they laid it aside till the morning, as Moses commanded them, and it did not stink, and there were no worms in it. Moses said, "Eat it today, for today is a Sabbath to the Lord; today you will not find it in the field. Six days you shall gather it, but on the seventh day, which is a Sabbath, there will be none."

On the seventh day some of the people went out to gather, but they found none. And the Lord said to Moses, "How long will you refuse to keep my commandments and my laws? See! The Lord has given you the Sabbath; therefore on the sixth day He gives you bread for two days. Remain each of you in his place; let no one go out of his place on the seventh day." So the people rested on the seventh day.

Now the house of Israel called its name manna. It was like coriander seed, white, and the taste of it was like wafers made with honey. Moses said, "This is what the Lord has commanded: 'Let an omer of it be kept throughout your generations, so that they may see the bread with which I fed you in the wilderness, when I brought you out of the land of Egypt.'" And Moses said to Aaron, "Take a jar, and put an omer of manna in it, and place it before the Lord to be kept throughout your generations." As the Lord commanded Moses, so Aaron placed it before the testimony to be kept. The people of Israel ate the manna forty years, till they came to a habitable land. They ate the manna till they came to the border of the land of Canaan. (An omer is the tenth part of an ephah.)

ROLLING OUT THE RED CARPET AND PARTING THE RED SEA

God's stories are the best stories. We know not to be too quick to pass judgment, because let's be honest, we are like the Israelites. Raise your hand if you've never complained. Cast the first stone if you've never missed the mark.[9] That's what I thought. We see in Exodus 16:1 that it had only been six weeks since Moses and Aaron had led the Israelites out of Egypt. Their Red Sea experience was fresh. God rescued roughly four million people out of slavery from a hard-hearted Pharaoh in a miraculous manner. And there they were—a little over a month later—and "all the congregation," the "whole congregation,"[10] of Israel "grumbled against Moses and Aaron in the wilderness."[11] They had the nerve to go on and say, "Would that we had

---

9   John 8:7.
10   Exodus 16:1–2.
11   Exodus 16:2.

died by the hand of the Lord in the land of Egypt."[12] Then they start pointing fingers at Moses and Aaron (in reality against God): "You have brought us out into this wilderness to kill this whole assembly with hunger."[13] I'm almost laughing out loud at this point in the story, because it sounds like something my kids would say in their complaining, zombie-moaning voices. I'd like to get a megaphone and read Exodus 12 to the Israelites, reminding them about that time when God passed over Egypt and provided a way to avoid death. The Passover was a prophetic Gospel-message banner flying overhead, and they completely missed it! Or I'd like to retell them their own recent story of God's red-carpet provision at the Red Sea.[14] This huge mass of water opened up for them to walk through.[15] And just so their Birkenstocks didn't get muddy, God even dried the ground![16] The Israelites had an extreme "out of sight, out of mind" grumbling reaction to God and His chosen leaders. At times, I am guilty of the same reaction.

Fast-forward to the New Testament story of Jesus feeding the five thousand: He miraculously fed the crowd (including left-overs for tomorrow's lunch), and the very next day they had the audacity to question/lecture Him about sending them a sign like God did to their forefathers with the manna![17] How quickly they forgot! How quickly we forget! We'd benefit from preaching these stories to our own complaining selves. You see, when we have a clear picture of the juice box Distributor, we are most likely to be content with the juice box He's given us.

When we have a clear picture of the juice box Distributor,
we are most likely to be content with the juice box He's given us.

---

12   Exodus 16:3a.
13   Exodus 16:3b.
14   Exodus 14.
15   Exodus 14:21–22.
16   Exodus 14:22.
17   John 6:31.

Now we have a clear picture of who the Israelites were as well as their view of God. So what did God do?

PHYSICAL AND SPIRITUAL SUSTENANCE

Yep, you guessed it, God provided. God's not just *in* the provider business. He *is* the provider business. His Hebrew name, *Jehovah Jireh*, means "the Lord will provide."[18] A version of this name, *Yahweh Jireh*,[19] was first used by Abraham for the place[20] where God provided a ram to slay instead of Abraham slaying his son.[21] (Don't miss the allusion here of God later doing to His only Son the very thing He spared Abraham from doing to his only son).[22] God responded to the Israelites' grumbling not just by promising bread and meat but by telling Moses these five things (Exodus 16:4–7):

1. I am about to rain bread from heaven.
2. The people shall … gather a day's portion every day, that I may test them, whether they will walk in my law or not.
3. You shall know that it was the Lord Who brought you out of the land of Egypt.
4. You shall see the glory of the Lord.
5. He has heard your grumbling.

God's not just in the provider business.
He is the provider business.

---

18   *Bible Hub*, https://biblehub.com/topical/j/jehovah-jireh.htm. Accessed April 30, 2021.
19   Ibid.
20   Genesis 22:2–3, 9, 14. One of the mountains in the land of Moriah (Genesis 22:2), associated with Jerusalem and the place where Solomon's temple would be built (2 Chronicles 3:1).
21   Genesis 22:8, 14.
22   John 3:16–17.

The text states four times that God heard their grumbling.[23] Imagine how the script might have changed if God's children thanked God for His provision and obeyed rather than complained. I bet their juice boxes would've looked different. "No eye has seen, nor ear has heard, nor the heart of man imagined, what God has prepared for those who love Him."[24] Oh, the provisionary mercy of God that surfaces here! When I, my family, or those around me are simultaneously complaining (which happens more often than I'd like to admit), my gut reaction is not to give us heavenly food, not to provide us with instructions and a life lesson, not to remind us of a wonderful time when God delivered, not to point us to see the glory of God, and not to remind us that God hears our grumbling. But isn't that what I should be doing? Is not this God's example to me—to us—in this common narrative? Teaching grumbling humans of all ages, including our own murmuring souls, is not yelling, "Shut up," or barking, "Quit your griping! Don't you know that there are starving kids all over the world?"

We must get the eyes of our hearts to see the glory of God in such a way that we love whatever juice box we get, because we love the juice box Distributor. This text isn't about magical bread and ornithological victuals. Rather, it's a clear picture of a loving God Who provided for His beloved children—not just the real sustenance of manna and quail, but also the spiritual sustenance of beholding His glory and knowing that He was their God. He's our God too—providing for our every need.[25] The truth of this juice box never expires. We should poke our straws into it and drink up the reality that God will always and forever take care of us and meet our needs.

We must get the eyes of our hearts to see the glory of God in such a way that we love whatever juice box we get, because we love the juice box Distributor.

---

23   Exodus 16:7, 8, 9, 12.
24   1 Corinthians 2:9; Isaiah 64:4.
25   Exodus 15:11–13.

Just after the sixth time the word *grumble* appears in the text, an unexpected tender moment surfaces when Moses and Aaron say, "Come near before the Lord."[26] In the original language, this sentence would have sounded more like, "Come close, face-to-face, with Yahweh, the one Whose name you're not worthy to even utter aloud." As a mother, this is such a humbling phrase to study, because I see that I have so much growth still to accomplish to be like Moses and Aaron in their gracious response to complainers. Moses and Aaron really brought the light into this moment! Yet their loving reminders fall on deaf ears. The people "did not listen to Moses."[27] Then God follows up and says, "How long will you refuse to keep My commandments and my laws?"[28] This text ends in a matter-of-fact way: "The people of Israel ate the manna forty years."[29] God continued to provide for His people through this difficult period. And this is good news for all of us ... that is, if you're a complainer like I am. Many times my life displays absolute dislike and disdain for my current juice box. I relate to God's people in the desert, whose exodus perfectly paints a picture, similar to mine, of bickering, discontent, complaining children who were never happy with their juice boxes. I mean, juice boxes were falling out of the sky, for crying out loud—manna and quail flavored! In their discontentment, they missed the juice box Distributor. Because they had not learned to enjoy God, they never enjoyed the perfect, divinely hand-picked, life-giving fruity boxes of goodness He provided for them. Which is why they turned a few months' journey into a forty year detour.

THERE'S NOTHING TO EAT

I'd love to tell you that all's well that ends well, but I'd be lying. I'd like to share that this story ends with God's people trusting and living in a close relationship with their Provider God, but no. They continued to lose their

---

26   Exodus 16:9.
27   Exodus 16:20.
28   Exodus 16:28.
29   Exodus 16:35.

patience and gripe. Let's read Numbers 21:4–9 to see another childish scenario followed by another provision from a patient God.

> From Mount Hor they set out by the way to the Red Sea, to go around the land of Edom. And the people became impatient on the way. And the people spoke against God and against Moses, "Why have you brought us up out of Egypt to die in the wilderness? For there is no food and no water, and we loathe this worthless food." Then the Lord sent fiery serpents among the people, and they bit the people, so that many people of Israel died. And the people came to Moses and said, "We have sinned, for we have spoken against the Lord and against you. Pray to the Lord, that He take away the serpents from us." So Moses prayed for the people. And the Lord said to Moses, "Make a fiery serpent and set it on a pole, and everyone who is bitten, when he sees it, shall live." So Moses made a bronze serpent and set it on a pole. And if a serpent bit anyone, he would look at the bronze serpent and live.

What did Moses record about the Israelites when he wrote Numbers, and what can we learn from them and of God? Time after time, God gave His precious children extra care, extra instructions, extra chances to turn to Him. Let us not forget that this is our Daddy too. He's the same for us now as He was for them then. Yet in verses four through five, we see that they were impatient and spoke against God and Moses. Impatience here means, "Down, to be short, cut down, much discouraged."[30] The way they spoke to God and Moses was assertive, commanding, threatening, and telling.[31] After God just saved them from Pharaoh and sustained them in the wilderness, they accused Him of trying to kill them. While bread and meat are still falling from the sky they said, "There is no food and no

---

30   *Bible Hub*, https://biblehub.com/hebrew/7114.htm#7114. Accessed April 30, 2021.
31   *Bible Hub*, https://biblehub.com/hebrew/1696.htm. Accessed April 30, 2021.

water" (Numbers 21:5).[32] Then they finished their harping by saying, "Oh, there is food and water. It's just worthless and we loathe it." Really?

Time after time, God gives His precious children extra care, extra instructions, extra chances to turn to Him.

So many times I have opened my fridge or pantry cupboard and thought or said, "There's nothing to eat," both literally and hypothetically. There is something to eat; we just don't like the choices. Perhaps we should read this story to our own hearts, to our children at the dinner table, and to our friends at church when life doesn't give us what we want. Don't miss the Israelites' internal heart response towards God's provision—they "loathed this worthless food."[33] Might this be an allusion back to Eden—a perfect place with perfect provisions where humanity was dissatisfied and questioned the Distributor of all blessings, including daily food? The Israelites abhorred it, dreaded it, were sick and tired of it, were vexed by it, and were disgusted.[34] This word comes from another word meaning "severing oneself from."[35] They called God's sustaining provisional food "worthless, miserable, and insubstantial."[36] Pretty much they wanted to fire the juice box Distributor! Leading is hard, especially for Moses and Aaron. Don't think for a single second that leading is hard for God. He's God. We are not too hard for Him. He's our Shepherd. He risks the ninety-nine to save the one.[37] "He will tend His flock like a shepherd; He will gather the lambs in His arms; He will carry them in His bosom and gently lead those that are with young."[38]

---

32   Numbers 4:5.

33   Numbers 21:5.

34   *Bible Hub*, https://biblehub.com/hebrew/6973.htm. Accessed April 30, 2021.

35   *Bible Hub*, https://biblehub.com/hebrew/6972.htm. Accessed April 30, 2021.

36   *Bible Hub*, https://biblehub.com/hebrew/7052.htm. Accessed April 30, 2021.

37   Matthew 18:13–14.

38   Isaiah 40:11.

Don't think for a single second that leading is hard for God.
He's God. We are not too hard for Him.

But choices have consequences. The Israelites continued to choose unwisely, and the provision did come, but only after some hefty consequences. God does two things. First, from Numbers 21:4–9, God sent fiery, or venomous, snakes. Say what? The Israelites had seen snakes before in their story. Do you remember where? Aaron's staff turned into a snake.[39] It was a physical weapon of defense as well as a symbolic reminder of God's protection. But here, the snakes are objects of reprimand and agents of deadly consequences. If you're a parent, you should be nodding your head right now in understanding God's point of view. The parent sees what the children do not see. The children miss the point or disagree with the instructions coming from their loving authority. The good news is that God didn't allow them to die.

Second, He gave them a way out.[40] He provided salvation from physical death. He told Moses to erect a pole in the middle of the camp. On top of the pole, Moses put a snake. God gave one easy command: just *look* at the snake on the pole and live.[41] That doesn't sound too difficult. Just one simple act of obedience. I find it ironic that through a serpent's tempting (Adam and Eve in Genesis 1), death entered into humanity, but here in this story, through a mere statue of a serpent, life was granted to God's people. A foreshadowing for sure: "As Moses lifted up the serpent in the wilderness, so must the Son of Man be lifted up, that whoever believes in Him may have eternal life."[42] The Bible tells us roughly how many people *didn't* look at the snake pole. 1 Corinthians 10:8 says, "Twenty-three thousand fell in a single day." The story just ends right there. The point of the narrative for the Israelites back then was *look* and *live*, sheer obedience—a contrast to

---

39   Exodus 7:8–12.
40   1 Corinthians 10:13. Note that the context of this well-known verse is idolatry.
41   Numbers 21:9.
42   John 3:14–15.

what they had been doing, which was sheer disobedience. The point from the narrative for us now is to look and live.

God calls us to sheer obedience in all areas He clearly reveals. Paul refers to this Biblical narrative in 1 Corinthians 10:8–13 as an "example"[43] to the Israelites not to grumble[44] and as "our instruction"[45] (*our* refers to the church in Corinth) not to indulge in idolatry and sexual immorality.[46] Sheer obedience (looking where God tells us to look and other clear commands) is hard at times, isn't it?

God calls us to sheer obedience in all areas He clearly reveals.

LOOK AND LIVE

It's a pretty simple equation—look and live. Now, I don't have a snake pole in my back yard, but I do have a Sword of the Spirit[47] in my hand, in my heart, and on every other surface in my home. As I lift my eyes[48] to the Lord via His Word, I am saved—saved in the vastest meaning of the word. I am saved eternally once for all, through the Person and work of Jesus Christ.[49] I am saved daily by the free refills of God's new morning mercies.[50]

---

43   1 Corinthians 10:11.
44   1 Corinthians 10:10.
45   1 Corinthians 10:11.
46   1 Corinthians 10:7–8.
47   Ephesians 6:17; Hebrews 4:12.
48   Psalm 121.
49   Romans 6:5–11; Hebrews 7:26–27, 10:10, 12; Acts 16:31.
50   Lamentations 3:22–23.

*I am saved eternally once for all, through the Person
and work of Jesus Christ.[51] I am saved daily by the free refills
of God's new morning mercies.*

The saving benefits we receive from our Provider God are attainable, but sometimes we position ourselves as far away as we can get from our "snake pole," and then we say, "I can't see God. I can't find Him working in my life. I can't feel His presence." At least I do at times. God has hard-wired the eyes of our hearts to look to Him.[52] Even unregenerate eyes, though blind, know the truth that God exists, because "what can be made known about God is plain to them, because God has shown it to them."[53] We must move our physical selves, our real eyeballs, our physiological minds closer to our Agent of life—God and His Word.

*We must move our physical selves, our real eyeballs, our physi-
ological minds closer to our Agent of life—God and His Word.*

God's Word is like a personalized snake pole, pointing our eyes to our saving Agent, Jesus. Pre-Calvary, I think God's people (all people, actually) would've killed to have the direct enlightenment of God's Spirit in them and His living Word in front of them. And when it (He) did arrive, many rejected, beguiled, and killed Him. Post-cross, we have God's written Word and indwelling Holy Spirit, which deliver salvation to the doorstep of our hearts. Accepting the Gospel and the One to Whom it points is what saves[54] us from being "without excuse."[55] It also curbs our daily discontentment. Can you imagine the Israelites being bitten by poisonous snakes and then

---

51   Romans 6:5–11; Hebrews 7:26–27, 10:10, 12; Acts 16:31.
52   Romans 1:19–20.
53   Romans 1:19.
54   Ephesians 1:3–7.
55   Romans 1:20.

NOT looking at the snake pole? That's absurd. They would've been without excuse. Yet some refused to look. To those who know what to do and do not do it, to them it is sin—game over.[56] I entreat all of us by the mercies of God[57] to look to the hypothetical snake pole (salvation through Jesus) and to the God Who set it (Him) there for us and present our bodies as living sacrifices[58] to the Most High God. We are now *living dead things*, as one of my dear friends likes to say. This side of heaven, the snakes will still bite; our choices have consequences. But our continual gazing at Jesus and position in Christ rest in the power that He already crushed the snake's head.[59] And His power over death does this EVERY SINGLE TIME for those who know Him and are saved by Him. Our life is now hidden in Christ;[60] we are divinely protected. Look and live, my friends, look and live.

WAITING FOR GOD'S BEST YES

Often as a teenager, I struggled with disappointment and consequent contentment. I *worshipped the why* and questioned the juice box Distributor's provisions for me. If I could just figure out why things happened, I could mentally accept them and/or adjust my life to cause them or prevent them from happening again. Yet the truth of Who He was covered the gaps of my young faith and fragmented theology. Then when storms came, I was able to see God's provision. He had saved His best yes (one of many) for me and for the people around me. For example, He placed a genetic mutation—filtered through His sovereign fingers of love—into my daughter's every cell. He continues to provide through the seemingly endless special needs wilderness and mental health hurdles that come with it. He provided His best yes by guarding her from all the debilitating symptoms for her first seven years, even though the physiological markers were there. And to this day, my Provider provides. He provides my daughter with vibrant

---

56   James 4:17.
57   Romans 12:1.
58   Ibid.
59   Genesis 3:15.
60   Colossians 3:3.

health, despite brain set-backs, so that she and I and the watching world can come near face-to-face to Him and His glory and always know that He is the Lord our God. I've raised her to look at the snake pole, to look to God her Provider. Friends, I can't lie: we've had AWFUL days and months. Together, my family trusts our Provider, even if it seems He swaps-out juice boxes and gives us one that we'd *never* choose for ourselves (which indeed happened when she started having seizures and related behavioral issues). I love the lessons from looking at the Israelites in the story of the manna and the quail. I see who the Israelites were, how they viewed God, and in contrast what I need to think and do based upon knowing that God is my Provider.

God always saves His best provision for us, for His glory, for our good. Make no mistake, His pinnacle best yes is His calling, drawing,[61] and saving you. So every time you think you hear Him saying "no" to you, try making a 180-degree about-face and remind yourself that He's saving another "yes" for you. That's a sure recipe for conquering complaining, dashing disappointment, and creating contentment, even if you don't see His provision in this life. So in the strength of the Spirit, drink up the wisdom and life experience right in front of you. Share your juice box—your story, your goods, your God—with those right in front of you. If your neighbor spills his or her juice box, help clean up the mess and whisper the reminder that God will provide another one. Quit asking God for a case-discount because you think you deserve it. Join me and learn lessons from a juice box. And hopefully along the way, we'll become more content people, and we'll begin to trust and fall more deeply in love with the juice box Distributor.

---

61   John 6:44.

PRAYER

Most High God,
Jehovah Yahweh, Jehovah Jireh,
I am in the wilderness at times.
I am often surrounded by complainers.
My own daily murmurings are just that—
murmurings against You, railings against You, my Provider.
Forgive me, Lord.
You hear my grumblings;
You rain down bread from heaven;
You instruct me what to do;
You test me.

May I obey You and gather just enough for my day's portion,
trusting my tomorrow to You.
When tested, may I pass.
When I sin and fall short,
may I look to You and to Your daily provisional help,
oftentimes seen from everywhere I'm camped-out in my own sinful pride.
I want to walk in Your ways.
I want to see Your glory.
I want to know that You are not just Israel's God
but that You are the Lord my God,
rescuing me from slavery and guiding me in the desert.
Amen.

DISCUSSION QUESTIONS

1. From the text, Exodus 16, what do you love most about God and His character?

2. To better know God's hand-picked leader of Israel, Moses, read Exodus 15:1–18. What sticks out to *Moses* about God and His character?

3. Are you coming near, face-to-face, with the glory of God on a consistent basis, let's say weekly? Specifically, how is God asking you to "walk in His ways" (Exodus 16:4)? How are you gathering nutrients (spiritual truth)? In what places are you looking for these? (Note: God, His Word, prayer, His people, and His bride are some of the right places.) See Exodus 16:27.

4. What false hypothetical snake staffs need to be chopped down from the yard in your soul? What tangible saving-ways has the Lord placed in your daily life to draw your eyes to Him? Stop right now and thank Him for the life-saving poles He erects in your life to magnify Himself, draw your eyes to Him, and give you life. See Numbers 21:8–9.

WHAT GOD DOES:
ENLIGHTENS/INDWELLS/UNVEILS

CHAPTER 4
THE PERFECT MIRROR

James 1:22–25; Exodus 38:8

I have a mirror in my home that I call my "skinny mirror." You know what I mean, don't you? A skinny mirror makes us *appear* different than we are. It shows us what we think we want to see rather than what really is. Some mirrors make us look taller or shorter than we are. Some mirrors distort us. Sometimes we ignore the mirror altogether … at least I do. I know each of us has an individual experience with mirrors: some of us don't care about mirrors either way, some of us are obsessed with them, and some of us avoid them. I humbly and tenderly address you whatever may be your relationship with mirrors. Let me throw this question out there: if we're looking into an imperfect mirror, are we going to get an accurate picture of ourselves? Nope. So what is it that makes mirrors effective or ineffective? And who cares anyway?

INTO THE LOOKING GLASS

For mirrors to be effective, "The key factor is a smooth surface, because rough surfaces scatter light instead of reflecting it."[1] The purpose of a mirror is for looking into it, which is why it's also called a looking glass. It's for seeing a perfect reflection—whether that's seeing ourselves (to make sure we look acceptable and catch anything out of place) or seeing things outside of ourselves (like other people, or objects in the rearview mirror, and all the way into outer space). This *seeing* in a mirror causes us to adjust, improve, move out of harm's way, etc. Or at least it should. Even the rearview mirror carries that famous reality: "Objects in the mirror are closer than they appear." So is there a perfect mirror? There is! It's so perfect that I'm going to capitalize it. Unlike my skinny mirror, or a circus mirror, this perfectly accurate Mirror shows us reality. The objects in this Mirror are neither closer nor further than they appear. The reflection and feedback from this Mirror are exactly where it says they are. This Mirror is God's Word.[2] Not only are we to be readers of the Word but also lookers into the Word … that is, *intently* reading it.

LOOK INTO GOD'S PERFECT MIRROR

According to James, God's Word is a hypothetical mirror. Let's look at what James is talking about in James 1:22–25.

> But be doers of the Word, and not hearers only, deceiving yourselves. For if anyone is a hearer of the Word and not a doer, he is like a man who looks intently at his natural face in a mirror. For he looks at himself and goes away and at once forgets what he was like. But the one who looks into the perfect law, the law of liberty, and perseveres, being no

---

1   "How Do Mirrors Work?" *Wonderopolis*, wonderopolis.org/wonder/how-do-mirrors-work/. Accessed April 30, 2021.
2   2 Timothy 3:16–17; Hebrews 4:12.

hearer who forgets but a doer who acts, he will be blessed in his doing.

God's Word is a mirror to see the internal reflection of our thoughts and attitudes next to Who God is; it's a mirror to help guide our external actions compared to Jesus' example; and it's a mirror to give us freedom and blessing revealed in this life and beyond. First, our internal reflection is the accurate current state of our thoughts, feelings, and motives. James is clear regarding the effect of intently looking into the mirror of God's Word. It will change us on the inside as it shows us the Most High God in Whose image we are made. Second, seeing our inner reflection in the perfect mirror of God's Word will change what we do and what the world sees. Just like the watching world saw Jesus' example of a Godly, shining life, the world will see us as true light-bringers. Last, we receive God's precious gifts of freedom and blessing as we *look* into His Mirror and *do* what it says. Let us not for a moment confuse our ideas of freedom and blessing with God's ideas of freedom and blessing.

God's freedom and blessing are much grander and holier than our finite minds could imagine. They were bought at the cross and they free us from the law of sin and death.[3] That's a lot different than the freedom worldly culture is selling us these days. Let's look a little closer into our perfect Mirror. I love personalizing the pronouns in Scripture for women (never forgetting that "context is king" as well as a prerequisite for application). Read this passage again as if you are James' recipient.

God's freedom and blessing are much grander and holier than our finite minds could imagine. They were bought at the cross and they free us from the law of sin and death.

---

3   Romans 8:1–4.

But be doers of the Word, and not hearers only, deceiving yourselves. For if anyone is a hearer of the Word and not a doer, [she] is like a [woman] who looks intently at [her] natural face in a mirror. For [she] looks at [herself] and goes away and at once forgets what [she] was like. But the [woman] who looks into the perfect law, the law of liberty, and perseveres, being no hearer who forgets but a doer who acts, [she] will be blessed in [her] doing.

James 1:22–25

SPINACH IN YOUR TEETH, SIN IN YOUR HEART

We check in the mirror because of what it tells us. *Or we turn away from the mirror because of what it tells us.* Are we checking the reflection of our heart in God's Word at every opportunity? Or are we turning away from the reflection of our heart that God's Word reveals? We see in this text in James that God's Word is a mirror, just like the one in our home or car. Note that James, the author, doesn't say it's *like* a mirror; he says it *is* a mirror (not literally, but functionally) as a means of legitimate self-looking ("for he looks at himself").[4] What do we do when we look in a real mirror and see spinach in our teeth? We do everything within our power to remove it. Only a fool would walk away from the mirror without cleaning his or her teeth. In the same way, God's Word creates an intimate relationship with God whereby we see the spinach of sin and deception in our hearts.[5] In seeing (if we are made of Him) our bane (sin, what causes death), we go after it and try to destroy it with all our Holy Spirit-infused

---

4 James 1:24.
5 Jeremiah 17:9.

might! We follow the Holy Spirit's conviction to get rid of it,[6] and He powerfully removes it.[7] This spinach removal boils down to a holy God and our right relationship with Him.[8] God's Mirror, His Word, gives us good news, hopeful news, solution-oriented news—tidings of deliverance,[9] justification,[10] and sanctification.[11] God's Mirror is where we need to set our gaze and examination[12] to soak up and live out the Good News.

God's Mirror, His Word, gives us good news, hopeful news, solution-oriented news—tidings of deliverance, justification, and sanctification.

---

6   "Getting rid of sin," for the believer, involves knowing one's own heart (1 Kings 8:38–39; Ephesians 4:22) and praying honest confessions such as this beautiful prayer: "God, show me all the sins of my life, reveal all of them, uncover every little corner of my life. Bring it up and may it become as detestable to me as it is to You, and may You give me the strength to see it go away." John MacArthur, "How to Kill Sin in Your Life," *Grace to You*, Sept. 10, 2009, www.gty.org/library/Articles/A180/How-to-Kill-Sin-in-Your-Life. Accessed April 30, 2021.

7   Psalm 51:10.

8   John 1:12–13.

9   *Deliverance* in the greatest sense is eternal salvation. It is "God's rescue which delivers believers out of destruction and into His [divine] safety." *Bible Hub*, https://biblehub.com/greek/4991.htm. Accessed April 30, 2021.

10   *Justification* is "the judicial act of God, by which He pardons all the sins of those who believe in Christ, and accepts, and treats them as righteous in the eye of the law. ... Justification is not the forgiveness of a man without righteousness, but a declaration that he possesses a righteousness which perfectly and forever satisfies the law, namely, Christ's righteousness." *Bible Hub*, https://biblehub.com/topical/j/justification.htm. Accessed May, 8, 2021. Psalm 32:1–2; 2 Corinthians 5:21; Galatians 2:16.

11   *Sanctification* "involves more than a mere moral reformation of character, brought about by the power of truth: it is the work of the Holy Spirit bringing the whole nature more and more under the influences of the new gracious principles implanted in the soul in regeneration... and extend[ing] to the whole [person]." *Bible Hub*, https://biblehub.com/topical/s/sanctification.htm. Accessed May 8, 2021. 1 Corinthians 6:11; Colossians 3:10; 2 Thessalonians 2:13.

12   Psalm 26:2; 1 Corinthians 11:28.

I've got news for you—the skinny mirror isn't accurate (nor is any other distorted looking glass). Though we may like what we see (or not), it doesn't show us reality. If we are to be the rooted and grounded, sound-minded,[13] wise,[14] prepared,[15] diligent,[16] wonderfully-made[17] people God calls us to be, then don't you think we should be looking into an accurate mirror, especially for our souls? Don't you think our mirror should be perfect and flawless? So let's get in front of *the* Mirror! It's the one we're told to look into *intently*. This Mirror makes us lean in closer to get a better look at ourselves. It's the Mirror that tells us how to look our best, the way God created us. This Mirror is our power tool. This Mirror promises freedom. This Mirror has a cause-and-effect relationship with what we *do* once we've *looked* into it. This isn't a circus mirror, folks. It's a supernatural Mirror that dives beneath the surface of the spinach in our teeth and bears witness to the spinach in our souls.[18] This internal roughage is sin, and it's got to be identified, confessed, and removed by God's grace if we're to accurately bear the image of our heavenly Father.[19]

If we are to be the rooted and grounded, sound-minded, wise, prepared, diligent, wonderfully-made people God calls us to be, then don't you think we should be looking into an accurate mirror, especially for our souls?

I feel so privileged and excited every time I get to look into God's Word. This is better than Disneyland. This is a "we-get-to" mentality. If the Spirit

---

13   To be *sound-minded* [*sophron*] means to be safe in one's inner outlook. *Bible Hub*, https://biblehub.com/greek/4993.htm. Accessed May 2, 2021.
14   James 3:13–17.
15   1 Peter 3:15.
16   2 Peter 1:10, 3:14.
17   Psalm 139:14.
18   Hebrews 4:12.
19   1 John 1:5–10.

of God lives in us, we should be jumping-at-the-bit to look into God's Mirror. His reflecting Word is two-fold in nature.

- It shows us what God really looks like.[20]
- It shows us what we really look like.[21]

We see this dual-reflective power in every single Biblical account. So take what we are about to study in James and apply it to everything you read in Scripture while asking these questions: What do I learn about God? What do I learn about the intended recipients? What am I to apply in my own life?

A MIRROR TO SEE OURSELVES AND TO SEE GOD

Our brother, James, knows this fact: God is holy; we are not. It's not my goal here to theologically exegete every jot and tittle of God's holiness, our sin, and the irreconcilable impasse. It's there; it's the reality; the Bible says we know it.[22] Rather, I want us to fall in love with this holy God, and in the process, fall out of love with our sinful selves. Through the Holy Spirit,[23] our spiritual smile is great, but the spinach has got to go. James, who refers to himself as a bond servant, is known for penning this very practical letter of wisdom to Jewish Christians.[24] As Jews, James' readers would have been extremely familiar with and knowledgeable of the Old Testament writings and the law. He assumes that they knew how holy God was and how unholy they were. God knew you and I would be reading James today. God—via this text, this author, this literary audience—has tremendous recommendations for us regarding our internal hearing and external doing.

---

20   Genesis 1:1; 2 Samuel 22:32–34; Psalm 68:19–20, Psalm 96; Micah 7:18–19; 1 John 4:7–9; Revelation 4:8. The entire Bible does a great job of showing us what God looks like.
21   Romans 3:10–23; Hebrews 4:12–13.
22   Romans 1:19–20.
23   1 Peter 1:14–16.
24   James 1:1.

Our Wonderful Counselor[25] gives us tips[26] to be wholly holy, not this hip holy that our current culture is selling. His holiness is timeless and oblivious to "likes," followings, and approval ratings. He tells us what to put on. He tells us what to put off.[27] The Lord is our spiritual stylist,[28] with unlimited alterations, commendations, and accessories. Do you honestly think the Lord Who designed you to wear His armor like a brand ambassador would give you cheap, unflattering garments and a faulty, warped mirror? Doesn't He promise to give us everything pertaining to life and Godliness?[29] Not the hand-me-downs. Not the sale-rack items. Not the colors no one wants.

---

*Our Wonderful Counselor gives us tips to be wholly holy,
not this hip holy that our current culture is selling.*

God wants us to look like Him. We cannot look like Him if we're not looking at Him. Have you taken a good, hard look at *I Am* lately?[30] Have you breathed-in His presence? *YHWH* … His very name means and sounds like living breath. We saw Him as the Redeemer in Philippians 2. We saw Him as the Provider in Lamentations 3. We saw Him as the Knower in Exodus

---

25   Isaiah 9:6; John 15:26.
26   "Tips," not in the sense of "useful pieces of practical advice," but "tips" as in "very reliable … inside information" ("inside" because we are God's children and have His Holy Spirit and "reliable" because the Most High God is instructing us with His infinite Truth that is accessible to believers by salvation through Christ). "Tip," *Dictionary.com,* www.dictionary.com/browse/tip. Accessed April 30, 2021.
27   Ephesians 4:22–24, 6:11–17.
28   Psalm 18:32.
29   2 Peter 1:3.
30   *I Am* is the meaning of God's name, Yahweh. The name of God used in a specific context informs the meaning of the text. For example, in Genesis 7:16, Yahweh (I Am) is the very name of God used to describe the last moment before the flood came. "And the Lord shut him in." When the entire human race as Noah knew it was on the brink of extinction, it must have been nice to know that *I Am* was the One shutting the door of the ark. Human existence is in jeopardy but God's existence, His "I-Am-ness" is present, certain, and saving. *Bible Hub,* https://biblehub.com/hebrew/3068.htm. Accessed April 30, 2021.

16. All of Scripture points to what God looks like and what we look like. The only way to look like Him is to see what He looks like, study His features, clothe ourselves in His raiments,[31] and walk the catwalk of life in true righteousness and holiness.

God wants us to look like Him. We cannot look like Him if we're not looking at Him.

God's Mirror never lies. He's not going to have us look into a false mirror of pumped-up, self-care injected, "I-am enough" mustered righteousness. Our righteousness is as filthy rags,[32] FYI. Our hustle lands us in hell. By the power of the Holy Spirit, we can begin the process of looking like and acting like our Father. By Jesus' death-defying hustle—reconciling us to God—we are to be ambassadors for Christ.[33] And at this very confession of our own self-loving deadness[34] and recognition of God's us-saving resurrection, we are looking at our brand new made-alive-in-Christ[35] reflection. In our deadness to self, we are now more alive than we've ever been. Talk about empowerment![36] This is way better than women's lib. This is Holy Spirit lib. This is the first step of us catching an accurate view of ourselves in God's perfect Mirror. As we stoop down on our hands and knees to look intently at Jesus, He raises Himself up powerfully within us, as He is seated at God's righteous right hand, *interceding for us.*[37] Hallelujah, what a Savior!

---

31   Galatians 3:12; Ephesians 4:24.
32   Isaiah 64:6.
33   2 Corinthians 5:20.
34   Ephesians 2:1; Colossians 2:13.
35   Romans 6:11; 1 Corinthians 15:22; Ephesians 2:5; Colossians 2:13; 1 Peter 3:18.
36   Ephesians 1:1, 3:20; Colossians 1:11; 2 Timothy 1:7; 2 Peter 1:3.
37   Psalm 48:10; Romans 8:34; Hebrews 12:2.

God's Mirror never lies. He's not going to have us look into a false mirror of pumped-up, self-care injected, "I-am enough" mustered righteousness. Our righteousness is as filthy rags, FYI. Our hustle lands us in hell.

SPIRITUAL TWISTER

In the original language, *looking intently*, from this passage in James 1, means "stooping down sideways with a bent body to carefully and curiously inspect something."[38] The goldsmiths would do this type of intense looking, all bent over, watching for the dross (impurities) and skimming it off and away from the pure gold. James calls his listeners, and us, to bend over backwards—to do a spiritual stretch of a sort. They are to look at themselves in such a way that they didn't "forget" (James 1:24). They are to *remember* what they looked like as non-doers,[39] as worthlessly religious,[40] as those not "quick to hear," as those not "slow to speak," as those not "slow to be angry," and as those living out "all filthiness and rampant wickedness."[41] The goal of this close examination is pure gold. As a believer, that means we (with the help of the Spirit) look into the Mirror of God's Word so that we look just like Jesus, Who pours off our sinful dross. James calls his recipients (and us) to look intently into God's Word, as much as they can (and we can). This is a game of spiritual Twister: it's getting us in the right position to better understand God and get *Him* right, and it's the power of Yahweh breathing the wonder of Who He is into our deepest parts. If we're not looking intently into the Bible consistently, we're missing Him, an accurate view of ourselves, and how to be the "active doers" that James 1:25 commands. We need nothing other than Holy Spirit-guided intentional

---

38 *Bible Hub*, https://biblehub.com/greek/3879.htmbiblehub.com/. Accessed April 30, 2021.
39 James 1:22.
40 James 1:26.
41 James 1:19–21.

Word-looking. It's not enough to cry and then wash our faces when what we really need is to cry over our sin and look into the face of the One Who washes our hearts, minds, and souls. Let's not settle for anything less than this James-infused wisdom.

We need nothing other than Holy Spirit-guided intentional Word-looking. It's not enough to cry and then wash our faces when what we really need is to cry over our sin and look into the face of the One Who washes our hearts, minds, and souls.

What if we look at ourselves and then go away and forget what we look like? Who forgets what he or she looks like? This seems like a silly question, but I know I forget what I look like sometimes, on the outside but especially on the inside. Close your eyes and envision what you look like from your head to your toes. Do you remember what you're wearing, what accessories you put on, and your overall facial structure? Spiritual self-analysis takes work and focus. Some of us may choose at times not to remember what we look like because it seems too painful. James implies a forgetfulness much deeper than our outward appearance. He says we forget what we are like, what we are in our essence—once image-bearers of the Most High God, now sinners in need of a saving. Jesus is much more than a facialist as He goes deep into the pores of our souls to make us new at our point of salvation and to sludge off the dross of sin in our daily sanctification. So why does James tell us not to forget what we look like? In modern times, we have mirrors galore, photographs, social media, and unlimited reflections of ourselves everywhere. Back in James' day, mirrors were less common, expensive, and sometimes rare. Not everyone had one. So when someone looked into a mirror, they most likely looked at their reflection much more intently than we do today. They had good reason to, as the text says, *not once forget*.[42]

---

42 James 1:24.

I FORGOT

In the original text, the word *forget* means "failing to notice, neglecting or overlooking, to lose out of your mind, especially of the effects that go with failing to notice. And with these forgetful effects come the consequences that build upon overlooking something."[43] James strongly urges them to remember what they looked like. I never want to forget, or fail to notice, God's Word[44] and where His wisdom is showing up. It's like a child who replies "I forgot" when asked, "Why didn't you look where I told you to look?" Through James, God says to us, "Why don't you look in the cupboard where I tell you to look … to find the Bread of Life?" We reply, "I forgot," and then wonder why we don't *feel* God's presence, *know* His peace, and *love* Him dearly. Let us not overlook something, or rather, Someone.

Dear friends, go get in God's cupboard, His Word. It's stocked full of Him and His goods. Staying in sin breeds forgetfulness. James reminds us to remember what our hearts and minds look like. We're looking to *see* and listening to *do*. Just like children, we need reminding. As a mom, I feel like a full-time professional Remind-er—that's my job-description. As I remind my children to look at and listen to me, I expect them to be *doers who act*. God, our heavenly Parent, expects the same.

Dear friends, go get in God's cupboard, His Word.
It's stocked full of Him and His goods.

A MIRROR TO GUIDE OUR ACTIONS TO LOOK LIKE JESUS

One day, I told my eleven-year-old son to clean his room. My son came back to me a few hours later and said, "I listened to what you said. I memorized what you said. I studied what it means to clean my room." I laughed

---

43   *Bible Hub,* https://biblehub.com/greek/1953.htm. Accessed May 8, 2021.
44   Psalm 119:16.

in his face. We all know how ridiculous this is! The bottom line is this: "Did you clean your room?" My words implied a specific action, a *doing*, on the part of my son. This is a hypothetical story to make an obvious point. James tells us to be "not hearers only" but to "be doers of the Word," like those who "persevere." In this context, perseverance is "a close-working relationship or partnership—a *stay-close remaining*."[45] The word "hear" comes from the Greek, *akouo*, which is where we get "acoustics."[46] Can we say that our current relationship status with God is a stay-close remaining one? If we're not within earshot of God's "acoustics," if we're not listening to God in such a way that is wedded to action, we are deceived.

Yuck, I don't want to be deceived. I don't want that state of living or label. That sounds bad. It is. We—you, I, everyone—got this name in the garden when Adam and Eve looked at, listened to, and followed the deceiver. James calls us out when he says, "… Deceiving yourselves…" (James 1:22). There it is … dropped like a truth bomb right in the middle of our *listening* and *doing*. The Apostle John says it this way, "If we claim to have fellowship with Him yet walk in the darkness, we lie and do not live by the truth" (1 John 1:6). Deception is a nasty thing. The second we recognize deception, it's no longer deception. It's the enemy—the master deceiver—standing there with his hands on his hips, taunting, "What are you going to *do*?"

---

*Deception is a nasty thing. The second we recognize deception, it's no longer deception. It's the enemy—the master deceiver— standing there with his hands on his hips, taunting, "What are you going to **do**?"*

---

45   *Bible Hub,* https://biblehub.com/greek/3887.htm. Accessed May 2, 2021.
46   *Bible Hub,* biblehub.com/greek/202.htm. Accessed April 30, 2021. James 1:22: "Do not merely listen to the Word, and so deceive yourselves. Do what it says" (paraphrased).

PARALYZED LOGIC

Paralogizomai is Greek for "deceive." *Para* means "contrary when compared side-by-side, and *logizomai* means "to reason."[47] One of the applications from this context is James telling us that we are reasoning contrary to God's Truth in such a way that we are misleading ourselves. This listening without doing seems plausible at first but later disappoints us and lets us down.[48] Do you see some English words emerging from the Greek? *Paralyze* and *logic* perhaps? We have self-inflicted logical paralysis! A silly example from my life: I tend to have paralyzed logic when I see a cute rug. (I have a rug addiction). My mind utters, "No, you don't need to buy that." And rather than acting in accordance with my internal Counselor—Who wants me to spend my collateral on Him versus another rug—I ignore the doing that I know is best, and I actually do the opposite: I purchase the rug! As if thirteen rugs come even close to investment in the free and unlimited soul-session and redeemed-lifestyle with my Wonderful Counselor! So what does our Therapist tell us to *do*?

There's a *doing* that's in our DNA. It's called *imago Dei*.[49] This is the image of God in each of us that reflects Him in all that we do and all that we are. The Holy Spirit counsels us to be who God created us to be—His workmanship. This is now possible once we're in Christ. I find it interesting that the root word for *do* is *poiema*, which is where we get the word "poem."[50] Beautiful! Do you see the connection between Jesus' Holy Spirit inside of us and what the watching world beholds? Jesus designed us to be living poems. That's His therapy for us. Over our lifetime, and through His

---

47   *Bible Hub,* https://biblehub.com/greek/3884.htm. Accessed April 30, 2021.
48   *Bible Hub,* biblehub.com/greek/3884.htm. Accessed May 1, 2021. James 1:22: "Do not merely listen to the Word, and so deceive yourselves. Do what it says" (paraphrased).
49   *Imago Dei* is Latin for "Image of God." It is a theological term referring "to the unique imprint God placed upon humanity, identifying people as a special creation." "Just the Facts on Religions," *ReligionFacts,* www.religionfacts.com/. Accessed May 1, 2021. "Imago Dei." The term has its roots in Genesis 1:27, "So God created man in His own image, in the image of God He created Him, male and female He created them."
50   *Bible Hub,* https://biblehub.com/greek/4163.htm. Accessed May 8, 2021.

skilled editing, a masterpiece, sculpture, poem, final product, performance emerges. Despite ourselves, because of our justified position in Christ, we showcase our Boss, Director, Artist, and Author.

---

*There's a **doing** that's in our DNA. It's called **imago Dei**. This is the image of God in each of us that reflects Him in all that we do and all that we are.*

We are His workmanship, His living poems. We do this best only by looking into the Mirror of His Word over and over and over again. When we're in love with Jesus, we will be in love with His Word. To love logos, we must read logos. When we read logos, we are logos. The much-intended play on words here is life-altering. Remember in the introduction, John 1:1–18 tells us that Jesus is the living Word, the divine Logos. He is the "I am from the beginning" Word; He is the "I am with God" Word; He is the "I am God" Word. He is the Word "Who became flesh;" He is the Word "Who dwelt among us;" He is the Word "Who gave us the right to be His children." What a hopeful mirror we've been given in which to gaze. What a good Director we have to follow to be living masterpieces on the stage of life. The icing on the cake is the freedom and blessing in Christ that James recorded.

A MIRROR TO FREEDOM AND BLESSING

James 1:25 says, "The one who looks into the perfect law, the law of liberty ... a doer who acts, he will be blessed in his doing." So this perfect mirror into which we are to intently look is likened to a perfect law that gives freedom and blessing. Wait a minute ... a law that gives freedom and blesses you? This sounds like a theological oxymoron combined with the genie from Aladdin. We *must* define the terms to see what James was saying to his recipients as well as to apply it to our lives today.

Webster's Dictionary defines perfection as, "the quality or state of being perfect: such as freedom from fault or defect; flawlessness, maturity; an unsurpassable degree of accuracy or excellence." In this text, the root word for perfect is *teleios*, from which we get the word *telescope*. So when James says *perfect law*, he means a general assigned principle, which when it reaches its end is complete, or full grown.[51] This is just like the extending aspect of a sailor's telescope. It "unfolds and extends in stages, one at a time, to function at full strength of capacity and effectiveness."[52] Liberty, or *eleutheria*, means freedom, especially from a state of slavery.[53] Do you see it? God's law is so perfect that it extends into our lives and gives us freedom to see, act, and live outside of our current slavery to sin. Being slaves to God's law gives us complete freedom. Literally, we are freely free. God's Word is the seatbelt that keeps us safe as spiritual babies but gives us freedom to drive anywhere as spiritual adults. Scripture is like gravity: it's a law that binds, and yet because of it we have the freedom to walk and move. This place of freedom is a position to be envied, which is exactly what *blessing* means! James' promise of God's blessing goes way beyond a jovial blue genie. Our blessing—resulting from our doing, resulting from our looking, resulting from the Holy Spirit's enlightening and daily sanctification—puts us in a fortunate position where we receive God's extended benefits. Notice that this goes well beyond what we do. It is a "position, an enviable (fortunate) one, for the believer for receiving God's provisions (favor), which literally extend His grace (benefits)."[54] How privileged we are that He has extended His grace-fueled benefits to us! Our position in Him is to be envied! This is the liberated life; this is the blessed life. We cannot confuse the world's view of liberation and blessing with God's freedom and benefits. Looking like Jesus *is* our freedom. Bearing the image of God *is* our blessing. Apart from Him, we have no good thing.[55] Any saving faith, resulting deeds, and blessed lives run on Holy Spirit fuel—start to finish, here on earth and on into eternity.

---

51   *Bible Hub,* https://biblehub.com/greek/5046.htm. Accessed May 8, 2021.

52   *Bible Hub,* https://biblehub.com/greek/5046.htm. Accessed May 2, 2021.

53   *Bible Hub,* https://biblehub.com/greek/1657.htm. Accessed May 2, 2021.

54   *Bible Hub,* https://biblehub.com/greek/3107.htm. Accessed May 2, 2021.

55   Leviticus 20:26; Psalm 16:2; Isaiah 45:5.

Looking like Jesus is our freedom. Bearing the image of God is our blessing. Apart from Him, we have no good thing.

THE PERFECT MIRROR

In conclusion to our study in James 1, I want us to go back in time, carrying our mirrors with us, to the women in Exodus 38:8. I want us to see where they positioned themselves, where they set their gaze, and what they did with their mirrors. I promise you, these women and what they did will blow you away. You might be convicted. You might fall in love with God's Word for the first time. You might even get saved (if you're not already). I hope so. Let's soak up this Godly example from the Exodus women.

Exodus 38:8 says: "He made the basin of bronze and its stand of bronze, from the mirrors of the ministering women who ministered in the entrance of the tent of meeting." In the Old Testament, the bronze basin and its bronze stand were used by the priests for washing with water before entering God's presence in the tabernacle. We'll discuss this topic and structure in more detail in the next chapter. The mirrors mentioned here, made of well-polished bronze plates, were rare and treasured possessions, most likely given to the Israelite women by the Egyptians at the Exodus.[56] So what is the significance of all this to us as we relate back to our study of James 1? I find it interesting that the women in Exodus were doing two crucial things: 1) serving, and 2) putting themselves in close proximity to God. They "ministered in the entrance of the tent of meeting." This was just outside the tabernacle where God lived in the Holy of Holies. *They were as close as they could get to God,* and *they were serving.* When the time came, they joyfully gave up their most treasured mirrors to be used in His

---

56 The first mirrors were bronze discs, finely polished until smooth and reflective. These first polished bronze discs date back as early as 2900BC to ancient Egypt. Not everyone had one; they were rare. The Hebrew exodus from Egypt is dated around 1300BC. "The History of Mirrors," *Mirror* History, http://www.mirrorhistory.com/. Accessed May 1, 2021.

tabernacle. Do you see what's happening here? These women in Exodus were looking at God to such an extent that they were willing to take their treasured mirrors and turn them over to be used for their cleansing and God's glory. Their eyes were fixed on the perfect image—God Himself. What a state they must have been living in!

The closer we are to God, the more willing we are to allow Him to transform our objects of self-reflection into objects of spiritual cleansing. God will take the very things that draw our eyes onto ourselves and transform them into the very tools that place our eyes on Him. I wonder what would happen if we exchanged gazing at our phones for gazing at the splendor and majesty of the Most High God. I wonder what would happen if we stop saying yes to every social invitation we receive and instead said yes to "what is better,"[57] to time in the presence of the Lord. What would happen if we stop comparing ourselves to everything that culture—even Christian culture—tells us to be and instead compared ourselves to whom God is telling us to be?

The closer we are to God, the more willing we are to allow Him to transform our objects of self-reflection into objects of spiritual cleansing. God will take the very things that draw our eyes onto ourselves and transform them into the very tools that place our eyes on Him.

Many people with whom I talk, especially in the church, tell me how badly they want to have a quiet time (commune with God through His Word) but just struggle to do it. A heart in love will move mountains to spend time with his or her Lover. A soul passionate for God will find time for Him. If you require some catchy, salesy pitch for the Lord to be attractive to you, I've got news for you: you're not attracted to Him. This is a red flag. So why aren't professing Christ-followers in love with Jesus? Humbly, I believe it's because they're spending way too much time in front

---

57   Luke 10:41–42.

of their flawed mirrors. I too am guilty of gazing into these false mirrors like: escapist shopping, fear-of-someone-seeing-my-messy-house cleaning, excessive volunteer work, unbridled internet trolling, prioritization of outside ministry over home/family ministry, unrestrained social media sponging, too many hours spent at the gym, plus whatever designer deterrents the devil deceptively holds in front of me. None of these hypothetical mirrors in and of themselves are bad. The point is we are not to prioritize them. Most people agree that social media *can* be the death of us.

If you require some catchy, salesy pitch for the Lord to be attractive to you, I've got news for you: you're not attracted to Him.

Social media sacrifices us on a dangerous altar that slowly sucks Jesus out of us. I have gazed into all of these poor mirrors, among numerous others, at different times in my life. Do you walk away from your screen feeling free and blessed? Do you go to and depart from events that *you* scheduled on *your* calendar experiencing freedom and blessing? Do you leave the mall, bags in hand, having tasted and seen that the Lord is good?[58] Does your obsession with accelerating on the corporate ladder draw you into oneness with Christ? I know I don't feel great when I routinely make those choices and sacrifice what is best, sitting at the feet of Jesus.

By constantly looking into the Mirror of Scripture, we allow God to convert our faulty mirrors into agents of sanctification.[59] This is when our minds become worthy homes and our hearts become holy of holies in which the Holy Spirit dwells and makes us lovers of Him and doers of His calling. Why not let God's divinely-breathed, life-changing words—colored with the Holy Spirit's presence—pen volumes of truth on our hearts and in our minds in such a way as to reveal wordless masterpieces?

---

58   Psalm 34:8.
59   Psalm 19:7–11, 40:8, 86:11, 119:9–16.

By constantly looking into the Mirror of Scripture, we allow God to convert our faulty mirrors into agents of sanctification. This is when our minds become worthy homes and our hearts become holy of holies in which the Holy Spirit dwells and makes us lovers of Him and doers of His calling.

PRAYER

Lord,
May I look so intently into Your perfect face
that I accurately see You and all that You are as the Most High God.
Use the mirror of Your Word to help me clearly see myself
and all that You created me to be as Your child.
Trade my forgetfulness for Your freedom.
Transform me from a paralyzed hearer into an active doer of Your Word.
Bless me, Lord, with the righteous life that You desire.
May I draw in so close to You that I give up my most valuable inner and
outer possessions as tools for You to use to refine me and to proclaim You.
May I remain so very near to You that I am content with
nothing else than Your presence.
Make my mind a worthy home and my heart a holy of holies in which You
can dwell.
You are my most prized possession.
Amen.

DISCUSSION QUESTIONS

1. Error in the mind can lead to error in the heart (James 1:22, 26). Go to www.biblehub.com and look up (in the interlinear Greek) the words "deceiving" (vs. 22) and "deceives" (vs. 26). According to James, what is the way to avoid this kind of religious error or deception? See all of James 1.

2. What is the focal point of your intentional daily looking (James 1:23)? If it's not Jesus, what aspects about the Lord's single-minded focus of doing the will of His Father can you claim and do in your own life in order to overcome your double-mindedness and instability (James 1:5–8)?

3. Are you a forgetful hearer or effectual doer? See Matthew 7:15–27. (The mirror into which you are looking influences you; may it always be the Word of God, not only well-intended books, podcasts, blogs, etc.). See Psalm 19:7–11. In your daily time with God, I encourage you to step away from all influences except God's direct Word for one month.

4. What items/patterns in your life are agents of self-focus and with what can you exchange them to be agents of holiness in your own life (Exodus 38:8)?

CHAPTER 5
PITCH A TENT

———

Exodus 29:42–46; Revelation 21:3

What if I told you to go out in the yard and pitch a tent? What would this involve? It seems like a pretty simple task. But anyone who's pitched a tent knows there's a science to it. A basic internet search includes multi-step instructions for pitching a tent. For example:

HOW TO PITCH A TENT[1]

1. Find an area that is as level as possible. Remove any stones, twigs, or other hazards. Avoid areas with dips, as these can fill with water.
2. Lay out a ground sheet.
3. Unpack your tent supplies.
4. Insert tent poles through the frame.
5. Raise the tent.
6. Hammer in the tent pegs.
7. Put up the rain-fly.
8. Move your things into the tent.

———

1   *Wikihow,* https://www.wikihow.com/Assemble-a-Tent. Accessed May 8, 2021.

I see a sermon in each step—you probably do as well. God told Israel to pitch a tent. This tent was no ordinary tent. It was much grander than a weekend pop-up or the Big Top. This tent had to be specific. There was a divine science behind it. It was to house something great—the presence of the Most High God. Eek! How exciting is this? Every measurement, every supply, every stake position, every seam, every clasp, every color, every general contractor,[2] every step along the way was exact. Everything in it was commissioned by the Most High God. Even the order in which this tent was to be erected was purposeful. Each item in it was handcrafted from specific raw materials for deliberate reasons. There were instructions for the people who needed access—*who* could enter the tent, *how* they had to enter, *what* they had to wear. These tent blueprints are vividly described for us by Moses in Exodus 25–30.[3] They are commonly skimmed over, skipped, or considered boring and tedious to read. But they are anything but that. Humbly, I entreat you to enter this Old Testament tent with me to study what serves as a "copy and shadow of the heavenly things."[4] I am no tabernacle scholar, just a woman in love with the Old Testament and with the God to Whom it points.

MEET WITH ME

Have you ever studied the Old Testament tabernacle, the Holy of Holies, and all the cleansing rituals? This is one of my favorite Bible topics. We'll study this historical tent, what it meant for the Israelites, and the symbolism that flows out of it to us today. In the Old Testament specifications of the structures, laws, and rituals, all I see is perfect love pointing to a perfectly loving God. All the holiness that we can never attain, God points to through the tabernacle and fulfills for us through the death and resurrection of His Son, Jesus.

---

2   Exodus 31:1–6.
3   There are many other references in the Bible describing God's dwelling with us. Exodus 15:17–18; Leviticus 26:11–12; Ezekiel 37:27–28; Zechariah 3:10–11.
4   Hebrews 8:5.

The precision and care God takes for the inhuman, inanimate sanctuary of His holiness that He's trying to establish outside our hearts tells us about how much precision and care He takes to bring His holiness to life inside us, His very human, animate temples. The God of the universe wants to *meet* with us and *dwell* with us. He says so: "That I may dwell in their midst," "there I will meet with you," "there I will meet with the people of Israel," "I will dwell among the people of Israel," "that I might dwell among them," and "I shall meet with you."[5] This will all come full circle as we end in Revelation 21:3, where God says He wants to dwell not only with Israel but with all believers for all of eternity. To what measures does He go in order to prepare us for moving day? God is moving in—into our hearts. He is worthy of the best. On our own, our best is never enough. The bottom line is this: God's presence is all we need. It was enough for God's people when He dwelled in a physical tent, the Holy of Holies, and it's enough when He pitches His eternal tent inside our souls.

The precision and care God takes for the inhuman, inanimate sanctuary of His holiness that He's trying to establish outside our hearts tells us about how much precision and care He takes to bring His holiness to life inside us, His very human, animate temples.

Let's be readers of the Word and camp out in this beautiful historical narrative of the tabernacle to see how God's very indwelling gives us more than we need to make us perfect bringers of His light as He tabernacles within us. I can't say it enough: we are never enough; He is enough. This might be a hard pill for some of us to swallow because of all that culture throws at us regarding our enoughness. Just so we're on the same page, Webster's dictionary defines *enough* as, "plenty to go around; enough of something for all the people who want or need it." This describes God and only God, not us. Anyone who tells you that you are enough is selling

---

5 Exodus 25:8, 22, 29:45–46, 30:36.

something. I'm here to tell you that God living in us is what we need; there's plenty to go around, and what He has for us is unlimited and free. His free gift is beautifully pictured in the tabernacle, perfectly completed in Christ, and permanently placed by Him in the soul saved by grace.[6] Go read Exodus 25–30 in one sitting. I love reading Scripture aloud as if I'm sitting in front of little kids. This expressive audible reading helps me get a grasp on conveying what is being said to my own listening ears.

God living in us is what we need; there's plenty to go around, and what He has for us is unlimited and free. His free gift is beautifully pictured in the tabernacle, perfectly completed in Christ, and permanently placed by Him in the soul saved by grace.

To give us historical context, God dictated the content of these chapters to Moses face-to-face on Mount Sinai.[7] It was only six weeks,[8] give or take, after the Israelites exodus-ed[9] out of Egypt. It was just over a month after "Israel saw the great power that the Lord used against the Egyptians"[10] at the Red Sea. Their newfound freedom from the bondage of ancient Egyptian slavery was fresh. Though without a physical home at this point in the story, the plans for their spiritual habitat were on their way. The physical tabernacle would point to the One Who provided stability in every sphere (Jesus). The tabernacle instructions are laid out in these categories (with corresponding references in the footnotes):

---

6   Ephesians 2:8.
7   Exodus 24:12–18.
8   Exodus 16:1.
9   Exodus 12:33–40, 14:1–30.
10   Exodus 14:31.

TABERNACLE INSTRUCTIONS (EXODUS 25-30)

1. The Contributions for the Sanctuary.[11]
2. The Ark of the Covenant.[12]
3. The Table for Bread.[13]
4. The Golden Lampstand.[14]
5. The Tabernacle Doors: The Screen and the Veil.[15]
6. The Bronze Altar.[16]
7. The Court of the Tabernacle.[17]
8. The Oil of the Lamp.[18]
9. The Priest's Garments.[19]
10. The Consecration of the Priests.[20]
11. The Altar of Incense.[21]
12. The Census Tax.[22]
13. The Bronze Basin.[23]
14. The Anointing Oil and Incense.[24]

I'll try to simplify from my personal reading and study what all this means. Think of it as *Tabernacle-Building for Dummies*. And, of course, let's pray that the Holy Spirit teaches us in our study. Pause and pray now.

---

11 Exodus 25:1–9.
12 Exodus 25:10–22.
13 Exodus 25:23–30.
14 Exodus 25:31–40.
15 Exodus 26.
16 Exodus 27:1–8.
17 Exodus 27:9–19.
18 Exodus 27:20–21.
19 Exodus 28.
20 Exodus 29.
21 Exodus 30:1–10.
22 Exodus 30:11–16.
23 Exodus 30:17–21.
24 Exodus 30:22–38.

1. THE CONTRIBUTIONS FOR THE SANCTUARY

Exodus 25:1–9

Before anything could be built, supplies were needed. These supplies were material offerings given freely by each person from their own means. Their possessions most likely came from plunder from the Egyptians when God's people left Egypt.[25] Do you remember that story? Pharaoh said, "Go!" and "the Egyptians were urgent with the people [Israelites] to send them out of the land in haste. For they said, 'We shall all be dead.' … And the Lord had given the people favor in the sight of the Egyptians, so that they let them have what they asked. Thus they plundered the Egyptians."[26] The Israelites had a lot of bounty to donate to the tabernacle, giving it back to God in worship. The tabernacle supply list puts back-to-school shopping to shame. But just like a teacher intentionally lists all the supplies needed for a successful education, so God purposefully hands Moses a *back-to-Yahweh* supply list for His people's sanctification location so they can have the best possible first-hand education of Him and intimacy with Him.

---

*God purposefully hands Moses a **back-to-Yahweh** supply list for His people's sanctification location so they can have the best possible first-hand education of Him and intimacy with Him.*

So what's on the list and why is it there? As we can see, this was no ordinary tent. Here's a tabernacle cheat sheet to make it easier.[27]

---

25   Exodus 36:3, 6.
26   Exodus 12:33–36.
27   *Bible-History.com*, https://www.bible-history.com/tabernacle/tab4preparing_for_the_tabernacle.htm. Accessed May 8, 2021.

TABERNACLE CHEAT SHEET

SUPPLY / COLOR / ANIMAL	MEANING / SYMBOLISM
Gold	Holiness, Deity
Silver	Redemption, Untarnished
Bronze	Judgement, Uncleanness
Blue	Heaven
Purple	Royalty
Scarlet / Red	Sacrifice
Linen	Purity, Holiness, Defense against Judgement
Goat	Cursed
Ram	Substitutionary Sacrifice
Lamb	Perfect Sacrifice, Jesus
Badger Skin	Unattractive, Outward Appearance
Acacia Wood	Durable, Hard to Work With, Doesn't Rot, Hard Human Heart, Jesus' Incorruptible Humanity
Oil	Holy Spirit
Incense	Fragrance of Worship, Pleasing to God
Gemstones	Value and Holiness in Christ, Points to Heaven as Our Future Home

2. THE ARK OF THE COVENANT AND 3. THE TABLE FOR BREAD

Exodus 25:10–30

Maybe you've heard of the Ark of the Covenant, thanks to Indiana Jones. But what the Bible says about the ark is entirely different than you might have seen in that movie. First and foremost, the ark represented God's presence in the midst of His people, specifically the lid, or the mercy seat. This was the first item God laid out to Moses, as it was central to gaining access to God and worshiping God as well as pointing to our need for a Messiah, Jesus. The ark was a box made from gold-covered wood. These two mediums were opposites yet mingled together to create this most exquisite and meaningful tabernacle furnishing. This box is everything to us in that it foreshadowed Jesus. The gold represented His deity, and the wood represented His humanity, both of which were essential for Him to be the perfect atoning sacrifice.[28]

The gold represented His deity, and the wood represented His humanity, both of which were essential for Him to be the perfect atoning sacrifice.

On top of the ark, or the lid, was the mercy seat and the cherubim, or angels of judgment—all made of gold. The two cherubim were on either end facing each other with outspread wings to cover the center of the lid, the mercy seat. These angels represented God's righteous rule and were executors of God's righteous judgment.[29] Once a year, on the Day of Atonement,[30] the High Priest sprinkled blood on the mercy seat[31] underneath the wings and gaze of the cherubim. God's holy wrath was satisfied

---

28   Colossians 1:15–20.
29   *Bible-History.com*, https://www.bible-history.com/tabernacle/tab4the_ curtain_coverings.htm. Accessed May 8, 2021.
30   Leviticus 16.
31   Leviticus 16:14.

through the symbolic gaze of these judgment angels as they looked upon the blood.[32] Back then, God saw the animals' blood, and His wrath was satisfied (once a year),[33] making an atonement (or way) for the Israelites to meet with Him. The same is true for us today as God sees the blood of Jesus, which satisfied God's wrath (once for all).[34] This atonement makes meeting with Him possible. Note that the tabernacle sacrifices were never once-for-all, therefore there were no chairs for the priests to rest because their work was never finished. Sounds exhausting, doesn't it? It was. We'll discuss this concept in the next chapter, as Christ's sacrifice was once-for-all, showcased by the fact that He sat down, as Hebrews 8:1 declares.

The tabernacle sacrifices were never once-for-all,
therefore there were no chairs for the priests
to rest because their work was never finished.

Do you grasp God's holiness, love, and pursuit of His people in all these details? It all pointed to the fact that He would sacrifice His only Son in order to gain us as His sons and daughters. God didn't just have His people slap together a tabernacle and all its fixtures, especially the Ark of the Covenant, like one of those premade kits we buy at the craft store. Neither does He slap us together to prepare us for His indwelling and daily relationship.

So what was in the Ark of the Covenant? What was on the table for bread? The ark contained the Ten Commandments written by God on stone tablets, manna (bread), and Aaron's rod. These items were reminders of God's covenant relationship with His people, conveyed through His law, His provision, and His power. The table for bread was made the same way as the Ark of the Covenant—acacia wood covered in gold. On the table sat

---

32 *Bible-History.com*, https://www.bible-history.com/tabernacle/tab4the_ark_of_the_covenant.htm. Accessed May, 8, 2021.
33 Leviticus 17:11.
34 Hebrews 10:10.

bread *at all times*, symbolizing the future Bread of Life,[35] the coming of the Messiah. After Jesus came, He left us His Spirit, Who like the bread on the table of the tabernacle was and always will be available to us. Spiritually speaking, God never calls us to be grain-free—that is, to do it on our own. The Bread of Life (Jesus) is vital nourishment to our spiritual gut. This is what Jesus said in His "Not Today, satan" speech (also known as the temptation) found in Matthew 4:4. Jesus quoted this from Deuteronomy 8:3: "But He answered, 'It is written, 'Man shall not live by bread alone, but by every word that comes from the mouth of God.'" Jesus' answers demonstrated His intentional and sole reliance on the very words of God, His living nourishment.

4. THE GOLDEN LAMPSTAND

Exodus 25:31–40

This iconic lamp is also known as a menorah. 1 Samuel 3:3 calls it the lamp of God … so beautiful. It had seven branches and was made of one solid piece of gold in an exact measured weight. It truly is a stunning piece of art. To the Jews, the menorah symbolized God's truth (wisdom).[36] For believers, Christ fulfilled all of this at Calvary. Jesus was the personified incarnation of all that the lampstand declared.

Jesus was the personified incarnation of all that the lampstand declared.

---

35   John 6:48, 51.
36   *Oneforisrael.org,* https://www.oneforisrael.org/bible-based-teaching-from-israel/the-meaning-behind-the-menorah/. Accessed May 8, 2021.

When the temple veil tore in two, "the miraculous center light of the menorah began to shine throughout the whole world"[37] in the person of Christ. What a stunning truth as the symbolism of the menorah's actual light became a reality in a very Person, Christ ("the Light of the world"). For us as Christ-followers and children adopted into God's family, Jesus' total work here on earth was foreshadowed in the lampstand.[38] To believers today, the menorah's light points to heaven's eternal lamp: the "lamp is the Lamb"[39] and "they will need no light of lamp or sun, for the Lord God will be their light."[40] Like this beautiful golden lampstand, we are mini versions of Jesus and His light. We are to be His little menorahs of a sort-lampstands of our Light-of-the-world, "mini-mes" of our Indweller.

37 *Hebrew4christians.com*, https://www.hebrew4christians.com/Scripture/Parashah/Summaries/Tetzaveh/Menorah/menorah.html. Accessed May 8, 2021.
38 John 8:12.
39 Revelation 21:23.
40 Revelation 22:5.

5. THE TABERNACLE

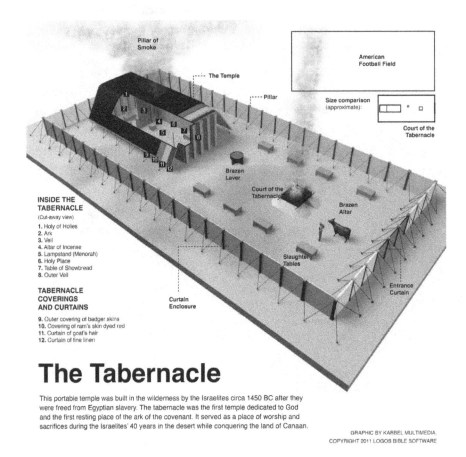

INSIDE THE TABERNACLE
(Cut-away view)

1. Holy of Holies
2. Ark
3. Veil
4. Altar of Incense
5. Lampstand (Menorah)
6. Holy Place
7. Table of Showbread
8. Outer Veil

TABERNACLE COVERINGS AND CURTAINS

9. Outer covering of badger skins
10. Covering of ram's skin dyed red
11. Curtain of goat's hair
12. Curtain of fine linen

The Tabernacle

This portable temple was built in the wilderness by the Israelites circa 1450 BC after they were freed from Egyptian slavery. The tabernacle was the first temple dedicated to God and the first resting place of the ark of the covenant. It served as a place of worship and sacrifices during the Israelites' 40 years in the desert while conquering the land of Canaan.

GRAPHIC BY KARBEL MULTIMEDIA.
COPYRIGHT 2011 LOGOS BIBLE SOFTWARE

Now it's barn raising time. The tabernacle was spectacular, both actually and transcendentally. This was no REI or North Face product. This tent had three sections: 1) the outer court, 2) the Holy Place, and 3) the Holy of Holies. These rooms were structured by curtains, clasps, coverings, frames, the veil, and the screen. Its ten inner curtains were made of blue/purple/red linen and woven with cherubim (pictures of angels).[41] Here, the symbolism foreshadowing Jesus the Messiah cannot be overlooked: blue shows Jesus as God, purple shows Jesus as King, red shows Jesus as human, and

---

41   Exodus 26:1.

linen shows Jesus' purity and holiness.[42] Next, the tabernacle's eleven outer curtains were made of goats' hair.[43] Clasps held these curtains together. Now, I know you didn't pick up this book to get a degree in Biblical clasp knowledge, but you're going to get one anyway. It's actually quite simple yet profound. The clasps on the outside were made of bronze.[44] The clasps on the inside were made of gold.[45] Here's why:

> Exodus gives instructions that the items inside the tabernacle (the [lampstand], incense altar, showbread table, and of course the Ark of the Covenant itself) were to be made of gold, but everything outside the tent was bronze. ...Gold is symbolic of God's kingship, glory, and holiness. ... Certainly there is a clear divide: gold inside, bronze outside. ... The sin and uncleanness were dealt with at the altar and the bronze [basin]. Bronze is where God's judgment deals with sin—only then can a person enter the pure and holy presence of God.[46]

The bronze clasps, being of lesser value and placed on the exterior, represented our sinful state outside of Christ, as well as the separation that sin created and consequential judgment due. On the other hand, the gold clasps, being of the highest value and placed in the interior, showed God's glory made available, especially now to us as we are "in Christ." The gold clasps are symbolic links to the Gospel. Once "clasped" in Christ, God no longer sees the judgment that is due us but rather the worth Christ gives us. [47] Christ's it-is-finished[48] moment symbolically comes out of the Old Testament tabernacle gold clasp. God never wastes a detail, does He? This

---

42 1 Peter 1:19.
43 Exodus 26:7.
44 Exodus 26:11.
45 Exodus 26:6.
46 Oneforisrael.com, https://www.oneforisrael.org/bible-based-teaching-from-israel/the-meaning-of-bronze-in-the-bible/. Accessed May 9, 2021.
47 2 Corinthians 5:21.
48 John 19:30.

Biblical account is yet another reason why we are joy-bearers and have Christ's shine-status. This is why we are hope-dealers and light-bringers. All the joy, hope, and light that adorn Jesus now adorn us as we point to Him.

The gold clasps are symbolic links to the Gospel. Once "clasped" in Christ, God no longer sees the judgment that is due us but rather the worth Christ gives us.

Next, the roof and top coverings of the tabernacle were made of rams' skins, goats' skins, and badgers' skins.[49] The further outward and upward away from the innermost room where God dwelled, the less valuable were the building supplies. The point—stay close to Him! Holding all these curtains and coverings together to make the tabernacle structure were frames and bars made of acacia wood.[50] They were covered in gold,[51] just like the Ark of the Covenant and the table for bread. Imagine all the gold in every direction! How grand and holy this place must have looked and felt. The closest thing I can imagine to this is Versailles' famous Hall of Mirrors. Imagine what the inside of our hearts look like once God has done His saving and sanctifying soul-raising inside us through His Holy Spirit.

THE TABERNACLE DOORS: THE SCREEN AND THE VEIL

Exodus 26

Now let's look at the two beautiful and meaningful partitions inside the tabernacle: the screen and the veil. Studying the screen and the veil leaves me speechless every time. Let's look at these curtains from an Old Testament

---

49   Exodus 26:14.
50   Exodus 26:15.
51   Exodus 26:29.

perspective—what God told Moses, who then told the Israelites. In my next chapter, "Perfect High Priest," we'll see the New Testament meaning of these ornate fabric doors. These fabric doors represented Israel's separation from a holy God. In the Old Testament tabernacle, to enter into the Holy Place (the first room) one had to pass through a beautiful linen door, embroidered with cherubim in vibrant blue, purple, and scarlet yarn.[52] This was called the screen. It was the front door (and only door signifying the truth that there is one way, not many ways, to God) into the tabernacle. Before passing through the screen,[53] the high priest and priests had to first wash themselves and make a blood sacrifice on the bronze altar[54] in order to meet with God. Exodus 29:42–46 describes this connection.

> It shall be a regular burnt offering throughout your generations at the entrance of the tent of meeting before the Lord, where I will meet with you, to speak to you there. There I will meet with the people of Israel, and it shall be sanctified by my glory. I will consecrate the tent of meeting and the altar. Aaron also and his sons I will consecrate to serve me as priests. I will dwell among the people of Israel and will be their God. And they shall know that I am the Lord their God, who brought them out of the land of Egypt that I might dwell among them. I am the Lord their God.

The Most High God wanted to meet with them, speak to them, and be their God! And He wants to meet with us, speak to us, and be our God! Back then, the people needed the priests or else they had no way to come through the door and prepare to meet with God. Today, the screen represents Jesus' perfect humanity and highlights Him as *the dividing line to keep all that is unclean outside of God's dwelling place.*

---

52 Exodus 26:36.
53 Exodus 30:17–21.
54 Exodus 40:6; Leviticus 1:5, 11.

Not only was there the screen into the Holy Place, but there was the veil into the Holy of Holies, the second room. The veil was made the same as the screen.[55] Only once a year, on the Day of Atonement, could the high priest pass through the veil into the Holy of Holies to meet with God.[56] For us, the veil represents Jesus' torn flesh (at His death) and divine power (over death) as *the opening for passage of all that is clean into God's dwelling.* We pass through Jesus, our screen, into the Holy Place, and then we pass through Jesus, our veil, into the Holy of Holies.[57] "God's goal is not for us to merely enter into the Holy of Holies, where we can enjoy something of God or of Christ, but for us to be brought fully into God Himself and have a direct contact with Him, in His glory, being one with Him, for the fulfillment of His heart's desire,"[58] and our heart's desire. As believers, this is our greatest moment! Fast forward with me into the New Testament.

---

*Today, the screen represents Jesus' perfect humanity and highlights Him as **the dividing line to keep all that is unclean outside of God's dwelling place.** ...The veil represents Jesus' torn flesh (at His death) and divine power (over death) as **the opening for passage of all that is clean into God's dwelling.***

Do you understand the life-changing significance of what happened to the temple veil in the New Testament when Christ died on the cross? Matthew 27:51 and Mark 15:38 both give an account: "The curtain of the temple was torn in two, from top to bottom." Just imagine if you and I were around when this happened. What if this had happened back in the Old Testament tent before God's glory left the Holy of Holies? What if the priests saw into the protected Holy of Holies without first being washed? What if they gazed into God's presence and didn't die? Like Isaiah, this

---

55   Exodus 26:31–35.
56   Exodus 30:10.
57   *Agodman.com*, https://www.agodman.com/spiritual-application-the-veil-screen-tabernacle-exo-26/. Accessed May 9, 2021.
58   Ibid.

should leave us *undone*.[59] Rather than God's holiness smiting us dead, it transfers out through the torn veil of Christ's flesh and delivers the highest-of-heights and deepest-of-depths of Christ's holiness in love to us. The symbolism of our reality cannot be missed!

> The veil was obviously thick enough to obstruct anyone from seeing into the Holy of Holies, so it would have been hard to rip, whatever thickness it was. But rather than emphasizing the miracle of it being rent because of its "thickness," the Bible draws our attention to the "height" of the veil. "And the veil of the temple was rent in twain from the top to the bottom." That was a long way up there (30'), and then all the way down to the bottom (floor level). No man has a reach that great, or the strength. It had to have been someone much higher and greater than man to rip it in two. And we know who that "Someone" is. Hebrews 10:19-20 says, "Having therefore, brethren, boldness to enter into the holiest by the blood of Jesus, by a new and living way, which he hath consecrated for us, through the veil, that is to say, his flesh."[60]

There's our way! He's our way. He actually calls Himself the Way[61] and the Door.[62] This fact alone, considering all we've just read from God's Word, should make us overflow with love for our Savior and gratitude for what our saving cost Him. I hope you will never again read these New Testament words the same: "The curtain of the temple was torn in two."[63] My eyes are watering with tears of gratitude and awe as I write this. It takes me to

---

59   Isaiah 6:5, NKJV.
60   *Libertygospeltracts.com*, http://www.libertygospeltracts.com/question/prequest/veiloftemple.htm. Accessed May 9, 2021.
61   John 14:16.
62   John 10:7–9; 2 Peter 1:11.
63   Mark 15:38.

the lines found in numerous Christian songs, "My anchor holds within the veil."[64]

Jesus is our Anchor Who holds us firm to Himself—away from our sin, in the midst of His holiness—within the veil. This means we can chuck the veil. The old covenant (the promised Messiah to Abraham)[65] is fulfilled; the new covenant (Jesus for all, Jews and Gentiles)[66] has come. It's God and us, face-to-face. This is what Moses experienced. "And there has not arisen a prophet since in Israel like Moses, whom the Lord knew face-to-face."[67] God's presence came out of the actual Holy of Holies and became available to tabernacle in us. His Holy Spirit now indwells our hearts, something the Israelites were desperately and exhaustively working towards all day every day, with no avail.

Jesus is our Anchor Who holds us firm to Himself—away from our sin, in the midst of His holiness—within the veil.

For to this day, when they read the old covenant, that same veil remains unlifted, because only through Christ is it taken away. Yes, to this day whenever Moses is read a veil lies over their hearts. But when one turns to the Lord, the veil is removed. Now the Lord is the Spirit, and where the Spirit of the Lord is, there is freedom. And we all, with unveiled face, beholding the glory of the Lord, are being transformed into the same image from one degree of glory to another. For this comes from the Lord Who is the Spirit.

2 Corinthians 3:14–18

---

64   Hymnsuntogod.org, https://www.hymnsuntogod.org/Hymns-PD/T-Hymns/The-Solid-Rock.html. Accessed May 9, 2021.
65   Genesis 12:2–3, 26:4; Jeremiah 31:31–33; Ezekiel 34:25–31.
66   Isaiah 61:8; Acts 3:25; Hebrews 13:20.
67   Deuteronomy 34:10.

We'll come back to this wonderful truth in the next chapter. Let's finish studying the remaining items in our study of the tabernacle.

6. THE BRONZE ALTAR AND 7. THE COURT OF THE TABERNACLE

Exodus 27:1–19

The bronze altar was in the outer court, called the court of the tabernacle. This courtyard was the place for atoning sacrifices to be made. The bronze altar was a large bronze platform for animal sacrifice. Note that its bronze material symbolized judgment and the sacrifice of a life that it required. As we continually focus on God wanting to dwell with His people, we see the impediment of their sin and their need for protection from its effects—atonement by blood. This is where the bronze altar came in as a temporary way to meet with God. The animal's blood temporarily satisfied the holiness of God and provisionally covered the unrighteousness of humans—until the final spotless Lamb arrived many years later on a starry night in Bethlehem.[68] Once the blood sacrifice was made in the court of the tabernacle, the priests could enter the Holy Place, or the high priest could go further into the Holy of Holies. Let's follow the priests inside God's tent to behold His glory and be sanctified by it.[69]

---

68 Jesus was born in a stable outside of Bethlehem near the place (Migdal Eder, the flock tower) where the spotless lambs were prepared for temple sacrifice in that day. The temple shepherds would have immediately recognized Jesus as the spotless Lamb. Thirty years later, John the Baptist recognized Jesus as the perfect lamb: *"Behold, the Lamb of God who takes away the sin of the world." Hub,* https://biblehub.com/topical/m/migdal-eder.htm. Accessed May 9, 2021. Micah 4:8, John 1:29.
69 Exodus 29:43.

8. THE OIL OF THE LAMP

Exodus 27:20–21

We've seen that what goes on inside this tent far exceeds glamping. The two rooms were made with curtains as explained above. Also, inside the tent was the oil burning in the golden lampstand in the Holy Place. This oil was made from olives, hand-beaten (crushed) rather than pressed. This process points to Christ being crushed on the cross, as Isaiah 53:10 says: "Yet it pleased the Lord to crush Him." The pureness of the oil that comes from this process symbolized God's Holy Spirit and His purifying work of habitating with us. Through His presence, He causes pure light to shine from our lives. Of course, displaying His glory inside our heart-scape is what's most valuable to God. And from a pure heart, lived-in by God Himself, we get our new eyes to see God as He meets with us. And where God is, He brings the light. From the inside out, the priests were continually purified and given the task to keep this physical lamp with all its symbolism always lit, always shining. From the inside out, we are continually purified and empowered to outwardly shine the light that is at work within us. Moving on, this is exactly what the priests' garments, their outerwear, exemplified. Let's see what they wore.

9. THE PRIEST'S GARMENTS

Exodus 28

The priest's garments included the ephod (waistcoat with shoulder straps), the breastplate, and a blue robe. This was a sacred wardrobe, exclusive to the priests. The priest's garments,[70] just like everything else in the tabernacle, were symbolic and sacred. The priest was the only one who wore these garments. He wore a blue linen robe, called an ephod, with a gem-covered

---

70   *Biblehistory.com*, https://www.bible-history.com/tabernacle/tab4the_
priestly_garments.htm. Accessed May, 9, 2021.

breastplate hanging on the front of it. I encourage you to look up a picture of this stunning, one-of-a-kind breastplate. The two clasps that held the ephod together were made of onyx stones and had engraved into them the names of the twelve tribes of Israel. Don't miss the significance here: one breastplate comprised of twelve stones showed one people comprised of twelve tribes, all working together in one collective masterpiece, led by God. The woven breastplate had a pocket in which were two stones, the Urim and Thummim, which stood for God's divine wisdom.

The high priest's designer outfit shouted, "Look at God. Look at God's glory. Look at God's beauty. Look at God's holiness. Look at God's precision and care." Obviously, the priest's garments were representations of God's glory. Believers today, similar to the Old Testament priests, showcase God's glory as His living raiments. In addition to the wardrobe, cleanliness was a virtue.

The high priest's designer outfit shouted, "Look at God. Look at God's glory. Look at God's beauty. Look at God's holiness. Look at God's precision and care."

---

10. THE CONSECRATION OF THE PRIESTS

Exodus 29

Ceremonial washings, consecration rituals, and offerings of animals and food were a daily part of the priests' lives. The consecration of the priests was some serious business. This wasn't God putting antibacterial hand-wipes in the outer courtyard with a sign that said, "Take one." Sin is a messy business. Bulls, rams, and lambs were sacrificed on the altar. Blood was everywhere, literally *everywhere*. The red was a constant visual reminder, a sobering one. This blood was a temporary covering over sin until the final sacrifice, Jesus, the Lamb of God, arrived.[71]

The red was a constant visual reminder, a sobering one.
This blood was a temporary covering over sin until the final
sacrifice, Jesus, the Lamb of God, arrived.

God wanted His people to see how serious sin was (and for us, still is). These ceremonies and rituals were painstaking. Sometimes they took days. Some of them came with a warning label: "So that they will not die."[72] Special unleavened bread was made and offered to the Lord. Heads were anointed with oil. Meat was cooked and eaten. Just outside the Holy of Holies was the Altar of Incense, which was used once a year on the Day of Atonement.[73] These instructions point to one thing and one thing only: HOLINESS, what God is and what we are not. The Good News is that truly holy things make other things holy.

HOLINESS, what God is and what we are not. The Good News
is that truly holy things make other things holy.

Jesus' cleansing is much more than the matriarchal holler out the open back door: "Kids, wash your hands and come in for dinner!" The call from our patriarch God is more like, "Dear children, let *Me* wash your heart, and then come in for the eternal meal of a lifetime—Living Water and Bread of Life to enjoy with Me forever." It's what Yahweh told Israel throughout the Old Testament. It's what Jesus told the woman at the well in John 4:10, 14: "If you knew the gift of God, and Who it is that is saying it to you, 'Give me

---

71 John 1:36.
72 Exodus 30:20–21.
73 Leviticus 23:26–32.

a drink,' you would have asked Him, and He would have given you living water." It's what Jesus told His disciples in John 6:51: "I am the Living Bread that came down from heaven." It's what our High Priest tells us today. We'll read about Jesus as our High Priest in the next chapter. When God gave Moses all these instructions for the ceremonial washing, consecration, and offerings of the priests, God was revealing His love as a Father and His goal to gather His unholy people back to His holy Self. He shows us this continual pursuit through the next tabernacle items.

11. THE ALTAR OF INCENSE AND
12. THE CENSUS TAX

Exodus 30:1–16

The altar of incense was smaller than the bronze altar, and it was made of gold, rather than bronze. We know why—it was closer to God's dwelling place and therefore had to be made of the purest element. It had a golden square crown with four golden horns on it and was located inside the Holy Place, just outside the Holy of Holies. The priests burned fragrant incense twice a day on it. Once a year on the Day of Atonement, the priest sprinkled blood on it: "Aaron [the high priest] shall make atonement on its horns once a year. With the blood of the sin offering of atonement he shall make atonement for it once a year throughout your generations. It is most holy to the Lord."[74] Atonement always comes with a price, a price too great for anyone to pay except for Jesus (go ahead, applaud Him for this). "Jesus paid it all, all to Him we owe; sin had left a crimson stain; He washed it white as snow.[75]

---

74   Exodus 30:10.
75   Elvina Hall, "Jesus Paid It All," 1865, *Timeless Truths,* https://library. timelesstruths.org/music/Jesus_Paid_It_All/. Accessed May 1, 2021.

Atonement always comes with a price, a price too great for anyone to pay except for Jesus (go ahead, applaud Him for this).

To remind the Israelites of their blood-bought redemption, God commanded them to pay a census tax. This was a small payment of half a shekel[76] per person to the tabernacle. The amount was negligible, so all were able to pay it. Again, it was yet another reminder of God's promised purchase of them looking forward to His assured Messiah, through Whom God purchases all who believe in Him.

13. THE BRONZE BASIN AND
14. THE ANOINTING OIL AND INCENSE

Exodus 30:17–38

The bronze basin—also called the laver—was a large bowl where the priests washed their hands and feet after sacrifice on the bronze altar, prior to entering through the screen and after exiting the Holy Place. Why all this washing? Notice the bronze basin came after the altar (sacrifice first); it came before the door (washing before entering); and it came after leaving the Holy Place (wash before going out).[77] This basin was to make God's priests worthy to come into His presence on behalf of His people. God also did this through the anointing oil and incense[78] to make everything about His Holy Place, including those in it, a sweet aroma consecrated to Him.

The anointing oil was the same as the oil of the lamp. The oil was used to anoint the tabernacle and its furniture and to light the golden lampstand. The incense, constantly rising up, never stopping, always burning "tells us of the ministry of Jesus as our Intercessor Whose prayers never

---

76 Exodus 30:13.
77 *Bible-History.com*, https://www.bible-history.com/tabernacle/tab4the_bronze_laver.htm. Accessed May 9, 2021.
78 Exodus 30:34-38.

stop ascending to God for us."[79] God was drawing them then, and He's drawing us now. This is a timeless, cross-cultural, principle of leaning into God … as close as we can get. The further away from the Divine and His cleansing, the more likely we are to be just what we are—a human mess.

God was drawing them then, and He's drawing us now. This is a timeless, cross-cultural, principle of leaning into God … as close as we can get.

The principle was the same throughout the entire tabernacle. The further you moved from the Holy of Holies the less valuable were the materials used. And the lesson for us is that in the presence of God there is beauty and purity (gold) and as you move away back out into the world there is only judgment (bronze) and a need of continual cleansing.[80]

Lean in, my friends, lean in. God's purifying presence is ever and always available to you. Come as you are, throw open the throne room doors and lay at His feet. He'll take care of the rest.

SACRED INTRICACIES

Please don't tell me the book of Exodus with all its tent-making details is dull. The intricacies of the Old Testament tabernacle are invaluable to us, just as our intricacies are invaluable as the scaffolding of our faith and testament of our God inside us. To reiterate, if God takes such precision

---

79   *Bible-History.com*, https://www.bible-history.com/tabernacle/tab4the_golden_altar_of_incense.htm. Accessed May 9, 2021.
80   *Bible-History.com*, https://www.bible-history.com/tabernacle/tab4the_curtain_coverings.htm. Accessed May 9, 2021.

and care for the inhuman, inanimate sanctuary of His holiness that He has established outside our hearts, what does this tell us about how much precision and care He takes to bring His holiness to life inside us, His very human, animate temples? God's below-the-surface details are our sacred intricacies. These are the details of holiness. God sees inside us; He sees our intricate scaffolding. If He hasn't yet met with us, He knows it and so do we. That means you are not made of Him. He longs to be your High Priest. Stop trying to duct tape the veil back together and do things on your own. He can level your broken ground and tabernacle in you. How about trading your fit-pitching for God's tent-pitching? How about exchanging your aroma of death for Christ's aroma of life?[81] We are the fragrance of God to the world!

TOGETHERING WITH THE MOST HIGH GOD

Conversely, for those who have boldly approached the throne of grace[82] and said, "Pitch your tent," God hears you and sees what you are made of—Him. He makes your heart a very holy of holies in which He can dwell. He is the Master of setting up camp. He has removed the stones, twigs, and hazards in your heart so the ground sheet of your very core is now built upon the Rock.[83] He has taken out the slack and hammered in the pegs, which doesn't always feel good. He has unpacked His unlimited tent supplies. The poles are up. The tent is raised. His glory is at work. His hand is your rain-cover when storms come.[84] He has moved in. Deuteronomy 33:27 says, "The eternal God is your dwelling place, and underneath are the everlasting arms."[85] This dwelling in us foreshadows heaven, as Revelation 21:3 reports: "Behold, the *dwelling place* of God is *with* man. He will *dwell with*

---

81 2 Corinthians 2:15–16.

82 Hebrews 4:16.

83 The wise man built his house upon the rock. Matthew 7:24–27.

84 "And the rain fell, and the floods came, and the winds blew and beat on that house, but it did not fall, because it had been founded on the rock." Matthew 7:24–27.

85 Deuteronomy 33:27.

them, and they will be His people, and God Himself will be *with* them as their God" (italics added). Guess what the words *dwelling place* and *dwell* mean in the original language? The first means a "tabernacle, tent, abode, dwelling, habitation, inmost sanctuary."[86] The second means to "have one's tent, dwell, have my tabernacle, pitch a tent, live in a tent."[87] Now let's look at what *with* means. It means "among, in company with, accompanied, companioning, togethering."[88] Allow me to rewrite Revelation 21:3, elaborating on the highlighted words from their original language:

> Behold, the dwelling place, the tabernacle, the tent, the abode, the dwelling, the habitation, the inmost sanctuary of God is in company with man and woman. He will dwell with, tabernacle, pitch His tent and companion with them, and they will be His people, and God Himself will be togethering with them as their God.

I love that the Greek language turns *together* into a verb and preposition of connection—*togethering*, like connecting *God* and *them* in a linguistic hug. Just think of the Most High God *togethering* with us! The best translation is the word *dwell*. We see that John, the author of Revelation who was also a disciple of Jesus, weds his knowledge of the Old Testament tabernacle with his first-hand experience of being with Jesus as well as being at Pentecost,[89] when God the Holy Spirit literally came to inhabit hearts. John witnessed this indwelling first-hand. He was first-gen indwelt! John, like Moses, knows the *companioning with* and *togethering with* that are a part of God pitching His tent and tabernacling in us. The Gospel comes straight out of the tabernacle, ripping the veil in two on its way to us.

The Word-reader in us sees that God the Father sent God the Son to give us God the Holy Spirit Who now dwells in us. The light-bringer in us knows that God's presence living inside us is all we need. So let's go shine *that* to the watching world: to our God-given spouses, to our God-picked

---

86   *Bible Hub*, https://biblehub.com/greek/4633.htm. Accessed May 9, 2021.
87   *Bible Hub*, https://biblehub.com/greek/4637.htm. Accessed May 2, 2021.
88   *Bible Hub*, https://biblehub.com/greek/3326.htm. Accessed May 9, 2021.
89   Acts 2:1–4.

children, to our work crew, to our tent-worthy family, to our tentless audience, to our Jesus-freak tribe, and especially to our own listening ears. No matter what comes our way, God living inside us is our confidence to help us in time of need.[90]

The Word-reader in us sees that God the Father sent God the Son to give us God the Holy Spirit Who now dwells in us. The light-bringer in us knows that God's presence living inside us is all we need.

---

90   Hebrews 4:16.

PRAYER

God,
Establish Your presence right here in me.
Use everything needed to consecrate me to You.
Exhaust Your supplies to clothe me in Your righteousness.
Exchange my clasps of bronze for clasps of gold, so that all You see is
the pure gold of Jesus living in me.
Make my heart solid ground upon which Your tent can be raised up,
held secure by the pegs of Your love, Your pursuit, Your promises,
Your atonement, Your grace, Your holiness,
Your faithfulness, Your indwelling.
Come companion with me as Your Holy Spirit tabernacles in me.
Throw back the torn veil so that I can experience all the togethering
You have for me, both on earth and in heaven.
You, dear God, are my everything.
Apart from You I have no good thing.[91]
May I always know and feel that
Your presence living inside me is enough;
I am covered by the blood of the Lamb.
Amen.

---

91   Psalm 16:2.

DISCUSSION QUESTIONS

1. What is your favorite aspect of the Old Testament tabernacle and why?

2. Are you able to step away from all the tabernacle details, zoom-out away from them, and see the big picture that God is painting? According to Exodus 29:42–46, what is that big picture?

3. As a post-cross believer, how does having God's presence in you influence your daily living (in contrast to the pre-cross laws and rituals)? See Romans 8:1–4.

4. Revelation 21:3–5 shows us (the perfect bride of Christ) and God (the Eliminator of pain and Maker of all things new) in our eternal relationship together. Is your reaction to this visual from Scripture "bring it" or "oh no, I'm not ready"? Spend time right now praying in gratitude, confession, and worship.

CHAPTER 6
PERFECT HIGH PRIEST

Hebrews

What is your first thought when you hear the term "traveling salesperson"? In modern day, a traveling salesperson is "a representative of a business concern who solicits orders usually in an assigned territory" (*Merriam-Webster Dictionary*). Our omnipresent Purveyor of free grace, Jesus our High Priest, represents the business of heaven, and the human heart is His assigned territory. Do not for a second think that He solicits orders. He does not *need* the sale. He needs nothing outside of Himself. He *wants* the sale. He wants us. In His infinite love, He longs to adopt us as His own. Hebrews 1 and 2 call Jesus *supreme, superior,* and *better*. First John 3:1 calls what He did *lavish love*. He's been trying to tell us this forever. The prophet Ezekiel spoke: "It is not for your sake, O house of Israel, that I am about to act, but for the sake of My holy name … I will sprinkle clean water on you, and you shall be clean from all your uncleannesses … then [you] will know that I am the Lord."[1]

For the sake of His holy name, our High Priest furnishes our souls with His supreme goods. This side of heaven, I don't think we'll ever truly comprehend His goods—that is, what we gain from His redeeming sacrifice on

---

1   Ezekiel 36:22, 25, 38.

our behalf, with all of its eternal ramifications. This experience of unlimited access into God's presence is so much *better* than the Old Testament tabernacle and temple experiences.[2] The best fact about this holy transaction is that the purchase is not just *of us*. The true acquisition is *of Him*—we acquire Him and all that goes with Him. And as we spend time with God in His Word, we fully begin to access holy fluidity in every area of our lives with our omnipresent Mediator at our sides.

For the sake of His holy name, our High Priest furnishes our souls with His supreme goods.

FROM TRANSIENT ACTION TO ETERNAL POSITION

At the same moment of Christ's death on the cross, the actual temple veil tore in two. At salvation, the spiritual veil of our hearts rips asunder as the Spirit of our High Priest enters into our hearts and now travels with us wherever we go. In the last chapter, we discussed the power of this symbolic connection of the renting of the veil and the literal tearing of Christ's flesh on our behalf. Anyone living before Christ's resurrection needed priests, or they had no way to come through the veil into the temple and stand before God. For us today, as we stand on this side of the cross, we have a High Priest opening the unopenable door to us into the life and rest He gives. Jesus is the Door to our salvation—salvation *from* our sin and salvation *to* eternally dwelling with Him. Jesus offers rest because of the peace He delivers. There can be no peace between us and Christ while there is peace between us and sin, says Charles Spurgeon.[3] Boom! This actualization of confession, atonement, forgiveness, and holiness mobilizes Jesus' excellence, enoughness,[4] and hopeful respite upon our saved souls. In this

---

2 Hebrews 7:19, 8:6–7, 9:11, 10:14, 10:34, 12:24.
3 *Spurgeon.org*, https://www.spurgeon.org/resource-library/sermons/the-reason-why-many-cannot-find-peace/#flipbook/. Accessed May 9, 2021.
4 Hebrews 10:18.

chapter, we'll read various words from Hebrews (and a few other texts) that describe Christ as our High Priest, the God-Man Who spiritually and literally unveils our way back to God the Father through His perfect ministry. We'll see that Christ's ministry as the divinely appointed and human High Priest to New Testament Jewish believers *and* to us is this:

- A ministry "much more excellent" based on "better promises" (Hebrews 8:6).
- A relationship in which "single sacrifice for sins" atones "once for all" (Hebrews 10:10, 12).
- A foundation for our "hope," "confidence," and "full assurance" (Hebrews 3:1, 6; 10:19–22).

This actual *and* spiritual unveiling by God (of Himself to us) as our High Priest is the culmination of the Gospel message since it was first preached to us in Genesis 3:15. Our hope is in the supremacy of our High Priest, Who stomps the head of the vile deceiver with His holy heel. Take that, satan! Christ's supremacy for us today means that forgiveness is no longer the *transient action* of Old Testament law but an *eternal position* of the "it is finished" New Testament covenant.

---

*Christ's supremacy for us today means that forgiveness is no longer the **transient action** of Old Testament law but an **eternal position** of the "it is finished" New Testament covenant.*

More will be coming on this matter. Because we're delving into bigger passages of Scripture in this chapter, rather than list all the verses at the beginning as we've done prior, we'll bite off verses bit-by-bit and chew on them as we go. I encourage you to sit down and read the entire book of Hebrews in one sitting. Personally, I did this at least eight times before sitting down to research and write this chapter. The blessing from reading God's Word is everything. First and foremost, put down every book (mine included) and read The Book (God's inspired Word). Since we're discussing a Priest and forgiveness, it's important that we remind ourselves why we need to be forgiven. After you read Hebrews, turn to Genesis 2 and 3 and read about original sin, which is why we need to be rescued in the first place.[5]

HIGH PRIEST TO THE RESCUE

Our culture falsely tells us that "being real" covers a multitude of sins. Our society tells us that "being who we are" is our greatest need and goal. The Bible says the exact opposite: Jesus is our greatest goal. Sin stands in our way of getting to Him; sin is what got us off the track of communing with God in the first place. I'm finding more and more that the word *sin* offends many people. The world softens and sanitizes sin and instead uses terms like "blind spots," "areas of growth," or "woods that need clearing." "Just be true to yourself," the world preaches, "that's the best you can do."

Really? That's not the Gospel. "Being real" lands us as far away from God as we can imagine. Our blind spot of sin, if not covered by the blood of the Lamb, sends us to hell in a handbasket. The best way to be true to ourselves is to vow allegiance to the One Who is *called True,*[6] Whose Word *is true,*[7] and Who writes the book of life.[8] Can we talk about what "being real" looks like? The true state of affairs is called original sin, a topic about which fewer and fewer people are talking. It goes like this:

---

5   Romans 3:23. "Original sin" is the theological way of saying, "all humans are born sinners, no exceptions." See chart on following page.
6   Revelation 19:11.
7   Psalm 33:4.
8   Revelation 20:12, 21:27.

ORIGINAL SIN

Scriptural Wording	Modern Wording
1. "You may surely eat of every tree of the garden." (Gen. 2:16)	1. Eat your heart out (says God).
2. "Of the tree of the knowledge of good and evil you shall not eat, for in the day that you eat of it you shall surely die." (Gen. 2:17)	2. Just don't eat from this one tree; it'll kill you (says God).
3. "She [Eve] took of its fruit and ate, and she also gave some to her husband [Adam] ... and he ate." (Gen. 3:6)	3. We are all disobedient (not limited to a single action in time and space, but an eternal position of humanity).
4. "They knew that they were naked." (Gen. 3:7)	4. We all know (on the inside) we are separated from God by our sin.
5. "The Lord God made for Adam and for his wife garments of skins and clothed them." (Gen. 3:21)	5. God provided coverings on the outside for them then (blood-bought animal skins) what now Christ's blood covers on the inside for us (trades our sin for His holiness).
6. "[God] drove out the man, and at the east of the garden of Eden He placed the cherubim and a flaming sword that turned every way to guard the way to the tree of life." (Gen. 3:24)	6. The consequence of our disobedience is separation from God.

Fast-forward in the Bible from the beginning to the end. The end, Revelation 20:11–21:8, posts two lists, and everyone's name is on one list or the other:

- List One: HEIRS OF GOD—"I will be his/her God and he/she will be my son/daughter" (Revelation 21:7, 27).
- List Two: ENEMIES OF GOD—"... the cowardly, the faithless, the detestable, as for murderers, the sexually immoral, sorcerers, idolaters, and all liars" (Revelation 21:8, 20:12).

Somewhere in between Genesis and Revelation lies my life ... your life ... our lives. We are, or were, on the latter list. But as the famous hymn proclaims, our souls feel their worth based solely upon our *Savior's appearance.*[9] Before Jesus, I was a cowardly, faithless, detestable soul. No, I haven't murdered, been immoral, partaken in sorcery ... on the outside. But I've been all these things Revelation 21:8 mentions and more on the inside. I've built inner idols with my own hands and lied. Like Adam and Eve, I know my internal nakedness that needs not an outer animal covering but an inner entry (through exposure of who I really am, a sinner) back into fellowship with God. I was on list two; now I'm on list one. Apart from God, I am hole-ly. With Him, I am holy.

Like Adam and Eve, I know my internal nakedness
that needs not an outer animal covering but an inner entry
(through exposure of who I really am, a sinner)
back into fellowship with God.

We see in Genesis that at the Fall, humanity reached an impasse. This is where the book of Hebrews comes in with a rescue plan, or rather, a rescue Person. The Man with the plan is this: "Christ [as High Priest] has

9   John Sullivan Dwight (trans.) "O, Holy Night," 1847, https://genius.com/Christmas-songs-o-holy-night-lyrics. Accessed May 1, 2021.

obtained a ministry that is as much more excellent than the old as the covenant He mediates is better."[10] It continues with, "Christ had offered for all time a single sacrifice for sins."[11] It rests on:

> Therefore, brothers [sisters], since we have confidence to enter the holy places by the blood of Jesus, by the new and living way that He opened for us through the curtain, that is, through His flesh, and since we have a great Priest over the house of God, let us draw near with a true heart in full assurance of faith, with our hearts sprinkled clean from an evil conscience and our bodies washed with pure water.
>
> Hebrews 10:19–22

Here's the *more excellent covenant* that Hebrews 8:6 talks about! Here's our *once-for-all* atonement that our High Priest made *permanent for those who draw near to God*![12] Here's our hope! Get up from the Edenic Fall. Turn from Adam and Eve's deadly unbelief, which led to disobedience. Jesus is *better*; don't just trust me—trust Him.

WHO DOESN'T WANT BETTER?

Back then, the recipients of the book of Hebrews were considering going back to the Old Testament ways of life,[13] which would've been a disobedient digression from their freedom in Christ. As if grabbing the forbidden fruit the first time didn't do enough damage. "We are dead in our trespasses" ... no feelings, no hope, until we are made "alive together with Christ" ... lots of feelings, lots of hope.[14] The author of Hebrews reminds us:

---

10 Hebrews 8:1, 6.
11 Hebrews 10:12.
12 Hebrews 7:24–27.
13 They considered going back to the old law because of persecution and hostility. Hebrews 12:1–3.
14 Ephesians 2:5.

- Of "a better hope ... through which we draw near to God" (Hebrews 7:19).
- That Jesus is "the guarantor of a better covenant" (Hebrews 7:22).
- That "Christ has obtained a ministry that is as much more excellent than the old as the covenant He,ediatess is better, since it is enacted on better promises. For if that first covenant had been faultless, there would have been no occasion to look for a second" (Hebrews 8:6–7).
- That "He is the mediator of a new covenant, so that those who are called may receive the promised eternal inheritance, since a death has occurred that redeems them from the transgressions committed under the first covenant" (Hebrews 9:15).

The Son of God, a human descendant of Abraham, the appointed High Priest, also turns out to be our atonement Lamb. This is indeed excellent news. When we compare it to what went down pre-book-of-Mathew, it's so much better. Abraham was living in the shadowlands[15] compared to what we get in Christ today.

The Son of God, a human descendant of Abraham, the appointed High Priest, also turns out to be our atonement Lamb. This is indeed excellent news.

... God made a promise to Abraham ... God desired to show more convincingly to the heirs of the promise the unchangeable character of His purpose, He guaranteed it with an oath ... We have this [oath] as a sure and steadfast anchor of the soul, a hope that enters into the inner place behind the curtain, where Jesus has gone as a Forerunner on our behalf, having become a High Priest forever.

Hebrews 6:13, 17, 19–20

---

15   Hebrews 10:1.

We are unearthed, literally taken from the grave by the One Who took the grave. We are placed back into God's presence, a seat we kicked ourselves out of in the Garden. His glory is unveiled to us in a way much more excellent than at creation. Back then, God walked *with* humanity; now God dwells *in* humanity. Wow, just wow. Let that sink in a minute. The cherubim now allow our entrance—not back into the Garden of Eden from Genesis, not back onto the Mercy Seat of the Old Testament Holy of Holies, but *into the inner rest of being known, forgiven, loved* by God's indwelling Spirit. Did you read that? Old Testament Eden and the Old Testament Holy of Holies are history! They are obsolete—something better, or rather Someone better, is our aim. The ancients would have traded places with us in a heartbeat to have *Jesus go before them on their behalf*.[16] THIS is what the writer of Hebrews kept trying to tell his audience and what he's trying to tell us: a personal relationship with Jesus (Who is the best) is our assuring reality. We must stop going back to reruns when the Star of the show is standing right in front of us.

WORK OR REST

Not only was there a lot of physical work (daily labor) for God's people in the ancient world, there was much spiritual work simply to be temporarily holy and not die from unrighteousness. We saw what all that work looked like in the last chapter about the tabernacle. Jesus as our perfect High Priest comes as a saving exhale for us, doesn't He? Through our intimacy with Christ as our High Priest, we can put to rest all of the outward "work" of the Old Testament rituals while at the same time allow the Holy Spirit to go to work on our internal righteousness. Our options are these: to cover ourselves up and physically work our tails off like Adam and Eve and their descendants did OR to shed our inner garments and expose our shame and find eternal soul-rest like anyone can do who becomes God's child. Hebrews 3 and 4 beautifully explain that our High Priest gives us His rest through the exposure of our thoughts and intentions to Him and His Word.

---

16   Hebrews 6:20.

Therefore, while the promise of entering His rest still stands, let us fear lest any of you should seem to have failed to reach it ... there remains a Sabbath rest for the people of God, for whoever has entered God's rest has also rested from his works as God did from His. ... Let us therefore strive to enter that rest, so that no one may fall by the same sort of disobedience. For the Word of God is living and active, sharper than any two-edged sword, piercing to the division of soul and of spirit, of joints and of marrow, and discerning the thoughts and intentions of the heart. And no creature is hidden from His sight, but all are naked and exposed to the eyes of Him to Whom we must give account.

Hebrews 4:1, 9–13

He is the Provider of the daily and eternal rest our souls crave. It's no accident that *rest* is mentioned thirteen times, choreographed beautifully between Hebrews 3:1 (our need for a High Priest) and Hebrews 4:15 (Jesus fulfilling the role as High Priest). So how do we experience this restful existence?

CONSTANT CONFESSIONAL

The purpose of a manmade confessional is to enter into a private room and bear our sin, expose our inner short-comings, to a human priest. With Christ, our divine Priest, we are in a constant exposed state, aren't we? If you're like me, this is uncomfortable *if* I have something to hide. As seen from the verses above, rest comes from being intimately known by our merciful[17] and sympathetic[18] High Priest. A heart softened by God's living and active Word[19] is the gateway of entering into His rest.

---

17 Hebrews 2:17.
18 Hebrews 4:15.
19 Hebrews 4:12.

*Rest comes from being intimately known by our **merciful** and **sympathetic** High Priest. A heart softened by God's **living and active Word** is the gateway of entering into His rest.*

God exemplified rest to us in His observance of the first Sabbath when He stopped working.[20] Resting follows God's example set for us. He didn't need rest, but He knew we would need rest. The "Sabbath on earth" (not working on a certain day) and the "Sabbath of our souls" (not working for our salvation) is a foretaste of the "divine Sabbath" that God's presence will bring us in heaven for eternity.[21] Note: rest and the Sabbath *precede* the Fall, the Ten Commandments, and the Old Testament laws. The Sabbath rest is not a preventative measure to shackle our freedom. It's a saving measure to free us from the divine work we couldn't complete in the first place, namely keeping ourselves pure and saving our own souls. The Sabbath rest points to eternal rest found in the saving faith in Jesus. The Ten Commandments, laws, and rituals were instituted to show us our utter lostness and to lead us to our total dependency on the One Whose work on the cross and resting place at the right hand of God sustains the universe as we know it.

The Ten Commandments, laws, and rituals were instituted to show us our utter lostness and to lead us to our total dependency on the One Whose work on the cross and resting place at the right hand of God sustains the universe as we know it.

Isn't that awesome? It's holy napping at its best! Jesus invites those who labor and who are heavy laden to have His soul-rest for eternity.[22] Our rest proclaims Christ's Lordship over our time and over our souls. Rest is one

---

20 Hebrews 4:9–10.
21 Revelation 21, 22.
22 Matthew 11:28.

of the ways we are freed by God making His home inside us. Rest is only possible through Jesus, our High Priest, Who makes our inner heart-scape malleable as we hear His voice. "Today, if you hear His voice, do not harden your hearts as in the rebellion."[23] Further, true rest exhibits itself in the form of praising God, as the writer of Hebrews in the above verse quotes Psalm 95:7b–8, which is a psalm of praise. But beware! With the gentle dealings and sympathies[24] come a warning—not to harden our hearts.[25] Our High Priest digs beneath the surface and "discerns the thoughts and intentions of the heart."[26] We're either entering God's rest or falling into disobedience, as Hebrews 4:11 says: "Let us therefore strive to enter that rest, so that no one may fall by the same sort of disobedience." This is a continuum on which we are constantly by the grace of God "being sanctified" (Hebrews 10:14). This puts all of our self-righteous hustle to death. The less full of ourselves and the more full of God we are, the closer we are to living out the reality of what is put into our minds and *written on our hearts*: God is our God, and we are His people.[27]

The good news of the constant confessional is that there's nothing new to share with God that God doesn't already know. If we don't know Him, this causes fear and shame. If we know Him, this brings about peace and rest. This concept has revolutionized my life. I love being known by Him, covered by Him, forgiven by Him. We see that our High Priest's ministry to us is a better deal indeed than the original one of the Old Testament. Let's do some simple spiritual math (I'm not so good at math, but *this* math I get) to see how exactly we receive Christ's ministry of the new covenant.

---

23 Hebrews 3:15.
24 Hebrews 5:2.
25 Hebrews 3:13, 15, 4:7.
26 Hebrews 4:12.
27 Hebrews 8:10; Jeremiah 31:33.

*The good news of the constant confessional is that there's
nothing new to share with God that God doesn't already know.
If we don't know Him, this causes fear and shame.
If we know Him, this brings about peace and rest.*

ONCE FOR ALL

As I read and reread the book of Hebrews, the phrase "once for all" (and variations on this theme) jump out at me. *One* and *all* appear contradictory, yet our salvation comes through this seeming contradiction that doesn't make sense to our logical minds. Scholars say if something is mentioned more than once in Scripture, it's important. *Once for all* is mentioned roughly twelve times in the book of Hebrews. Listen up.

- Hebrews 2:9—"But we see Him Who for a little while was made lower than the angels, namely Jesus, crowned with glory and honor because of the suffering of death [once], so that by the grace of God He might taste death **for everyone** [all]" (emphasis added).
- Hebrews 2:11—"For He Who sanctifies and those who are sanctified **all have one** source" (emphasis added).
- Hebrews 2:14-15—"Through death He might **destroy the one** [one time, once] who has the power of death, that is, the devil, and **deliver all** those who through fear of death were subject to lifelong slavery" (emphasis added).
- Hebrews 5:9—"And being made perfect, He became the source of **eternal salvation to all** who obey Him" (emphasis added).
- Hebrews 7:27 - "He has no need, like those high priests, to offer sacrifices daily, first for His own sins and then for those of the people, since He did this **once for all** when He offered up Himself" (emphasis added).
- Hebrews 9:11–12—"But when Christ appeared as a High Priest of the good things that have come, then through the greater and more

perfect tent (not made with hands, that is, not of this creation) He entered **once for all** into the holy places, not by means of the blood of goats and calves but by means of His own blood, thus securing an eternal redemption" (emphasis added).

- Hebrews 9:26–28 - "He has appeared **once for all** at the end of the ages to put away sin by the sacrifice of Himself. And just as it is **appointed for man to die once**, and after that comes judgement, so Christ, having been **offered once** to bear the sins of many, will appear a second time, not to deal with sin but to save those who are eagerly waiting for Him" (emphasis added).

- Hebrews 10:10–12, 14—"... We have been sanctified through the offering of the body of Jesus Christ **once for all**. And every priest stands daily at his service, offering repeatedly the same sacrifices, which can never take away sins. But when Christ offered **for all time a single sacrifice** for sins, He sat down at the right hand of God. For by a **single offering** He has perfected for **all time** those who are being sanctified" (emphasis added).

Keep in mind that not all of these verses directly say *once for all*. I want us to see the big picture of the recurring terminology *one/once/single* and *all/ everyone*. Our High Priest delivers a "single sacrifice for sins" that atones for all time. Hebrews 10:12 says, "When Christ had offered for all time a single sacrifice for sins, He sat down at the right hand of God ... For by a single offering He has perfected for all time those who are being sanctified." Don't miss a very crucial element: *He sat down*, an experience that none of the Old Testament priests could ever have because their job was never finished. But the finality of the debt paid at the cross is bolded, underlined, written in red, and powerfully displayed in Christ's sitting down. Nothing else was needed. Let's break-down this "once for all" power move of our High Priest into its simplest form.

The finality of the debt paid at the cross is bolded, underlined, written in red, and powerfully displayed in Christ's sitting down. Nothing else was needed.

#ONCEFORALL

In Hebrews 7:27, Hebrews 9:12 (describing Jesus entering the Holy Place on our behalf), and Hebrews 10:10, the phrase *once for all* is not three words but rather one word. In English, it reads *once for all*, but in the original language, it reads *onceforall*. Not to be trite—it's God's most revolutionary hashtag, #onceforall. The Greek word is *ephapax*, which is made up from combining two simpler root words, *epi* and *hapax*.[28] The following chart further explains this concept.

---

28   *Bible Hub,* https://biblehub.com/greek/2178.htm, https://biblehub.com/greek/1909.htm, https://biblehub.com/greek/530.htm. Accessed May 9, 2021.

ORIGINS OF *ONCE FOR ALL*

epi (for)	*hapax: alpha + hapas* (once)
On, upon, implying what is appropriate given the fitting contact; naturally looks to the response (effect) that goes with the envisioned contact (Jesus); connected to the appropriate results/spin-offs/effects; the exact meaning is determined by the context, in this case "direction toward."	One time; used of what is so done as to be of perpetual validity and never needs repetition. *Hapax* originates from these two words: • *alpha:* the first letter of the Greek alphabet. FOOD FOR THOUGHT: any Greek word beginning with *alpha* cannot be made into an antithetical version of itself; it requires a separate negative participle or additional Greek letters. For example, we can never say *un-once-for-all* regarding our forgiven state. What Christ did was either *once for all* or it was *not once for all*. • *hapas:* the whole; each and every one as a comprehensive unit; focuses on the individual parts and their totality.

This sounds complex and economically impossible. It is. But not for Jesus. It's atonement algebra; I'm not good at math. Good thing I can count to one. Good thing this one counts for all.

ATONEMENT ALGEBRA IS OUR LIFE-SAVING EQUATION

When I do something *once for all*, let's be honest, I'm not really sure whether or not it's really once for all (due to my limits of being human). To use a shallow example from my own life to show the difference between me and God, if I get to my ideal pant size (where I feel comfortable) and say, "I'm staying this size for the rest of my life," my statement is more of a goal, motivated by my human desire and effort to be healthy and have energy. What I'm really saying is, "I *hope* I stay at this pant size for the rest of my life, and I'm going to do my best to accomplish this." It's a different matter when the Son of God says "once for all," especially regarding salvation. Within the endless bounds of His nature, He cannot express these words any other way than exactly what they mean. In the most objective, algebraic way, Jesus' atonement was once for all. There's no "let's sit around and see how this pans out" type of thinking. For us, He is Who He says He is.

In the most objective, algebraic way, Jesus' atonement was once for all. There's no "let's sit around and see how this pans out" type of thinking. For us, He is Who He says He is.

Then we take Him at face value and we LIVE FORGIVEN, we BREATHE FORGIVEN, we FORGIVE FORGIVEN. Our eggs are in one basket as we realize there is no other basket (name) whereby we must be saved.[29] It was about thirty-five years into my personal faith journey that I truly started to understand forgiveness and the implications it has for me personally. There's nothing worse than the feeling of owing someone something, especially when that Someone is God. I used to always feel like I was forgiven until the next time I messed up. Let me explain.

FORGIVEN UNTIL

Forgiveness is most certainly at times an action granted from one party to another. How we feel about forgiveness depends upon the territory of our hearts, specifically our belief. If our High Priest has eradicated the sin in our souls, we will experience forgiveness as an action *and* a state, regardless of how it feels, because we believe. In the Old Testament, forgiveness

---

29   Acts 4:12.

was often an action. In the New Testament, forgiveness is a whole other story—it begins with an action and carries on forever as a position. Don't miss this! In Christ, the whole of our being (soul, mind, body) is *perfected for all time [we] who are being sanctified.*[30] But we feel, think, and act forgiven as if we are "forgiven until"…

- the next Sunday we skip church.
- the next time we give free-reign to the negative committee in our head.
- the next time we cuss.
- the next time we gossip.
- the next time we lie.
- the next time we explode in anger.
- the next time we … (fill in the blank).

Forgiveness is not a "this for that." Forgiveness is not a "let me return the favor." Forgiveness is a place in Christ. Let me say that again—forgiven is a *place* in Christ. As a believer, you have arrived at your destination, and no one can snatch you out of it.[31] Do you believe this? Then start living like it. From our forgiven standing, we can forgive others and show them what a forgiven position looks like. This is what Hebrews 10 describes:

> For since the law has but a shadow of the good things to come instead of the true form of these realities, it can never by the same sacrifices that are continually offered every year, make perfect those who draw near. … For it is impossible for the blood of bulls and goats to take away sins. … We have been sanctified through the offering of the body of Jesus Christ once for all. … For by a single offering He had perfected for all time those who are being sanctified … "I will remember their sins and their lawless

---

30 Hebrews 10:14.
31 John 10:28–30.

deeds no more." Where there is forgiveness of these, there is no longer any offering for sin.

Hebrews 10:1, 4, 10, 14, 17–18

Forgiveness is not a "this for that." Forgiveness is not a "let me return the favor." Forgiveness is a place in Christ.

The following chart shows this point: through the shed blood of Christ (represented by the center line), we pass from the left side of the chart (where we owe an unpayable debt) over to the right side of the chart (where our debt is paid).

OLD TESTAMENT HIGH PRIEST VS. NEW TESTAMENT HIGH PRIEST

Law (to-do list)	Needs to be Forgiven (action required)	Once For All (done list)	Forgiven (requirement met)
Law	Blood owed	All sins	Paid
Ten Commandments	Blood owed	Of all time	Paid
Rituals	Blood Owed	From all people	Paid
Accidental sin[32]	Blood owed	Intended / unintended	Paid

⋮
↓

⋮
↓

Constant Discouragement

Impossible Assignments

Can never be perfect (Heb. 10:1)

Constant Empowerment

Nothing Else Needed

Perfected for all time (Heb. 10:14)

The law is there to show us something better.[33] *Once for all* is not merely our better moment; it's our best moment. Stop living a "to-do-list" mentality when all God sees is your "done-list" worth in Christ. You are forgiven... never to be unforgiven (see footnote).[34] With God, unforgiveness is impos-

---

32   In the Old Testament, God made a way for accidental sins, both of ourselves and of others. This concept is called "the scapegoat." Today, Christ's death and resurrection cover ALL the sins of those saved. See Leviticus 16:6–10.

33   Hebrews 7:19, 8:6–7, 9:11, 10:14, 34, 12:24.

34   A Greek word beginning with *alpha* cannot have an antonym version without a separate negating word or additional Greek letters being added. The Greek word for forgiveness begins with *alpha,* which means there is no single word for unforgiveness.

sible. There is no single word for "unforgiveness" in the New Testament, because the first letter of forgiveness (in Greek) is alpha ... which means a negative separate word has to be used separately like, "not forgive."[35] Again, when it's God doing the granting, forgiveness is final.

Stop living a "to-do-list" mentality when all God sees is your "done-list" worth in Christ.

HOMOGENOUS MIXTURE

As High Priest and as the eternal Son of God, Jesus doesn't just dole out His forgiveness like an item He stocks in the pantry of our souls. Our internal pantries are now structurally, through and through, made up entirely of Him and His righteousness. The priests of the Old Testament had to repeatedly restock Israel's internal shelves with atonement and forgiveness because the human priest's office, unlike Christ's, had limits. Under the old covenant:

> The former priests were many in number, because they were prevented by death from continuing in office, but He holds His priesthood permanently, because He continues forever. Consequently, He is able to save to the uttermost those who draw near to God through Him, since He always lives to make intercession for them.
>
> Hebrews 7:23–25

Our High Priest makes forgiven a part of who we are ... a homogenous mixture:

forgiven + us = inseparable.

---

35   *Bible Hub*, https://biblehub.com/greek/1.htm. Accessed May 9, 2021.

Of course, this is so much more than a solitary concept mingling with an individual human being in the hypothetical beaker of eternity. This is a Forgiver and a past-sinner becoming an heir, so deeply that the watching world knows "we're with Him," we're family. Our Forgiver Father is so visible in us, and our response to daily sin and our triumph over it sets us apart (shows Christ's holiness and the presence of His Spirit at work in us). Marinate in that fact for a moment. My resounding response, like Francis Schaffer, is how should I then live?[36]

OUR HOPE AND ASSURANCE

We've read about our High Priest's ministry to us being much more excellent and based on better promises than the old covenant. We've posted #onceforall on the walls of our hearts. Now let's take the unveiled holy space with us wherever we go with confident assurance. We best comprehend the nature of our Forgiver as well as our forgiven state in the context of God's omni-present nature as our foundation. In Christ, we are "on location" all the time. He is omni-present. He's everywhere all the time. Our spiritual movement in relation to God's divine presence is outside of metaphysical space and linear time. The material and immaterial are bridged by the divinity and humanity of Christ. Oh, the hope of this truth! Blessed assurance, Jesus is mine, ALL.THE.TIME.

> *We best comprehend the nature of our Forgiver as well as our forgiven state in the context of God's omni-present nature as our foundation. In Christ, we are "on location" all the time.*

---

36   Francis A. Schaeffer, *How Should We Then Live?* (Wheaton, IL: Crossway Books, 1976).

> Therefore, brothers, since we have confidence to enter the holy places by the blood of Jesus, by the new and living way that He opened for us through the curtain, that is, through His flesh, and since we have a Great Priest over the house of God, let us draw near with a true heart in full assurance of faith, with our hearts sprinkled clean from an evil conscience and our bodies washed with pure water.
>
> Hebrews 10:19–22

I have listened to, prayed over, and counseled way too many women who live in constant fear (including myself). Their lives seem to function in a permanent fight-or-flight state. Friends, you don't have to live this way. Jesus fought your fight. Jesus ran toward all that you're running away from. Be assured in Christ. Have hope in your High Priest. He came to save you, not to shame you.[37] The place into which even a glance would've killed you, you are now told to enter with confidence.[38] You're allowed behind the tabernacle veil. You can draw near to the Most High God with full assurance of your faith. God cleans your evil consciences and your bodies. This is your "full assurance of hope until the end."[39]

Current culture tells us to put our confidence in everything except the actual Source of our confidence. Our confidence has a name, and His name is Jesus. "Therefore do not throw away your confidence, which has great reward. … But we are not of those who shrink back and are destroyed, but of those who have faith and preserve their souls."[40] In the church age, I don't think we realize how good we have it. If I lived back in the days of the Old Testament tabernacle, I would have constantly been second-guessing myself with thoughts like: Did I bring my best lamb? Did I remember every sin I committed? Did the priest perform the ceremony correctly today? Confidence in our atoning Mediator and atoned position is a luxury of being this side of the cross and under His roof of Lordship. "And we are His house, if indeed we hold fast our confidence and our boasting in our

---

37   John 3:17.
38   Ephesians 3:12; Hebrews 4:16; 1 John 2:28, 3:21.
39   Hebrews 6:11.
40   Hebrews 10:35, 39.

hope."[41] "... Let us then with confidence draw near to the throne of grace, that we may receive mercy and find grace to help in time of need."[42] Preach this to your fears.

Confidence in our atoning Mediator and atoned position
is a luxury of being this side of the cross and under
His roof of Lordship.

THE INCLUSIVE CONCLUSION

To sum up the good news of the book of Hebrews: Christ offers us much more than a human priest can offer us. Our High Priest supremely and lovingly unveils the Holy of Holies to us by fulfilling a new covenant and better promise, He draws us into a relationship with Him through His once-for-all sacrifice, and He confidently assures us as our Foundation. At salvation, He forgives us. For eternity, we are forgiven. Simply rest in this promise, reality, and assurance. Then let's raise our hands in utter praise of "the Founder and Perfecter of our faith, Who for the joy that was set before Him endured the cross, despising the shame, and is seated at the right hand of the throne of God."[43] Let's spiritually tag all of our contacts with God's all-inclusive saving post. Let's pick up our mats and walk this message right out of our hearts and into our homes and our world. How do we do that?

---

41   Hebrews 3:6.
42   Hebrews 4:16.
43   Hebrews 12:2.

BRINGING THE LIGHT MEANS EXTENDING FORGIVENESS

With all our free time, since we don't have to spend endless hours doing rituals, fulfilling laws, and slaughtering animals, how can we be light-bringers of the very mercy, grace, and help that we have ourselves received? Can we share with others that once forgiven means always forgiven, and that unforgiven is spiritually and linguistically impossible? This position of nearness (through our High Priest) into God's presence will most certainly affect our souls, thoughts, feelings, prayers, decisions, tones, words, facial expressions, actions, etc. There doesn't have to be a dichotomy between the spiritual and physical realm when it comes to us walking with God in the most holistic way that we can.

I leave you with the constant empowerment that if you have a personal relationship with Jesus and He is your High Priest, the requirements have been met. Nothing else is needed. You are perfected for all time, and you are forgiven. I call it Priest-empowerment. Now go forgive that person who needs your forgiveness. Christ doesn't hold it back from you, so you shouldn't hold it back from anyone. He set the example on the cross when He said of those who sinned against Him, "Father, forgive them, for they know not what they do."[44] Go ask for forgiveness of that person you've sinfully harmed. This may be the hardest light-bringing I ask you to do in our study together. But you will better know God, your Forgiver, as you forgive others and are forgiven by others.

You will better know God, your Forgiver, as you forgive others and are forgiven by others.

Please, oh please, don't fall for the lie that you need to forgive yourself. God's forgiveness of you is enough. Mobilize this "better promise" of your forgiven state from the vertical realm into the horizontal realm. Put legs on your once-for-all standing. Invite others into your confident state in Christ.

---

44   Luke 23:34.

Hang out with people who don't yet know and love Jesus and show them real love before you God-talk them to death. This is what Jesus did; He did life with people just like you and me. Jesus always shared His message in life and in words. He treasured and protected the fragile pieces of people's souls. Then He opened His arms wide in the greatest hug of all time and died for us. He is the perfect Forgiver, never to unforgive those Whom He has forgiven. He is the perfect Lover, never to unlove those Whom He has loved.

---

*Jesus always shared His message in life **and** in words.*
He treasured and protected the fragile pieces of people's souls.
Then He opened His arms wide in the greatest
hug of all time and died for us.

Forgiveness = *aphesis* [αφεσις] ... never to be unforgiven, always forgiven.

Love = *agape* [αγαπη] ... never to be unloved, always loved.

PRAYER

Lord Jesus,
Thank You for loving me to the extent that
You gave Yourself up for me, the sinful person.
Thank you for opening a new and living way for me
to say "it is finished" to the veil that separates me from You,
to meet with You, and to be forgiven—once for all.
Because of Your mighty power, I am saved forever;
I am forgiven forever.

Jesus, You are my Door …
to enjoying God the Father,
to fellowshipping with Him,
to being one with Him.
Lord, give me the experiences I need
to break and terminate my sin,
to live-out my redemptive standing,
and to walk in the holiness you've already granted me.
Thank you for loving me with Your everlasting love;
Because it's You doing the loving, I will never be unloved.
I can always be confident
because of Who You are—the Most High God
and what You've done—died to save me.
Amen.

DISCUSSION QUESTIONS

1. How does God put His laws into our minds and write His command-
    ments on our hearts (Hebrews 8:6, 10, 13)? Why is this better and
    more excellent than the old tablets of stone?

2. Define *atonement* according to Hebrews 10:12. How does "atone-
    ment algebra" make a difference to believers today versus pre-
    cross God-followers?

3. Hebrews 10:19–25 can be referred to as a "salad passage" in that it con-
    tains a lot of "let us." Highlight in your Bible the three "let us" phrases,
    including what you are now able to *confidently* do since Jesus is your
    High Priest.

4. The state of permanent forgiveness for all believers is life-altering; for-
    given is a state that is impossible to lose. Spend time praising God for
    this gift because it means that "there is no longer any offering for sin"
    (Hebrews 10:18); just sit in God's presence. Take this truth with you
    next time you celebrate communion.

WHO TO BE:
MENTAL/SPIRITUAL/PRAYERFUL

CHAPTER 7
DECISION MUSCLE

———

Romans 12:1-3; 2 Corinthians 10:3-6

Only two people can get in your head: you and God. No one else besides God is omniscient or omnipresent, not even satan. God alone has access to what you think and feel before a response ever visibly emerges. There is so much power here. Every time we mumble, even under our breath, satan and his army *may* hear it. Though he and they are not omnipresent, *if* they hear our complaint, they can use it as ammo against us. But satan can't hear our thoughts. He can't feel our feelings. What if we blitzkrieg our minds the very moment our thoughts think towards enemy lines, enemy ways, enemy emotions? What if we take God up on His promise that He has given us everything we need for life and godliness through our *knowledge* of Him?[1] What if by *knowing* Him (as He reveals Himself to us through His Word, His Spirit, prayer, and other believers) He brings His light into our own minds? On our own strength, we cannot cut off sin at the mental pass—that is, we cannot think righteously without help. But with the Spirit of God in us, God can change our minds and hearts, which is the place where sin begins. "Every sin is an inside job. The devil comes and entices you to evil, but every time you and I sin, it's because we made

———

1   2 Peter 1:3.

the decision to sin, on the inside."[2] Trumping that fact about sin is the fact that God is an inside God. Can I hear an amen? When we fill our minds with Christ, we have the "mind of Christ."[3] This allows the Holy Spirit to train our decision muscles and route our feelings heavenward. His job is minding and reminding.

Only two people can get in your head: you and God.

In Romans 12:1–3, Paul lays-out a mental training program through *transformation, renewal, testing-discerning,* and *thinking with sober judgment.* These Biblical exercises are a few of the many activities our minds need to be repping consistently in order for our outward lives to be holy. Yes, I just dropped the "h" word. Holiness makes a lot of people feel uncomfortable. It's supposed to, because it's everything we naturally are not.

Holy lives predicate once-wicked souls who are now saved and sustained by a holy God. When we think of pursuing holiness, it's always in the framework of Christ granting His set-apartness to us. For us to be set apart from Him is a bad thing. Him being set apart from us is a good thing.[4] Training our decision muscle after God is like isolated muscle training. It's "leg day" for our mind/heart/soul. Strengthening our decision muscle ensures who we are to be—not just as cognitive beings, but as total and spiritual beings. The Bible oftentimes collectively groups the ideas of mind, heart, and soul into one concept.

Holy lives predicate once-wicked souls who are now saved and sustained by a holy God.

---

2   *Truthforlife.org,* https://www.truthforlife.org/store/products/cd-individual-messages/temptation/. Accessed May 9, 2021.
3   1 Corinthians 2:14–16.
4   Leviticus 11:44, 19:2; 1 Samuel 2:2; 1 Peter 1:16.

Kardia, the Greek word for heart, is defined as "mind, character, inner self, will, intention, center ... the affective center of our being and the capacity of moral preference ... our desire-decisions that establish who we really are."[5] *Phronema*, the Greek word for mind, means "the thought, aspiration ... inner perspective as it determines ... outward behavior."[6] Training our *desire-decisions* is an important part of our spiritual training. Of course, this is insanity-talk if we go at it apart from a redeemed vantage point.

Paul succinctly describes the connection between lives-lived-out and minds-thought-out; it's all based on hearts-changed-out. Listen to what he says:

> For those who live according to the flesh set their minds on the things of the flesh, but those who live according to the Spirit set their minds on the things of the Spirit. For to set the mind on the flesh is death, but to set the mind on the Spirit is life and peace. For the mind that is set on the flesh is hostile to God, for it does not submit to God's law; indeed it cannot.[7]

Did you hear that? To set the mind on the flesh, on human desires, is death! But everything we read or watch, both culturally and naturally in our human experience, tells us to move towards human desires, to love of self, to embrace inner and outer fulfillment. That's hogwash. And we all surely know that no one sets out to die. But giving our minds over to worldly venues (inside and out) rather than to the One Who created and sustains life is soul-suicide. I want the "no condemnation life" found in Christ; I want the "set me free" promise that the Spirit of life delivers.[8]

---

5   *Bible Hub,* https://biblehub.com/greek/2588.htm. Accessed May 1, 2021.
6   *Bible Hub,* https://biblehub.com/greek/5427.htm. Accessed May 1, 2021.
7   Romans 8:5–7.
8   Romans 8:1–2.

---

*Paul succinctly describes the connection
between lives-lived-out and minds-thought-out;
it's all based on hearts-changed-out.*

Apart from the Holy Spirit, no lasting advancement can be made in choosing to think about what is true, honorable, just, pure, lovely, commendable, excellent, or worthy of praise.[9] Unleashed thoughts can kill;[10] unguarded thoughts suppress truth.[11] Our internal maturity (mental, emotional, and spiritual) was designed at our very beginning to mirror God; we fell away from our divine design. So how did Paul rep God-thoughts? Especially with his intense life of persecution, imprisonment, and eventual martyrdom?

---

*Apart from the Holy Spirit, no lasting advancement can be made
in choosing to think about what is true, honorable, just, pure,
lovely, commendable, excellent, or worthy of praise.*

To endure what the apostle Paul endured (slander, imprisonment, hunger, cold, shipwreck, persecution, death, etc.), we find him fleshing-out his mindset at every turn in the accounts found in his writings. If you haven't read Acts, go do that now. Go read the whole book of Acts in one sitting. The poor conditions of Roman prisons into which Paul was thrown would've made headlines today. Yet it's out of these deathly dungeons that many of his life-giving letters emerge. We see Paul flexing mentally, getting strengthened by his Savior. Though the Bible doesn't record apostolic thoughts, it does record the results of such world-changing brain waves. Paul preaches how to think.

---

9   Philippians 4:8.
10   James 1:14–15.
11   Romans 1:18, 21–23.

I appeal to you therefore, brothers, by the mercies of God, to present your bodies as a living sacrifice, holy and acceptable to God, which is your spiritual worship. Do not be conformed to this world, but be transformed by the renewal of your mind, that by testing you may discern what is the will of God, what is good and acceptable and perfect. For by the grace given to me I say to everyone among you not to think of himself more highly than he ought to think, but to think with sober judgement, each according to the measure of faith that God has assigned.

Romans 12:1–3

As we break down these simple yet profound concepts—transformation, renewal, testing-discerning, thinking with sober judgment—we will best grasp the author's meaning in this passage and get the mental goods that God, through Paul, says are ours. Romans is such a hefty-holy book. It's truly our one-stop-shop when it comes to theological mental training. So if you haven't read Romans, go read that now.

Prior to the above passage in Romans, Paul addresses sin, God's judgment, our need, salvation through faith, living in the Spirit, and God's love and sovereignty. Directly after this passage, Paul discusses spiritual gifts within the church body, marks of a Christ-follower, our relationship with others, and Christ's example. (These last two sentences don't do justice to the book of Romans. My apologies; again, go read the whole book yourself.) The *transformation, renewal, testing-discerning,* and *thinking with sober judgement* come right after *presenting ourselves to God as living sacrifices* (which is also called our *spiritual worship*),[12] and they come right before the reality of *spiritual gifting.*[13] Wow, do you see that? Spiritual worship relates to what we think, and then it overflows in how we minister to the local body of believers using our spiritual gifts.

---

12 Romans 12:1.
13 Romans 12:4–8.

Spiritual worship relates to what we think, and then it overflows in how we minister to the local body of believers.

More often than I'd like to admit, I hear people (both in the church or leaving the church) telling me that their church is spiritually dead. To me, these people's words are most likely a dead giveaway that their mind is not centered on Christ, Who is seated at the right hand of God the Father. I compassionately, and from personal experience, offer that their spiritual worship might be more dead than their church. Ouch. I didn't say it … the apostle Paul did. He's stepping on our toes here, isn't he? At least he's stepping on mine. Word-readers shine the light of Christ not only in a dark world but also in non-exciting churches, broken churches, dark-at-times churches, and splitting churches. I've been in these kinds of churches more years than I've seen healthy, exciting churches. The perfect church is the one in which I am the only member—ha!

Word-readers shine the light of Christ not only in a dark world but also in non-exciting churches, broken churches, dark-at-times churches, and splitting churches.

Within the local church, praise precedes preference. Read that last sentence again if what you prefer about church precedes your praise of the Most High God. Perhaps like me, you've left church thinking the worship wasn't great. I've got news for you, we weren't worshipping you. Word-readers know and feel the call to minister where they are without mindsets and comments that are complaining, arrogant, jabby, and snarky. I hope you're convicted like I am, because I've complained and jabbed against church, my own included, with the best of them. Forgive me, Lord. Even as I've edited my own words in writing this book, I've had to remove some jabs, because they're not worthy to be hung on the walls of heaven. Word-readers boldly speak the truth in humility and love. This starts with our mindset. This is the type of decision muscle Paul is telling us to train for power-lifting … but it's power-thinking. Paul tells us to **bold**, underline, enlarge these mental exercises in order to strengthen the affective center of our being. First, let's think about transformation.

TRANSFORMATION

Transformation sounds like such a great, positive, productive idea. It is. But I've always wondered what's going through the caterpillar's head once bound up in its cocoon and unknowingly waiting to become a butterfly. Does it know it's metamorphosing? Is it uncomfortable? Can it breathe well in there? Does its fight-or-flight instinct kick in? Does it sense its inner-butterfly? When the Holy Spirit leads me to change my thoughts, or morph my mind (which is what *transformation* means), many times I feel more like Frodo in *The Lord of the Rings* as he's bound-up in the Shelob's webby cocoon, injected with poison, barely hanging on to consciousness, rather than a butterfly.

Rarely is transformation comfortable. But Christ knows transformation too. His change at the Transfiguration was for His glory and our good: "He was transfigured before them, and His face shone like the sun, and His clothes became white as light."[14] His change on the mountain to Peter, James, and John was to reveal Who He already was—God. Our change in the Spirit is to restore our Imago Dei. Comfort is never the way of the cross. The way of the cross always leads to transformation. The product of transformation is indeed our ultimate good, as it shows-off God. If it doesn't end in God's glory, it probably was never a butterfly (symbolically) in the first place.

Comfort is never the way of the cross. The way of the cross always leads to transformation. The product of transformation is indeed our ultimate good, as it shows-off God.

---

14   Matthew 17:2.

Transformation is our hope as we wrestle our stubborn sinful thoughts.[15] "Being transformed by the renewal of my mind," as Paul commands, "looks towards the after-effect" which "embodies a particular inner essence;" Biblical transformation (or metamorphosis) is a "change of outer form in keeping with the inner reality."[16] When our mind-soul-spirit is *with Jesus* (via His Word, prayer, and the Holy Spirit's presence), there is a *meta-*, or change, after being *with Him.*[17]

Transformative change is tangible change. If there's no change, I doubt we've been with Jesus. Ouch, but that's the truth. Those five loaves and two fish from Matthew 14:13–21 are still just five loaves and two fish if our inner beings haven't first been justified by faith. Christ alone changes things. He changed loaves and fish; He changes us. What's harder to say and fulfill—"Your sins are forgiven" or "Pick up your mat and walk"?[18] A butterfly is evidence of what precedes it: a caterpillar. The light we bring to those around us is evidence of what precedes that light, a once-sinner now living with the mind of Christ.[19] Our transformation occurs by renewing our minds. Think on that.

Transformative change is tangible change. If there's no change, I doubt we've been with Jesus.

RENEWAL

Renewal is more than a face cream or extra time with a book from the library (which eventually must go back). Christ's renewal never has to go back. The renewal Paul describes in Romans 12 comes from a root word meaning "new in quality ... fresh in opportunity," because what's in our

---

15 2 Corinthians 10:5.
16 *Bible Hub,* https://biblehub.com/greek/3339.htm. Accessed May 1, 2021.
17 *Bible Hub,* https://biblehub.com/greek/3326.htm. Accessed May 1, 2021.
18 John 5:1–17.
19 1 Corinthians 2:16.

minds was "not found exactly like this before."[20] When Christ comes into our personal think tank, spiritual renovation occurs as He works in us to will and to act according to His good purpose.[21] Simply put: while transformation is the result, renewal is the action. We didn't always need renewal. In Eden, we were already headed in the right direction. Renewal came about from a global gardening issue.

ONCE UPON A TIME

Once upon a time, we walked in the light with God Himself. No renewal was needed, because we were as we should be, in daily relationship with God, moving towards oneness with Him, ultimately in heaven one day. "From the very beginning, Eden was not meant to be static; it was headed somewhere. We could say that there was an eschatology of Eden. God's intentions for His creation have always been headed toward consummation, toward glory."[22] We needed no outer covering for sin, because we needed no internal covering for sin (enter nasty snake). Adam and Eve listened to a lie, made a rebellious choice, and now we must all die-to-self (via the Spirit) in order to stop our daily dying.[23] This is the priceless paradox of the Gospel. "Death brings life"—a red banner painted on the doorposts of the Old Testament covenant pointing to the New Testament promise of a Messiah, and the cloth door that was rent in two. Dying to self is made possible in Christ. He took the hit. He did what we could not do. He was the beauty resurrecting from the global ash heap of sin. From our once dead-to-self state, we are now more alive than we've ever been. It's God's glory to which our Edenic state always pointed and to which our heavenly home now calls us in our daily renewal.

---

20 *Bible Hub*, https://biblehub.com/greek/2537.htm. Accessed May 1, 2021.
21 Philippians 2:13.
22 Nancy Guthrie teaches the Bible at her home church. "10 Things You Should Know about the Garden of Eden," *Crossway*, 30 Aug. 2018, www.crossway.org/articles/10-things-you-should-know-about-the-garden-of-eden/. Accessed May 1, 2021.
23 Galatians 2:20.

"Death brings life"—a red banner painted on the doorposts of the Old Testament covenant pointing to the New Testament promise of a Messiah, and the cloth door that was rent in two. Dying to self is made possible in Christ. He took the hit. He did what we could not do. He was the beauty resurrecting from the global ash heap of sin.

Renewing: "to resume after an interruption," "to begin again." Do you see it? That means we were once doing it! We were once headed for glory, but then we stopped or got interrupted, but are all at once called to begin again. I don't mean to be a stream of consciousness, but our renewal is like run-on sentences ... it keeps going and going until completion.[24] Sweet Jesus, talk about a compression of time between the Garden, the Fall, rebirth in Christ, and future hope. Sin is the interruption. Salvation by our gracious Savior is our "begin again" moment. When the Holy Spirit enters the picture, renewal is all we now *know*, literally. It's what our minds long to experience and are empowered to think in Christ. I fist-pump at this!

SANCTIFIED REASONING

Mental renewal is also mentioned in Ephesians 4:21–23 in the context of our new life in Christ. "You ... were taught ... to put off your old self, which belongs to your former manner of life and is corrupt through deceitful desires, and to be renewed in the spirit of your minds." This mental renewal combines "up" and "new" to take us "... to a higher stage (level of sanctification) by God's power. Here believers are reminded of God's continuous offer to bring new strides in our sanctification through 'sanctified reasoning'—raising the meaning *up* to *new levels of spiritual comprehension and reality*."[25]

---

24   Philippians 1:6.
25   *Bible Hub*, https://biblehub.com/greek/365.htm. Accessed May 1, 2021.

We have antagonists to our sanctified reasoning: comparison, coveting, jealousy, fear, selfish ambition, anxiety, pride, doubt to name a few. The list is endless. It's no easy task to bench people's opinions and our own sinful thoughts. Like subbing players, once we pull a negative thought off the starting line-up in our head, we must then send in a stronger player, as Paul coaches the church in Ephesus to do. We must send in the strongest Player, the Holy Spirit. He permanently holds the VIP role. Once in the gym of our minds, He reps renewal, He power-lifts God's perfect will in us. He reveals our cerebral atrophy: the futility of our minds, the darkness of our understanding, the alienation from God, the ignorance in us.[26] Changing mindsets apart from Christ is crippled mind games. In Christ, our minds now reason differently; former manners and desires are laid aside, destined away[27] from us. Stop right now and take a moment, lift up your hands, and praise the Lord for sanctified reasoning. Personally, I need it daily.

TESTING-DISCERNING: SORTING LOOSE CHANGE

After transformation and renewal comes testing-discerning, "that by testing you may discern what is the will of God, what is good and acceptable and perfect."[28] Ooh, I don't like tests, and perfection sounds a little scary. I *do* like discernment, though. Different versions of the Bible say it like this:

- ESV: testing to discern.
- NASB: prove.
- NKJV: prove.
- NIV: test and approve.
- NLT: learn to know.
- Amplified: prove to yourself.

---

26   Ephesians 4:17–19.
27   *Bible Hub*, https://biblehub.com/greek/659.htm, https://biblehub.com/greek/5087.htm, https://biblehub.com/greek/575.htm. Accessed May 9, 2021.
28   Romans 12:2.

As living-dead things, Romans 12:2 exhorts us to *test that we may discern*. Those five English words are just one Greek word—*dokimazo*.[29] Testing our minds is part of being the living sacrifices this passage exhorts. This word *testing* means "I am fit." Did your decision muscle just flex when you read that? Mine did! We are to have fit minds. Also, we are to *examine* and *prove* our minds/spirits to discern all that is genuine.[30] There's nothing worse than someone who's a fake. We love and are drawn toward authentic, real people, aren't we? The same is true for our thoughts. This type of testing is never intended to prove wrong but always intended to prove right. It's as if the hands of our minds grab the extra change rolling around in our heads (we all have hypothetical change rolling around) and immediately we approve (test and discern) which coins (thoughts) are genuine and which ones are counterfeit, just by touching them. Chuck E. Cheese coins don't go very far in the real world; and our fingers can feel that they are counterfeit. By the mercies of God, we can save up holy currency, starting with our thought patterns. Holy mental currency, having the mind of Christ, helps us discern real gold from fool's gold.[31]

WATER IS WATER

How are we to bring the light when current culture is selling us the lie that spirituality is a feeling, a mystical nuance, an obsession with analyzation of self? Spiritual worship begins with a heavenly-groomed thought life. The vacuum-lines of the Spirit's constant passing over our noggin-rugs should be grooved deep. The distance between my mind and heart is thousands of miles. I need a spiritual zip tie for my heart and head to come together and stay together. That zip tie is God's truth. Only God's Word can close the gap between heart and head. Pumping our brains with self-reliance is like dropping excrement into the perfect brownie mix God's preparing in us. Why are we mentally hooked up to a septic tank when our Biblical

---

29   *Bible Hub*, https://biblehub.com/greek/1381.htm. Accessed May 1, 2021.
30   Ibid.
31   1 Corinthians 1:17–2:16.

fire hose lies on our bedside tables getting dried out from non-use? The Word doesn't go out void. I think the Bible appears to be void these days, because it's not going out like it used to. It's been banned from schools and the workplace. It's been set aside even in some churches. Culture has cancelled it. Sadly, we are more world-woke than Word-woke. Also, reading someone else's take on Scripture is not reading Scripture. Reading blogs and listening to podcasts is not reading Scripture. Reading Scripture is reading Scripture. Scripture informs Scripture. If you're already a Word-reader, put this book down and read God's Word, not mine.

Reading Scripture is reading Scripture.

When I'm teaching nutrition, I constantly hear people tell me in response to my asking how much water they drink, "I drink two cups of coffee, a glass of water, a tea, one diet coke, and a glass of water with dinner." I respond by saying, "Water is water." Coffee is not water; tea is not water; diet coke is not water. Light-bringers first douse their minds with God's Word. *Then* they pick up Biblically-engineered works of fellow saints to shed light and commentary upon the vast and complicated truths of God's Word. I had to do a lot of this when researching the tabernacle in chapter five. I read and reread Scripture and then checked secondary sources. Only the writers of the Bible were divinely inspired. Let Scripture explain Scripture, *then* seek commentaries and other helpful writings. We don't worship the Bible; we worship the God to Whom it points. We don't fall in love with the "Love Letter" but with the One Who authored it. I must say this, because I've seen people worship the Bible at the expense of an inner relationship with God and outer relationship with others. They are legalists and hypocrites, the ones Jesus called-out: holding law above love,[32] resounding their phylactery[33]-encased gongs[34] and clanging their white-

---

32   Matthew 23:1–35.
33   Matthew 23:1–12.
34   1 Corinthians 13:1.

washed[35] cymbals.[36] Rely on the Holy Spirit to help you test and discern the will of God. Pray before you read Scripture. Pray while you read Scripture. Pray after you read Scripture. Through the Holy Spirit, God's Word, and prayer, your brain-train is sure to head down the tracks of sober judgment.

Rely on the Holy Spirit to help you test and discern the will of God. Pray before you read Scripture. Pray while you read Scripture. Pray after you read Scripture.

THINKING WITH SOBER JUDGMENT

At first glance, this might read "don't make mental decisions when drunk." Sounds good to me. I've had drunk-like judgment. Have you? I've been unsober mentally, spiritually, and emotionally. The more the Lord transforms us, renews our minds, and teaches us to test and discern His good, acceptable, and perfect will, the more we'll think with sober judgment. I think we might look intoxicated with Him, like Hannah in 1 Samuel 1. We'll delve into her story in chapter nine. Sober judgment is not thinking more highly of ourselves than we ought.[37] This takes some mental handcuffing.

HANDCUFF YOUR MIND

"The eyes are not responsible when the mind does the seeing."[38] Is this saying that rather than gouging out our eyes we should get a lobotomy? Ha, of course not. One of my children struggled through a phase of hitting siblings. Over and over again, this child would apologize and ask forgiveness,

---

35 Matthew 23:27–28.

36 1 Corinthians 13:1.

37 Romans 12:3.

38 Publilius Syrus. *Brainyquote.com*, https://www.brainyquote.com/quotes/publilius_syrus_155304. Accessed May 9, 2021.

but the hitting continued. My husband always says, "Don't be sorry ... be different." But *how* to be different? I happened to be studying Scripture and researching for this very chapter on who we are to be mentally. I asked my daughter (who claims to know Christ) if I should handcuff her hands or handcuff her mind? She looked a little concerned. You see, if we handcuff the hands without addressing the heart-mind issue that caused the hitting, the problem will not be fixed. I discussed with my daughter that she should, through the strength of the Holy Spirit, handcuff her mind, taking her thoughts captive, prior to her hands losing self-control and harming others. We discussed practical ways to wrestle unwanted, unholy thoughts that led to hitting. Captives never go down without a fight, especially when the captives are ungodly thoughts.

Captives never go down without a fight, especially when the captives are ungodly thoughts.

We agreed that my daughter should pray for God to identify anger, selfishness, and impatience early, before they emerge as swings. Always pray first. Then, knowing she struggled with hitting, she should walk out of the room and pray for self-control and to respond wisely. To make this scenario more complicated, her neurological disorder brings on irrational episodes, so I'm teaching her that there will be moments when she is unable to handcuff her mind, and that in these moments, Jesus always carries her.

This isn't a parenting equation that's one-size-fits-all; any parent or human knows this not-so-fun fact. Of course my daughter's hitting problem didn't vanish overnight, and neither did her sin, her chemical imbalances, or the physical growths in her brain. Handcuffing our minds is a Biblical command from 2 Corinthians 10:3–6 that Paul says in the context of punishing disobedience (fleshly sin and mental strongholds).[39] Although you're probably familiar with it, read this famous passage about

---

39 2 Corinthians 10:3–6.

taking your thoughts captive and pray for the Holy Spirit to reveal mental strongholds that need to be cuffed and taken down.

> For though we walk in the flesh, we are not waging war according to the flesh. For the weapons of our warfare are not of the flesh but have divine power to destroy strong-holds. We destroy arguments and every lofty opinion raised against the knowledge of God, and take every thought captive to obey Christ.
>
> 2 Corinthians 10:3–6

This passage ties in with putting on the armor of God that we'll discuss in the next chapter. Stop those arguments and lofty options in their tracks before they rant, rave, destroy, and steal. Here are some examples of my mental handcuffing:

- "Don't look at that website/magazine/show, look at Jesus."
- "Assume the best of your friend; you don't have the whole story. Pray for truth."
- "Put your phone down. Pick up your hotline to heaven, your Bible and prayer."
- "Bite your tongue … literally clench your teeth right now. Practice silence."
- "Walk away, Adelynn, walk away. Breathe and thank God for space."
- "Turn off the television because those commercials are worse than the show. Turn on a Christian podcast or worship music."
- "Look the rude cashier in the eyes and engage in love."
- "That friend of seventeen years wasn't trying to hurt you; ask questions, clarify, love."
- "You can't control that person who donated to an ungodly organization; pray for him or her."
- "Your husband is not the enemy. Keep a list of rights, not wrongs."
- "Smile at the curt neighbor who rubs you the wrong way."

- "You're forty-five … get a grip and think and act like it. Call in sisters for back up."

Don't worry, if I'm sounding really Godly and close to perfect, I'm not. I struggle in relationships just like all of us. I have to wrestle-down my harsh tone of voice first in my mindset. If it makes you feel better, early in our marriage I told my husband that I hated that we were Christians and couldn't get divorced. Not my best moment. My mouth spoke what my mind told it to. Many times I need to ask my spouse or a trusted friend to help me know how to handcuff my mind before my mouth and actions explode. Even then, I still allow unhelpful or negative people and ideas to be on the starting line-up in my head game daily—people and ideas who were never invited! But I let them in; they don't just come in of their own accord. I invite them. We invite them. We read stuff; we watch stuff; we listen to conversations; we ask probing harmful questions; we troll; we scroll. We let the junk inside our heads, and then we wonder why T-shirts that say "hot mess" sell like crazy. We train the hot mess that original sin has been touting since its conception (or shall I say ingestion).

Sometimes taking our thoughts captive needs professional, medical, and chemical help. In this day and age, when mental health issues are REAL (I have a front row seat for this with my daughter's genetic condition), God calls us to preach sound-mindedness and radical thinking to our spiritual health; and sometimes the best way to start doing that is by getting God-honoring counseling, stabilizing medication, and practical daily tools when necessary. These can be tools that help some people best stock truth in their minds. Mental health issues are not sin. We're foolish not to take needed medications while singing "Jesus paid it all." One of the ways He washes us "white as snow" is by getting professional help, accountability, and a loving community around us. I love going to counseling. I wish I could go all the time. It makes me feel partnered-with, gospel-equipped, and togethered-with. Thank God we have Him as a personal Counselor to help overcome sin and to make God-honoring choices, like getting professional help when needed. Our saving faith is a beautiful thing—initiated by Him,[40] persevering through Him,[41] sealed by Him.[42] The captives of our mind must obey the One Who conquered them once for all[43] at the cross. This hope is more than just a feeling. We can *know* hope; we can *know* power; we can *know* we belong to God.

---

*The captives of our mind must obey the One Who conquered them once for all at the cross. This hope is more than just a feeling. We can **know** hope; we can **know** power; we can **know** we belong to God.*

THINK THE LIGHT TO BRING THE LIGHT

If we don't train and sustain them, bad ideas get weak and die. In Christ, we all have the power to call the shots in our own personal head games. Don't ever give other people this sacred power. I believe it's a divine gift from God. Our think-tank of two (God and us) can change the world around us as we walk in the light as He is in the light.[44] I find it interesting that God's first spoken sentence in Genesis is "Let there be light."[45] Then in the last two chapters of Revelation, the sun is gone,[46] it's not essential. It's almost as if God says, "You know that light, the sun, I spoke into being at the beginning of the world? You know how it sustains everything? It was only pointing to Me. You don't need it anymore. I am what's essential. I am the Sustainer. I am the true Light." Revelation 22:5 says it like this: "And night will be no more. They will need no light of lamp or sun, for the Lord God will be their light." As believers in Christ, let's strengthen our

---

40   Romans 9:11.
41   Philippians 1:6.
42   Ephesians 4:30.
43   Hebrews 10:12.
44   1 John 1:7.
45   Genesis 1:3.
46   Revelation 21:22–24, 22:5.

decision muscle to think towards God's truth and glory, so that in turn we feel, speak, and act towards God's truth and glory. Thanks to Paul, we see who we are to be mentally as we transform, renew, test-discern, and think with sober judgement. My prayer is that you have *decided* to follow Jesus; no turning back, no turning back.

PRAYER

God,
By Your mercy I come before You
as a living sacrifice,
presenting myself, through Christ, as holy and acceptable to You.
In Christ, this is my daily reality, my spiritual worship.
Transform me, change me from the inside out,
starting with my heart-mind-soul.
Help me to test, discern, and know Your will
in order to think soberly and live soberly.
According to Your divine power,
grant me increased faith as I wage war on my wrong thinking.
Exchange enemy strongholds for Your safe steadfasts.
Destroy arguments and build-up my knowledge of You.
In the name of Jesus, captivate all my thoughts
and replace them with total obedience,
followed by living obedience,
for Your glory.
Amen.

DISCUSSION QUESTIONS

1. In Romans 12:1, the "mercies of God" are the judgments He held back that were justly coming. How does "appealing to these mercies of God," as Paul does, affect your daily living? Does your life display God's gift of mercy or does it at times display what He held back in His mercy?

2. How has your decision-muscle gotten the best of you? How can you strengthen it so that visible change is seen and felt, just like the clear change from a caterpillar into the butterfly that Paul depicts in Romans 12:2?

3. There is no substitute for studying the authentic currency of God's Word. Pick an Old Testament and New Testament book to binge-read this week—both in one week. According to Romans 12:2, how does reading Scripture help you test and discern what is God's will?

4. According to 2 Corinthians 1:1–6, what does Paul say precedes complete obedience? How can you be "ready to punish every disobedience" in your daily life?

CHAPTER 8
SUIT UP

Ephesians 6:10-18

Standing against the schemes of the devil; wrestling against cosmic powers; *struggling against spiritual forces of evil in the heavenly places.*[1] This sounds like a Marvel comic or a sci-fi novel. The truth is, these warring concepts are straight out of reality; there's an unseen fight against the Most High God and it's for our testimony to the watching world. I think it's ok for that to scare us a little bit, in a holy fear sort of way. The Bible describes many different kinds of battles—physical ones, mental ones, emotional ones, spiritual ones. Oftentimes our battles are woven together and consume the whole of us … at least they do for me. Some struggles are out in the open, while others are hidden. Don't be deceived by what you cannot see. Many realities exist in our world that we cannot see, like gravity, wind, anger, and spiritual warfare, to name a few. But we see the results of them, don't we?

The struggle is real; satan is real. Spiritual warfare is real. We put on armor, *because* our struggle is against "cosmic powers over this present darkness."[2] Life is no quixotic sword-flailing whim against inanimate

---

1   Ephesians 6:11–12.
2   Ephesians 6:12.

windmills.[3] The enemy is after everyone—especially those of us bringing the light. The enemy is called lucifer.[4] Though his name in Latin means light-bringer, he's actually the father of darkness. The contrast of his name and what it means is stark. It's there as a warning sign. It shows the deception of what we think we're getting into when we first follow him or his ways, and then the exact opposite turns out to be our reality. Though he cannot steal our salvation, we better make sure the devil and his crew have a lot of Scripture to climb over when they tempt us to sin;[5] that Scripture is our armor.

GOD'S ARMORY

Much of the devil's activity is noted in Scripture.[6] It's there because God wants us to know the devil is real and what will become of him.[7] I sure don't want to give him one more inch of real estate in my life than I have to. The question is: Are we spiritually armed? If not, it's time to do so. The only place that stocks the armor we're looking for is Scripture. God has a rack of protective gear that we can't get anywhere else. It's His spiritual armory. Have you been to a museum, toured a castle, or seen a documentary about an armory? Picture a room full of everything needed to equip you for everything you'll ever go through in your entire life. As brand ambassadors[8] for Christ, this is our dress code. As aliens and strangers in this world, this is our space suit. As children of God, this is the plaid of our lineage-laced kilt. It's line-itemed in Ephesians 6:10–18. This is the famous passage about the armor of God. We know that all of Scripture is our protective weapon, as it points to Christ Himself Who is our true weapon

---

3   Don Quixote was the infamous literary knight, created by Cervantes, who delusionally fought windmills.

4   Isaiah 14:12–14.

5   Simply, meditation on and memorization of God's Word gets it *in* us; then when satan attacks, he is no match for the power of God's spoken Word against him and our own sin.

6   Job 1:6–2:7; Isaiah 14:12–15; Matthew 4:1–11; Luke 8:12; 1 Peter 5:8.

7   Matthew 25:41; Revelation 20:10.

8   2 Corinthians 5:20.

against evil and Victor over sin. The Bible as a whole is a living, active weapon, sharper than a two-edged sword.[9] Paul, the author of Ephesians, has battle-insight and warfare experience. In the book of Ephesians, Paul directs us put on the armor of God, including the belt, breastplate, shoes, shield, helmet, and sword.

As we sit down and read Ephesians as a whole, note how it's all about relationship, including the armor of God. This context cannot be missed. Relationships are the Biblical context of the armor of God, as seen in Paul's letter to the church in Ephesus. In the beginning and middle of the letter, there's a whole lot of *walking*[10] going on— it's a concept of offense as we're going after others and living in unity with them. Then, all of the sudden, the walking stops and we're told to *stand*— a concept of defense.[11] We're called to a life of Godly treading with our Maker and with others, followed by the command to halt and "*stand* against the schemes of the devil,"[12] "withstand in the evil day ... stand firm,"[13] and "stand."[14] Standing implies we're ready to do battle.

As we look at each piece of our spiritual armor, we'll naturally see how it functions against "the spiritual forces of evil in the heavenly places."[15] This passage may be familiar to many of you. I invite you to read it aloud or write/type it in order to see things you've never seen before. Note: Paul ends this text on the topic of prayer, as it is essential in the battle. Because prayer is such an expansive topic, I give it its own chapter, which follows this one. Let's look at our main text, Ephesians 6:10–18. As always, take a breath, pray, and then read.

> Finally, be strong in the Lord and in the strength of His
> might. Put on the whole armor of God, that you may be
> able to stand against the schemes of the devil. For we do

---

9   Hebrews 4:12.
10   Ephesians 2:2, 10; 4:1, 17; 5:2, 8, 15.
11   Ephesians 6:11, 13 (2xs), 14.
12   Ephesians 6:11.
13   Ephesians 6:13.
14   Ephesians 6:14.
15   Ephesians 6:12.

not wrestle against flesh and blood, but against the rulers, against the authorities, against the cosmic powers over this present darkness, against the spiritual forces of evil in the heavenly places. Therefore take up the whole armor of God, that you may be able to withstand in the evil day, and having done all, to stand firm. Stand therefore, having fastened on the belt of truth, and having put on the breastplate of righteousness, and, as shoes for your feet, having put on the readiness given by the gospel of peace. In all circumstances take up the shield of faith, with which you can extinguish all the flaming darts of the evil one; and take the helmet of salvation, and the sword of the Spirit, which is the Word of God, praying at all times in the Spirit, with all prayer and supplication. To that end, keep alert with all perseverance, making supplication for all the saints.

The armor of God is no stranger to books and stories outside the Bible. One of the most beloved literary characters of all time is given the armor of God. In John Bunyan's *Pilgrim's Progress*, Christian, the main character, is taken into the armory. Written in 1678, the allegorical story unfolds:

The next day they took him [Christian] and had him into the armory, where they showed him all the manner of furniture, which their Lord had provided for pilgrims, as sword, shield, helmet, breastplate, all-prayer, and shoes that would not wear out. And there was here enough of this to harness out as many men for the service of their Lord as there be stars in heaven for multitude.[16]

---

16   John Bunyan, *The Pilgrim's Progress: from This World to That Which is to Come*, (Chicago IL: S.I. Bell, 1891), chapter forty-eight.

Christian wears the armor and so should we. Paul succinctly explains our spiritual battle-wear:

1. Belt of Truth.
2. Breastplate of Righteousness.
3. Shoes of Readiness of the Gospel of Peace.
4. Shield of Faith.
5. Helmet of Salvation.
6. Sword of the Spirit.

The armor is referenced in the Old Testament in Isaiah 59:17: "He put on righteousness as a breastplate, and a helmet of salvation on His head." David proclaimed that the battle belongs to God;[17] it always has; it always will. We'll look at Roman armor back when Paul wrote Ephesians to best comprehend the spiritual armor to which he's pointing his original audience. Let's look at these pieces of defense, starting with the belt of truth.

The battle belongs to God; it always has; it always will.

BELT IT

God, through Paul, tells the church in Ephesus to "belt it." What does a belt do and why should we put one on? It strengthens and secures—strengthens what is of value and secures objects, such as a sword or tunic. As a source of protective strength, a belt holds up an outer covering so that what's beneath isn't exposed. The implication is that what is beneath is of great value. The inner parts that need covering and protection are the very epicenter of inherent value and the source for growth, multiplicity, progression, offspring, and lasting-evidence of the existence of the entire being or object as a whole. Hypothetically, the belt (whatever that

---

17   1 Samuel 17:47; Revelation 19:11–21.

is for the topic at hand) ensures that the base inner component is never compromised. The belt protects the hard drive, the germ-line, the soul. I did some fascinating study on germ-lines when I found out about my daughter's neurological condition. I talked to a geneticist and discovered fancy concepts like germ-line cells versus somatic cells, and mosaicism. Look up those terms if you have a lot of time on your hands. Bottom line: a faulty belt, one that comes off and leads to exposure, compromises future potential (germ-line), which in spiritual terms is our sanctification and gospel-influence on others.

A belt also secures weapons. A Roman soldier's belt was called a *balteus*, which means "little belt."[18] It was a leather waist-belt with leather strips hanging from it in front of the soldier's midline and frontal thighs. Oftentimes, these hanging strips had metal ornaments on them. A soldier always wore his belt, even when he wasn't working. From his belt he could secure his sword, a dagger or other small weapon, and his cloak. In order to run without constriction, he would tie up his cloak into his belt. This occurrence, commonly noted in Scripture, is also referred to as girding up one's loins.[19]

Do you see all the beautiful implications of what the belt provides? So many options of God's strength and security are made available to us as we fasten the belt of truth around the waist of our hearts and minds. We are able to secure all other spiritual weapons He provides for us as well as be spiritually nimble when dodging the arrows of the evil one.[20] The belt of truth is the structural foundation of our epicenter (our souls), which ensures our progress, influence, and success. Again and again, I can't say it enough: this is not a works-based dress-up game.

Truth is a Person ... Jesus.[21] Spend time in relationship with Him. Spiritually, our belt is to be made up of Him, our life is modeled after Him, our legacy is doused in His truth. The significance of a belt that Jesus,

18 *Theromanobritain.org*, https://www.romanobritain.org/8-military/mil_roman_soldier_belt.php. Accessed May 9, 2021.
19 2 Kings 9:1; Job 38:3; Jeremiah 1:17; 1 Peter 1:13.
20 Ephesians 6:16.
21 John 14:6.

Paul, and all of Scripture drives home is this: "stay dressed for action"[22] and be mentally ready for action.[23] If your belt is not on, you'll jump up to fight, no weapons to be found, and be exposed to the attacks of the devil and the sin he holds in front of you. The belt of truth is the first item on the list, thus highlighting its utmost importance. Next is the breastplate of righteousness.

Truth is a Person ... Jesus.

BREASTPLATE OF RIGHTEOUSNESS

Back in the first century A.D., breastplates were form-fitted metal plates that covered the breast/chest/heart area. They weighed between four and nine pounds. The breastplate protected the soldier's life-force, the heart. Notice that the spiritual breastplate is one of righteousness. The heart is the place where righteousness resides and resonates through faith.[24] The heart is deep within, and though unseen, we know it's there and functioning by nature of the life of its carrier. Righteousness itself is judicial approval—God's approval of us.[25] I can't say it enough: this divine eye of examination is between us and God. Each of us knows our verdict before the Judge. If we're still running around trying to prove that we're good people, then we must ask ourselves if we're really saved through grace and faith.[26] Good people go to hell; sinners go to heaven. Our eternal status solely rests on a personal relationship with Jesus Christ. We are made righteous by a personal relationship with the perfect Lamb, in Whose book our names are written.[27] Then the verdict is in: we are proved innocent, not guilty. This is

---

22   Luke 12:35.
23   1 Peter 1:13.
24   Romans 9:30–33.
25   *Bible Hub*, https://biblehub.com/greek/1343.htm. Accessed May 1, 2021.
26   Ephesians 2:8–9.
27   Revelation 21:23–27.

our breastplate of righteousness: Jesus' perfect state stamped all over us. The stamp says, "As if you have not sinned ... ever."

We are made righteous by a personal relationship with the perfect Lamb, in Whose book our names are written.[28]

Now go live like it. But this is hard; living the righteous life when satan is "going to and fro on the earth, and ... walking up and down on it"[29] looking for whom he may devour.[30] And in one righteous man's story (Job's), God allowed satan to directly attack. God seemingly bragged about Job: "Have you considered my servant Job, that there is none like him on earth, a blameless and upright man, who fears God and turns away from evil?"[31] God boasted about Job's righteousness because it was based on God, not Job. God banks against Himself every time we're in a spiritual battle. And God never loses. Wow! No human is exempt from spiritual warfare. But so many are exempt from God's presence when facing the schemes of the devil. It's like they're fighting without a breastplate when one is readily available to them. Take-on His stamp of approval; put on Christ; be found in Him.[32]

God banks against Himself every time we're in a spiritual battle. And God never loses.

I want to be one of the ones about whom God brags about His glory as He protects my righteousness. I still have a long way to go. When we get to heaven, we want to see the breastplate of righteousness that we wore

---

28   Revelation 21:23–27.
29   Job 1:7, 2:2.
30   1 Peter 5:8.
31   Job 1:8, 2:3.
32   Philippians 3:9.

here on this earth hanging on heaven's walls, don't we, right next to Job's righteous life? Wouldn't that be cool? Again, anything in heaven will exclusively point to God, not us, including the breastplate of righteousness we once wore.

Unrighteousness is a spiritual cancer that kills from the inside out. We must protect the epicenter of our righteousness at all costs. Weaponry assumes there will be a fight. Expect one. The devil wants to unright our right-ness. Even though he cannot unseat our saving faith, he can damage the fruit of our faith, which many times is our testimony to others. "Out of the overflow of the heart the mouth speaks."[33] And the verse just prior says the same: "The tree is known by its fruit."[34] God will get His glory, but the question is: Are we guarding our hearts with the breastplate of righteousness so that we're victors with our fearless King? In his every living cell, Paul wants to be "found in Christ, not having a righteousness of [his] own that comes from the law, but that which comes through faith in Christ, a righteousness from God that depends on faith."[35] In essence, Paul is saying that when satan attacks our righteousness, he's coming up against Christ Himself. Paul knows he is nothing apart from Christ--satan is on his own, left to his own devices, going to hell in a self-made handbasket. End of story.[36] Putting on our breastplate of righteousness always comes with a victory dance celebrating Christ's victory. Praise God for His protective presence that allows us to stand firm. Praise His holy name as we seek His holy armor daily.

The devil wants to unright our right-ness. Even though he cannot unseat our saving faith, he can damage the fruit of our faith, which many times is our testimony to others.

---

33 Matthew 12:34.
34 Matthew 12:33.
35 Philippians 3:9.
36 Revelation 20:10.

SHOE COLLECTION OF ONE PAIR

If we're standing firm, what kind of kicks are we to wear? As shoes for our feet, we're to "put on the readiness given by the Gospel of peace," as Ephesians 6:15 says. I know many people who are shoe people—that's their "thang." They have special closets built-to-order for their many pairs of shoes. Personally, I'm a slipper girl. Paul instructs the Ephesians to be shoe people as well. And their shoe menagerie is to be a collection of one, designed with the marks of readiness and the Gospel of peace. These shoes are custom-made by our Maker for us. So what are shoes of readiness?

Readiness is a Pauline word. He uses it almost ten times in his writings. The Greek word for readiness means "fitting; ready because prepared; standing by; ready because the necessary preparations are done (or are sure to happen as needed)."[37] The old noun (*heteos*)[38] for readiness means fitness. What? Did you get that? Before running shoes, tennies, and Air-Jordans, there were God's "Ready Runners." As a fitness trainer, I just love this. We all know what fitness encapsulates—frequency of training, intensity of training, time spent training, type of training.[39] The Bible instructs us not to be by-standers but *ready*-standers.

Readiness is the glitter of Paul's exhortation for our spiritual footwear; it's shining and it's everywhere:

- *Ready* to receive the Word—The Christians in Berea studied Scripture daily and pined away to receive more (Acts 17:11).
- *Ready* to give—The Christians in Corinth were called to follow the example of those in Macedonia, who generously donated love and material goods (2 Corinthians 8:1–11).

---

37   *Bible Hub*, https://biblehub.com/hebrew/2091.htm. Accessed May 1, 2021.
38   *Bible Hub*, https://biblehub.com/greek/2092.htm. Accessed May 1, 2021.
39   FITT principles. A. Barisic, S.T. Leatherdale, and N. Kreiger, "Importance of Frequency, Intensity, Time and Type (FITT) in Physical Activity Assessment for Epidemiological Research," *Canadian Journal of Public Health = Revue Canadienne De Sante Publique*, U.S. National Library of Medicine, pubmed.ncbi. nlm.nih.gov/21714314/. Accessed May 1, 2021.

- *Ready* to punish every disobedience—Paul says this readiness is essential in the defense of ministry (2 Corinthians 10:6).
- *Ready* to gift and set an example—The Christians in Corinth collected money for those in Jerusalem, and this was seen by many (2 Corinthians 9:1–5).

Does our readiness given by the Gospel mean we're running-around like crazy women? No. Being everything to everyone? No. Rat-racing? No. Our readiness is given by the Gospel of *peace*. The Gospel itself *brings* peace, doesn't it? I wouldn't put readiness and peace together first-off, especially when it's in the context of spiritual warfare. But God knows what He's doing. He knows what kind of readiness with which He's calling Paul to lead … peaceful prep and peaceful souls that He provides, even when the outer world is caving in.

This should ring a familiar bell, echoing Isaiah's words about feet and peace: "How beautiful upon the mountains are the feet of him who brings good news, who publishes peace, who brings good news of happiness, who publishes salvation, who says to Zion, 'Your God reigns.'"[40] Good news—Gospel news—wraps up all the loose ends in our lives into completion and wholeness; it always will. This is the kind of peace to which Paul directs his recipients: wholeness, the joining together of all the essential parts. And we *know* God's peace, because we're still in one piece—not destroyed by the enemy. In the original language, here peace is not a feeling but a tangible wholeness.[41] Peace is God's gift of wholeness, and our feet are best ready when fitted with the very thing that brings it—the Gospel.

SHIELD OF FAITH

We've belted it. Our feet are shod. The next piece of our spiritual armor is the shield of faith. This is no ordinary shield; this one "extinguishes all the

---

40   Isaiah 52:7.
41   *Bible Hub*, https://biblehub.com/greek/1515.htm. Accessed May 1, 2021.

flaming darts of the evil one."[42] What? This sounds crazy? I have so many questions: What kind of shield is Paul talking about? Why is it a shield of *faith*? What are the flaming darts? Who is the evil one? Why is he shooting at them? This sounds really crazy.

Shields in Roman times were ginormous. They were the size of small doors and made of wood so that the soldiers could completely hide behind them. They weighed around twenty pounds. The neatest thing about the shield was its design to be used in unison with other shields. Lined-up next to each other, the shields formed a 360-degree barrier, including a roof over those who held them. This formation was called a tortoise formation.[43] A band of Roman soldiers could advance forward, protected by wall-to-wall shielding; it looked like a moving turtle shell. Even arrows had a hard time penetrating this mobile bunker. To the spiritual forces of evil, the corporate body of Christ all lined up together must look like a divine transformer (like the transformer toys). In Christ, our shield of faith is so much "more than meets the eye," as Hebrews 11:1 states.[44] The connection is easily made: our spiritual shield—our faith—is a refuge in our spiritual war. Our faith, though individually attained and secured, is strongest in numbers. Side-by-side with fellow believers, we best advance against sin and the enemy and extinguish his destructive arrows as we stand firm and live out our faith stories, proclaiming Christ's reign. One shield alone is weak compared to our faith-collective. This is one reason why we are encouraged to gather with other believers in the local church: "Not neglecting to meet together, as is the habit of some, but encouraging one another, and all the more as you see the Day drawing near" (Hebrews 10:25).

---

42   Ephesians 6:16.

43   *History Hit*, https://www.historyhit.com/kinds-of-ancient-roman-shields/. Accessed May 9, 2021.

44   "Now faith is the assurance of things hoped for, the conviction of things not seen."

Our faith, though individually attained and secured, is strongest in numbers. Side-by-side with fellow believers, we best advance against sin and the enemy and extinguish his destructive arrows as we stand firm and live out our faith stories. One shield alone is weak compared to our faith-collective.

Why does Paul call it the shield of *faith*? If we look at the opening and closing words in the book of Ephesians, these people had noteworthy faith and noteworthy love: "... I have heard of your faith in the Lord Jesus and your love toward all the saints."[45] Paul ends his letter encouraging the Ephesians towards love with faith.[46] Biblical faith is absolute belief in God—that He exists and that He saves. Faith is one-hundred percent knowing that Christ is "a plan for the fullness of time, to unite all things to Him, things in heaven and things on earth."[47] Also, our faith in Christ, sealed by the Spirit, shields us from ever going back to our once dead state. Think about it: we have nothing for a shield to protect if we're dead. But once alive in Christ, man oh man, do we have something worth fighting for! And "the prince of the power of the air, the spirit that is now at work in the sons of disobedience" knows this.[48] As Christ-followers, we are children of obedience. That's why satan never wants us to believe in the first place. But the prince of this world is no match for the Prince of Peace.[49]

The prince of this world is no match for the Prince of Peace.

---

45   Ephesians 1:15.
46   Ephesians 6:23.
47   Ephesians 1:10.
48   Ephesians 2:2.
49   Isaiah 9:6.

"And what is the immeasurable greatness of His power toward us who believe,"[50] who have faith? Our faith gives us a front row seat to witness and experience the power of Christ's right-hand seat.[51] Talk about being armed! Right-armed … heh, heh. As a child of God, I feel so strong when I read about and study these truths of my spiritual armor. It's hard enough to walk in a manner worthy of my calling,[52] especially within the context of the many challenging human relationships like the ones that Paul discusses in Ephesians 4–6. But my shield of faith helps me to stand firm against all that is not "of flesh and blood."[53] The flaming darts of the evil one have one purpose—destruction. That's satan's job description.

Isaiah 14:13–14 records satan's back story: "I will ascend to heaven; above the stars of God I will set my throne on high; I will sit on the mount of assembly in the far reaches of the north; I will ascend above the heights of the clouds; I will make myself like the Most High." Here we have the highest-ranked angel serving the Most High God and delusionally thinking he can be like God. This was the lie he sold to Adam and Eve in the garden and that he's still trying to sell people today.[54] Clearly from the context, he's trying to annihilate our testimony, because he hates God and our faith in Him. The "angel of light" is trying to get rid of the Light; satan knows where his personal choice landed him. If he had the gall to tempt Christ,[55] how much harder will he try to tempt humanity? He desperately wants us to "go down" with him and choose to sin. Yikes. Time to put on our helmets. It's going to be a bumpy ride until God puts satan in the lake of fire.[56]

50　Ephesians 1:19.
51　Ephesians 1:20.
52　Ephesians 4:1.
53　Ephesians 6:12.
54　Genesis 3:5.
55　Matthew 4:1–11.
56　　Revelation 20:10.

HELMET OF SALVATION

As a thirty-year veteran snowboarder, I love my helmet. I wear my helmet. I need my helmet. I value my helmet. My confidence to ride, "catch air," and charge the steeps (especially at Mammoth Mountain) rests in my helmet and the protection it provides. The Roman helmet did the same. With its cheek guards and reinforcement at the front of the head, it protected against injury to the head. A helmet is pretty self-explanatory. Helmets save lives; so does God's eternal salvation.

Helmets save lives; so does God's eternal salvation.

God's helmet keeps our thoughts grounded in His truth and promises. The enemy will indeed try to attack us. He knows if he can tempt us to think crooked, we'll act crooked. Note how Paul places the armor of God right after relationship-heavy chapters. He discusses our relationship with God, with fellow believers, with Gentiles (people with different beliefs or worldviews), as prisoners, as believers, as spouses, as children, as parents, as employers, and as employees.[57] In the last chapter, we discussed how important it is to dwell on right thinking. All of our armor is important, but I know that most of the ground I lose, especially in relationships, is because of the territory I first give up on the battlefield in my mind. Mentally at times I distrust God; I grumble about my spouse; I internally feed my fear in parenting; I simmer in hurt when mistreated at work. I don't know about you, but with the helmet of salvation, the best way I protect my mind is with the Sword of the Spirit. I wield it at my warped and sinful mindset and heart-scape over and over again. We must be Scripture ninjas in order to defeat sin and the enemy.

---

57 Ephesians 4:1–6:9.

SWORD OF THE SPIRIT

Who here knows how to wield a sword? A real one? I sure don't. But from a very young age, by the grace of God, I was taught how to wield a spiritual sword, the Word of God, the Bible. I remember doing sword drills, Scripture memorization, and studying nouthetic Greek. I could recite a few epistles (in whole) from memory (thank you, Mom and Dad). I was well-versed in the names of God. I didn't know what it all meant in my youth, nor the power I was infusing into my spiritual IV, but my parents and spiritual mentors did. And for this I am eternally grateful. As said before, the Bible is sharper than a two-edged sword, as the famous verse from Hebrews says.[58] In this verse, the context of the Bible as a sword speaks of our internal terrain, as God's Word penetrates the thoughts and intentions of our hearts. The context of the Bible as a sword in Ephesians 6 speaks of a weapon we are to wield against the devil, just like Jesus did when he was tempted. The temptation of Christ is a one-on-one self-defense class for us. Here's how it went down.

> Then Jesus was led up by the Spirit into the wilderness to be tempted by the devil. And after fasting forty days and forty nights, He was hungry. And the tempter came and said to Him, "If You are the Son of God, command these stones to become loaves of bread." But He answered, "It is written, 'Man shall not live by bread alone, but by every word that comes from the mouth of God.'"
>
> Then the devil took Him to the holy city and set Him on the pinnacle of the temple and said to Him, "If You are the Son of God, throw Yourself down, for it is written, 'He will command His angels concerning you,' and 'On their hands they will bear you up, lest you strike your foot against a stone.'" Jesus said to him, "Again it is written, 'You shall not put the Lord your God to the test.'"

---

58 Hebrews 4:12.

Again, the devil took Him to a very high mountain and showed Him all the kingdoms of the world and their glory. And he said to Him, "All these I will give You, if You will fall down and worship me." Then Jesus said to him, "Be gone satan! For it is written, 'You shall worship the Lord your God and Him only shall you serve.'"

Then the devil left Him, and behold, angels came and were ministering to Him.

Matthew 4:1–11

There you have it. Christ used Scripture (He cited from Deuteronomy 8:3, 6:13, 6:16) as a sword to strike down every blow satan delivered. We should do the same. I speak many Scriptures out loud to my battles. I tell my battles how big my God is, and I speak God's character, truths, and promises at them. When a stand-off occurs between my troubles and my heart, I boldly worship God. Most of the time, my battles have no choice but to submit to the Lordship of Christ. I struggle with them longer than I'd like to admit. I make it sound easy. It's not. As a dear friend of mine says, it's those sick-to-my-stomach-trusting-Jesus moments. Have you ever had those? I've preached the Gospel to myself many times when I felt physically ill for days yet had immense mental/soulful peace that transcended my knowledge.[59] Just because we don't emotionally enjoy hardships doesn't mean that the Lord isn't ministering to us. Look at Christ's example: after fasting forty days, being in the desert, and fighting against satan, He had angels come minister to Him. And don't think for a second that God would hold back His divine army from ministering to you. You can't wield the Sword of the Spirit if you aren't holding it. Faith itself comes from hearing the Word of God.[60] If the Word of God really is our best weapon, then we'll be practicing it all the time before the real battle ensues. Training day is every day when it's God's Word we're training into our souls. Grab a friend and your Swords and let iron sharpen iron.[61]

---

59 Philippians 4:7.
60 Romans 10:17.
61 Proverbs 27:17.

You can't wield the Sword of the Spirit if you aren't holding it.

Back in the day when Paul wrote Ephesians, the swords used were short. Soldiers, from behind their shields, stabbed from close range rather than hacked. Ancient Roman soldiers used various weapons but swords were arguably the most important weapon. Our Sword of the Spirit is unarguably the most important weapon we carry. The devil should have a whole lot of Scripture to go through when trying to get to us. He doesn't stand a chance when we stand firm in God's truth as found in His Word. If you truly believe this, you'll spend time, lots of it, honing your Sword skills.

The Word of God is supernaturally used in our lives and through our lives. The Holy Spirit does His biggest work right here. This is where it all happens—battles are won, failures are grown-through, sin is beaten, and the Spirit speaks over and over again as we dig deep into the truth. We can't be "in the Spirit" if we're not in the Word. When God speaks to me, it's always when I've fire-hosed myself with Scripture. When He's silent, it's when my Sword is dusty. There are plenty of times that I'm just not "feelin' it." But I've learned to shy away from the presence of or absence from feeling when God speaks to me through His Word. It's in me, and it battles out of me … even when I'm mentally amuck, which is more often than I'd like to admit. Scripture fights our battles. Sometimes I awake at night reciting Scripture. Train in God's Word, on good days and bad days. Fill hours, minutes, and moments with Him. Training day is every day. Slowly we'll see it—we're soldiers for God. We're undefeatable, because He is undefeatable.

We can't be "in the Spirit" if we're not in the Word. When God speaks to me, it's always when I've fire-hosed myself with Scripture. When He's silent, it's when my Sword is dusty.

PRAYER

We have quite the armor—the belt of truth, the breastplate of righteousness, the shoes of readiness of the Gospel of peace, the shield of faith, the helmet of salvation, and the sword of the Spirit. Even with all this spiritual steel, one thing remains. Paul finishes describing our spiritual armor and then camps out on the concept of prayer: "… Praying at all times in the Spirit, with all prayer and supplication. To that end, keep alert with all perseverance, making supplication for all the saints, and also for me, that words may be given me in opening my mouth boldly to proclaim the mystery of the gospel."[62] Volumes have been written on the subject, and my next chapter is entirely given to it. What I want to hone in on is this: just after Paul instructs us to take up the sword of the Spirit, he tells us to pray *all the time* and *in the Spirit*.

How do we pray all the time? How do we pray in the Spirit? My simple definition of prayer is worshipful communication with God. It requires relationship, intimacy, reverence, and trust. Prayer can be spoken, thought, breathed, felt, written, shouted, or subconsciously uttered, just to name a few. Today, I don't want us to focus on *how* to pray but rather that we *are* to pray. It's that we indeed pray, "At all times," as the text says, *and* that it's "in the Spirit," according to God's will. Praying at all times is essential, like subconscious breathing, but trained like any regular conscious habit. The more we pray, the more we pray. Did you get that? It's compounding. Once we pray at all times, we start to notice fewer and fewer times we're not praying. I'll break down what this looks like in my life in the next chapter.

The more we pray, the more we pray.

I'm new to praying (real praying) and still learning. Clearly, Paul is beseeching the Ephesian church to pray for him because he knows the power of prayer—not just in his life but in the lives of those praying. His

---

62   Ephesians 6:18–19.

humility in what he asks them to pray for is astounding: "That words may be given to me in opening my mouth boldly to proclaim the mystery of the gospel."[63] If Paul, unarguably the most bold Christian in the New Testament, is asking for boldness (from a prison cell!), then what should we be asking in prayer for ourselves? I am speechless as I study Paul's example. I want to ask for bold prayers like he did. Don't you? He asks for boldness because he knows to Whom he's praying—the Most High God. I hope you're seeing this recurrent theme over and over. Yet praying like Paul scares me a little bit. What if God answers those bold prayers? What if I'm imprisoned or, more likely, rejected by people for my boldness? Let's risk our reputations in praying boldly so that God's reputation is loud and clear to us and through us.

Let's risk our reputations in praying boldly so that God's reputation is loud and clear to us and through us.

"In the Spirit" … the truth is, if we are in Christ, the Holy Spirit is constantly interceding for us with groans we cannot decipher.[64] After all, He is our Counselor.[65] The Holy Spirit will teach us God's will so that we pray God's will. To pray in the Spirit is to acknowledge His power, movement, and work right here in our day-to-day lives. He carries out the will of the Father in us. I know this often and am starting to feel it more and more. There are plenty of times I don't feel the Spirit, and that's ok. I'm still holding out for the promise that my mustard-seed-sized faith will someday move mountains.[66]

The more I take-up the sword of the Spirit and pray as often as I can, the more I literally feel the Spirit's presence, know I'm praying in Him, and am confirmed in Scripture on how to live my daily life. If we're ever going to be light-bringers, it's only with the Spirit's presence and by humbly staying

---

63   Ephesians 6:19.
64   Romans 8:26–27.
65   John 14:16.
66   Matthew 17:20.

on our knees. Sadly, some people read the Word, remain unchanged, and never bring the light. They are "futile in their thinking, and their foolish hearts [are] darkened."[67] Or they are saved, read the Word, and must be reminded to "fear not."[68] This verse is written about me, you know. I struggle with fear. It's applicable for all people for all time so that being in the Spirit becomes all we seek after—to the glory of God.

All of this armor means nothing if we haven't first been strengthened with power through His Spirit in our inner beings ... being rooted and grounded in love to have strength to comprehend "what is the breadth and length and height and depth, and to know the love of Christ that surpasses knowledge," that we may be filled with all the fullness of God.[69] We cannot be light-bringers apart from God's gift of the indwelling Spirit and our union with Him in prayer. Period. Good people are going to hell. Please, please, please let's check ourselves to make sure that we belong to Jesus *and* that we're wearing His armor. Then we will be bold like Paul to live out the truth that we're not enough, that we're mark-missers, that Jesus is enough, and that He wins.

How I wish that the apostle Paul was alive and well, living among us today. How cool would that be? We'd see the boldness he asked for in prayer right in front of our very eyes! How would our current culture respond to him? It's pretty safe to say that they'd respond to him the same way people responded to him and to Christ in the flesh—they'd reject his life-saving, light-bringing words and lifestyle. The book of Ephesians, specifically the armor of God, is just as applicable today as it was when it was written, especially considering the context of relationship hardship. For each piece of armor, Paul spiritually guides us in our relationship against evil and sin—we are to put on all of it! This side of heaven, the evil day is every day. Are we ready to stand? Christ-follower, train with that Sword, with everything you've got, with your every breath. Put on all of God's armor and stand firm. He's already won.

---

67   Romans 1:21.

68   Luke 12:32.

69   Ephesians 3:16–19.

PRAYER

God,
I know You are over all.
I know You see everything,
including the unseen spiritual world.
I trust that You fight for me.
I trust that You protect me with Your divine armor.
You know the enemy's every move,
and I will stand firm because You are in control.
I look to You to protect me from the evil one.
Thank You for giving me armor to fight against this present darkness.
I need Your holy help to continue putting on Your armor daily.
May all my days consist of using
Your belt of truth,
Your breastplate of righteousness,
Your peaceful ready-shoes,
Your shield of faith,
Your helmet of salvation,
Your sword of the Spirit,
and worshipful prayer.
Keep me alert with all perseverance.
Give me boldness to proclaim You as I ought.
I love you, Jesus.
Amen.

DISCUSSION QUESTIONS

1. What is the Biblical context of the Armor of God (Ephesians 6:10–18)? What do you think Paul is saying about how hard relationships can be and the importance of God's weapons for defending relationships?

2. What piece of God's armor is easiest and what piece is most difficult for you to put on? Why? Does struggling to fight evil and sin necessarily mean you're not winning? Why or why not? (Think about Whose might with which we fight, from Ephesians 6:10).

3. How does Jesus use Scripture to fight the devil in Matthew 4:1–11 (think context of each passage He quotes)?

4. What other passages in Scripture confirm the reality of an unseen spirit world? Use your concordance if needed. Why do Christians get frozen in "suiting-up" God's spiritual armor and shrink-back from boldly showing it to the watching world? Are you willing to go the distance and be Christ's armed ambassador, even if in chains or when you face trials (Ephesians 6:20)?

CHAPTER 9
STOP, DROP, AND PRAY

---

1 Samuel 1, 2:1-11, 3

"I'll be praying for you." How often do we hear this? Even more so, how often do we say it to others? Do we pray for them? Do we even remember we told them we'd pray for them? Countless times I've said this phrase and never prayed for that person who so desperately needs prayer. Honestly, I did it last week. It convicts me to my core. This is because I desperately need prayer all of the time. The apostle Paul tells us that our armor is incomplete without prayer.[1] I have worked for years to train myself to say "I'll be praying for you" if and only if either I stop, drop, and pray for the person right then and there *or* I pray for him or her as I walk away. I'm still a work in progress on this prayerful front. As one author puts it, "… Pray right then and there. Why wait? You can certainly still put any need on your prayer list. And you can still review your day as you slip into bed. But praying in the moment invites God's intervention that much sooner."[2] As we are confident in the God to Whom we pray, we will be confident to pray anytime for anyone. Try it. I dare you.

---

1   Ephesians 6:18.
2   Jay K. Payleitner, *What If God Wrote Your To-Do List? 52 Ways to Make the Most of Every Day*, (Eugene, OR: Harvest House Publishers, 2018) 71.

I stop-drop-and-pray over people a lot these days—not because it saves face when I say "I'll pray for you," but because I've seen prayer work. Prayer is serious business with God. Rather than throwing prayer around like a sentimental verbal wish, let's callous the knees of our hearts with it. Let's fill the airways of heaven with it, as Revelation 5:8 depicts: "…the twenty-four elders fell down before the Lamb, each holding a harp, and golden bowls of incense, *which are the prayers of the saints*" (emphasis added). Did you hear that? Our prayers, collectively throughout history, will all arise together in a holy aroma pleasing to God.

We should have more moments where we pray than moments where we don't pray, because our prayers mingle with the eternal. Prayer, offered through finite expression of the limits of humanity, has vast eternal effects. We see how Jesus prayed as both God and man. He told His disciples how to pray and how to not pray.

---

*We should have more moments where we pray
than moments where we don't pray, because our prayers
mingle with the eternal.*

- **Pray Like This:** "Our Father in heaven, hallowed be Your name. Your kingdom come, Your will be done, on earth as it is in heaven. Give us this day our daily bread, and forgive us our debts, as we also have forgiven our debtors. And lead us not into temptation, but deliver us from evil" (Matthew 6:9–13).

  "But when you pray, go into your room and shut the door and pray to your Father Who is in secret. And your Father Who sees in secret will reward you" (Matthew 6:6).

- **Don't Pray Like This:** "And when you pray, you must not be like the hypocrites. For they love to stand and pray in the synagogues and at the street corners, that they may be seen by others. Truly, I say to you, they have received their reward" (Matthew 6:5).

"And when you pray, do not heap up empty phrases as the Gentiles do, for they think that they will be heard for their many words. Do not be like them, for your Father knows what you need before you ask Him" (Matthew 6:7–8).

I want to sit at Jesus' feet like the disciples and ask Him, "Lord, You make prayer sound so simple, easy, and well-defined. Then why, Lord, is prayer so complex, mysterious, and hard at times?" I see exactly why the disciples said, "Lord, teach us to pray."[3] I think I would've asked Him the same question if He was standing next to me. We're going to dig a little deeper into the soul-prayer of a woman in the Old Testament named Hannah. I just love Hannah. She shows us whom to be prayerfully. She inspired another famous pray-er—Mary, the mother of Jesus, who voiced one of the most famous prayers of all time, The Magnificat.[4] Mary prayed like Hannah. I want to pray like Hannah too.

Talk about prayer pose, Hannah perfected it. In 1 Samuel 1, 2:1–11, 3, Hannah teaches us about prayer as she consistently prayed, expectantly prayed, and obediently followed through on her prayers. Through prayer, Hannah entered the throne room of God in such a way that the throne room actually came to her son, as God directly spoke to him. Let's read our three chapters from 1 Samuel. There's a lot of reading here; as always, I encourage you to read it aloud in one sitting. These words from Scripture carry such detail and truth that we don't want to miss any of it. Being women of the Word means we read the Word—a lot of it, over and over again—so as not to miss a thing.

Being women of the Word means we read the Word—a lot of it, over and over again—so as not to miss a thing.

---

3   Luke 11:1.
4   Luke 1:46–55.

Our aim in this chapter is prayer, and I will keep us on that course despite the many other life lessons presented in this story (like Hannah having six more children after Samuel, AND Eli the priest and his humility and trust in God even when his sons were awful and condemned, AND the fact that Hannah isn't in a perfect marriage and comes from a twisted cultural norm of polygamy and favoritism, AND Hannah's family though not perfect is dedicated to worshiping God). Think back to the chapters about the tabernacle, the priest, and his role (chapters five and six). I won't deliver a complete Old Testament history class on the prophets, Israel's covenant disobedience, and God's delivered wrath (nor could I), though a basic knowledge of these concepts will help us comprehend Hannah's understanding of God and willingness to submit to Him. Here's the story of Hannah's consistent, expectant, life-altering prayer life. Pause and pray for God's mighty Spirit to speak to you as you read this passage.

HANNAH TALKS TO THE LORD

There was a certain man of Ramathaim-zophim of the hill country of Ephraim whose name was Elkanah the son of Jeroham, son of Elihu, son of Tohu, son of Zuph, an Ephrathite. He had two wives. The name of one was Hannah, and the name of the other, Peninnah. And Peninnah had children, but Hannah had no children. Now this man used to go up year by year from his city to worship and sacrifice to the Lord of hosts at Shiloh, where the two sons of Eli, Hophni and Phinehas, were priests of the Lord. On the day when Elkanah sacrificed, He would give portions to Peninnah his wife and to all her sons and daughters. But to Hannah he gave a double portion, because he loved her, though the Lord had closed her womb. And her rival used to provoke her grievously to irritate her, because the Lord had closed her womb. So it went on year by year. As often as she went up to the house of the Lord, she used to provoke her. Therefore Hannah wept and would not eat. And Elkanah, her husband said to her, "Hannah, why do you weep? And why do you not eat? And why is your heart sad? Am I not more to you than ten sons?"

After they had eaten and drank in Shiloh, Hannah rose. Now Eli the priest was sitting on the seat beside the doorpost of the temple of the Lord. She was deeply distressed and prayed to the Lord and wept bitterly. And she vowed a vow and said, "O Lord of hosts, if You will indeed look on the affliction of Your servant and remember me and not forget Your servant, but will give to Your servant a son, then I will give him to the Lord all of his days, and no razor shall touch his head."

As she continued praying before the Lord, Eli observed her mouth. Hannah was speaking in her heart; only her lips moved, and her voice was not heard. Therefore Eli took her to be a drunken woman. And Eli said to her, "How long will you go on being drunk? Put your wine away from you." But Hannah answered, "No, my lord, I am a woman troubled in spirit. I have drunk neither wine nor strong drink, but I have been pouring out my soul before the Lord. Do not regard your servant as a worthless woman, for all along I have been speaking out of my great anxiety and vexation." Then Eli answered, "Go in peace, and the God of Israel grant your petition that you have made to Him." And she said, "Let your servant find favor in your eyes." Then the woman went her way and ate, and her face was no longer sad. They rose early in the morning and worshiped before the Lord; then they went back to their house at Ramah. And Elkanah knew Hannah his wife, and the Lord remembered her. And in due time Hannah conceived and bore a son, and she called his name Samuel, for she said, "I have asked for him from the Lord."

The man Elkanah and all his house went up to offer to the Lord the yearly sacrifice and to pay his vow. But Hannah did not go up, for she said to her husband, "As soon as the child is weaned, I will bring him, so that he may appear in the presence of the Lord and dwell there forever." Elkanah her husband said to her, "Do what seems best to you; wait until you have weaned him; only may the Lord establish His word." So the woman remained and nursed her son until she weaned him. And when she had weaned him, she took him up with her, along with a three-year-old bull, an ephah of flour, and a skin of wine, and she brought him to the house of the Lord at Shiloh. And the child was young. Then they slaughtered the bull, and they brought the child to Eli. And she said, "Oh, my lord! As you live, my lord, I am the woman who was standing here in your presence, praying to the Lord. For this child I prayed, and the Lord has granted me my petition that I made to Him. Therefore I have lent him to the Lord. As long as he lives, he is lent to the Lord." And he worshiped the Lord there.

1 Samuel 1

HANNAH'S PRAYER

And Hannah prayed and said, "My heart exults in the Lord; my horn is exalted in the Lord. My mouth derides my enemies, because I rejoice in Your salvation. There is none holy like the Lord; for there is none besides You; there is no rock like our God. Talk no more so very proudly, let not arrogance come from your mouth; for the Lord is a God of knowledge, and by Him actions are weighed. The bows of the mighty are broken, but the feeble bind on strength. Those who were full have hired themselves out for bread, but those who were hungry have ceased to hunger. The barren has borne seven, but she who has many children is forlorn. The Lord kills and brings to life; He brings down Sheol and raises up. The Lord makes poor and makes rich; He brings low and He exalts. He raises up the poor from the dust; He lifts the needy from the ash heap to make them sit with princes and inherit a seat of honor. For the pillars of the earth are the Lord's and on them He has set the world. He will guard the feet of His faithful ones, but the wicked shall be cut off in darkness, for not by might shall a man prevail. The adversaries of the Lord shall be broken to pieces; against them He will thunder in heaven. The Lord will judge the ends of the earth; He will give strength to His king and exalt the horn of His anointed." Then Elkanah went home to Ramah. And the boy was ministering to the Lord in the presence of Eli the priest.

1 Samuel 2:1–11

THE LORD TALKS TO SAMUEL

Now the boy Samuel was ministering to the Lord in the presence of Eli. And the word of the Lord was rare in those days; there was no frequent vision. At that time Eli, whose eyesight had begun to grow dim so that he could not see, was lying down in his own place. The lamp of God had not yet gone out, and Samuel was lying down in the temple of the Lord, where the ark of God was. Then the Lord called Samuel, and he said, "Here I am!" and ran to Eli and said, "Here I am, for you called me." But he said, "I did not call; lie down again." So he went and lay down. And the Lord called again, "Samuel!" and Samuel arose and went to Eli and said, "Here I am, for you called me." But he said, "I did not call, my son; lie down again." Now Samuel did not yet know the Lord, and the word of the Lord had not yet been revealed to him. And the Lord called Samuel again the third time. And he arose and went to Eli and said, "Here I am, for you have called me." Then Eli perceived that the Lord was calling the boy. Therefore Eli said to Samuel, "Go, lie down, and if He calls you, you shall say, 'Speak, Lord, for Your servant hears.'" So Samuel went and lay down in his place. And the Lord came and stood, calling as at other times, "Samuel! Samuel!" And Samuel said, "Speak, for Your servant hears." Then the Lord said to Samuel, "Behold, I am about to do a thing in Israel at which the two ears of everyone who hears it will tingle. On that day I will fulfill against Eli all that I have spoken concerning his house, from beginning to end. And I declare to him that I am about to punish his house forever, for the iniquity that he knew, because his sons were blaspheming God, and he did not restrain them. Therefore I swear to the house of Eli that the iniquity of Eli's house shall not be atoned for by sacrifice or offering forever."

Samuel lay until morning then he opened the doors of the house of the Lord. And Samuel was afraid to tell the vision to Eli. But Eli called Samuel and said, "Samuel, my son." And he said, "Here I am." And Eli said, "What was it that He told you? Do not hide it from me. May God do so to you and more also if you hide anything from me of all that He told you." So Samuel told him everything and hid nothing from him. And he said, "It is the Lord. Let Him do what seems good to Him." And Samuel grew, and the Lord was with him and let none of his words fall to the ground. And all Israel from Dan to Beersheba knew that Samuel was established as a prophet of the Lord. And the Lord appeared again at Shiloh, for the Lord revealed Himself to Samuel at Shiloh by the word of the Lord.

1 Samuel 3

CONSISTENT PRAYER

"Steadfast adherence to the same principles [or] course": this is the dictionary definition of consistency. To pray consistently is to cling unwaveringly to identical principles—to God Himself and all that He reveals Himself to be in Scripture. There's an "over and over and over again" patterning canopied in consistent praying. It's God's preeminence both *as* we pray and *in* our prayers. Hannah explicitly "stays the course" regarding consistency in her prayers. They are made of the same matter, over and over and over again—of God Himself. She is but a conduit pointing everyone, even the priest, to the Lord. Picture a teacher at the front of the classroom using a pointer. The teacher uses his or her pointer to get our attention off self and on to what lies at the end of that point, or what's written on the board or PowerPoint. Listen to Hannah as she does this in her prayer found in 1 Samuel 2.

- "My heart exults in the Lord (inner triumph based not in self but in God); my horn is exalted in the Lord (outer amplification and magnification of God)" (1 Samuel 2:1).
- "I rejoice (am very happy) in Your salvation (God's victory gifted to us)" (1 Samuel 2:1).
- "There is none holy like the Lord (she reverently knows her place and God's place on the holiness scale); for there is none besides You (God *is* the scale; Hannah isn't even on it); there is no rock like our God (the only thing that remains firm is God, period)" (1 Samuel 2:2).
- "For the Lord is a God of knowledge (omniscience, He knows the whole story and every perspective), and by Him actions (Hannah's as well as those who purposely provoked and irritated Hannah) are weighed (addressed by a just Judge)" (1 Samuel 2:3).
- "The Lord kills and brings to life (He ends and authors life; He's in the position to do so)" (1 Samuel 2:6).
- "The Lord makes poor and makes rich; He brings low and He exalts. He raises up the poor from the dust; He lifts the needy from the ash heap to make them sit with princes and inherit a seat of honor (He

is in the position to place people wherever He wishes, because He is the Most High God; He knows true needs and He knows the timing and manner of publicly honoring us)" (1 Samuel 2:7–8).

- "For the pillars of the earth are the Lord's and on them He has set the world (He owns, or rather *is*, the foundational support of all creation—Hannah, her family life, her womb, her legacy rest on Him)" (1 Samuel 2:8).
- "He will guard (keep safe) the feet (life and direction) of His faithful ones (those whose center is Him)" (1 Samuel 2:9).
- "The Lord will judge (one of His names is Judge and He perfectly does so) the ends of the earth (there is no territory that is not His); He will give strength to His king and exalt the horn of His anointed (ultimately, all of the Old Testament, with which Hannah was obviously familiar, points to the Messiah, Jesus; her son Samuel was part of the process to usher-in the human royalty, which eventually leads to Jesus)"[5] (1 Samuel 2:10).

I think it's safe to say this is one example of many prayers Hannah uttered long before she desired a child, long before she received a child, and long after permanently lending her child to the Lord. When the Bible says, "she continued praying before the Lord,"[6] this most likely was not a one-time ditch effort. I have a feeling that Hannah heaped (which is what *continued* means)[7] prayers at the Lord's feet quite often, perhaps more often when at home. The text doesn't say, but maybe her husband saw her; her children (to come) would see her; her servants saw her. She reminds me of Susannah Wesley, who's well known for pausing in the middle of chaotic family life, throwing her apron over her head, and praying under it.[8] Who's got an apron I can borrow?

---

5 Psalm 2:1.

6 1 Samuel 1:12.

7 *Bible Hub*, https://biblehub.com/hebrew/7235.htm. Accessed May 2, 2021.

8 Jackie Green and Lauren Green Mcafee, *Only One Life: How A Woman's Every Day Shapes an Eternal Legacy*, www.bible.com/reading-plans/11880-only-one-lifea-womans-every-day-shapes-legacy/day/6. Accessed May 2, 2021.

One doesn't just show up at the doorpost of the temple[9] and pray like a crazy lady if she hasn't been praying like a crazy lady at the doorposts of her own heart and home. Eli the priest thinks she's drunk! She responds, "I have drunk neither wine nor strong drink, but I have been pouring (dumping) out my soul before (face-to-face) the Lord."[10] She never wanders away from God as the principal Cause in the world. There's no option in her mind for God not to answer her in His way and in His time, even in "killing and bringing life."[11] We see her belief in God's sovereignty as she says, "For the pillars of the earth are the Lord's and on them He has set the world."[12] Post this view of God smack dab in the middle of your prayer life and see how you change. See how big God gets. Our experience will be like Lucy's in C.S. Lewis' *Prince Caspian*:

> "Aslan" said Lucy "you're bigger."
> "That is because you are older, little one" answered he.
> "Not because you are?"
> "I am not. But every year you grow, you will find me bigger."[13]

The more we know God, the bigger He seems. With much time spent talking to Him, we start to see that He upholds the pillars, not just of the earth, but of the sinews in our souls.

The more we know God, the bigger He seems. With much time spent talking to Him, we start to see that He upholds the pillars, not just of the earth, but of the sinews in our souls.

---

9   1 Samuel 1:9. The doorpost of the temple was as close as women could get to God in that culture.
10   1 Samuel 1:15.
11   1 Samuel 2:6.
12   1 Samuel 2:8.
13   C.S. Lewis, *Prince Caspian*, (New York, NY: Macmillan Publishers, 1970), 136.

We are built to rest on Him. Hannah does this all the time. She breathes her prayers out of a polygamous marriage, marital favoritism, barrenness, family rivalry, deep distress, and being misunderstood by spiritual leadership. Her story in some ways is mine, yours, and ours, as we too experience all but perfect lives. I can relate to Hannah. Can you? How do our prayers look in the "good, the bad, and the ugly" moments? Are they consistent, just like God Himself is consistent? One of the strands of Hannah's prayers is consistency; another strand is expectancy.

EXPECTANT PRAYER

There's a play on words here, for sure, when we visualize Hannah's expectant prayer life in the very midst of her expecting her long prayed-for firstborn son. As women, we can feel her heart pangs while seeing her birth pangs—all rooted in God and blooming into fruit that praises Him. How does Hannah exhibit expectant prayer?

- She went "often" to pray in the house of the Lord; that's where He was to be found.[14] You don't go somewhere often unless you're expecting to find something, or Someone.
- When "deeply distressed," she prayed, expecting God to change her circumstances (note the text does not say she expected God to give her what she requested).[15]
- She vowed to the Most High God. (Vows in general are serious dealings; vows to God are nothing shorter than intense expectant faith in the One to whom she's vowing.)[16]
- She expected the promised Messiah.[17]

Hannah's prayer in 1 Samuel 2 came after she received her precious boy. Here's the thing: I believe Hannah would've prayed the same prayer

---

14   1 Samuel 1:7.
15   1 Samuel 1:8, 10.
16   1 Samuel 1:11.
17   1 Samuel 2:10.

even if Samuel hadn't come along. She knows that the "seat of honor"[18] is found not in *having* a child of her own but in *being* a child of God. As I've said before, everything after that is gravy. Expectancy, when it comes to prayer, is an excitement about God and what He's about to do. If we expect our prayers to be answered the way we want, then our prayer life hasn't even begun. Expectant prayers bring us so close to the Lord, especially when we get what we don't want or don't get what we do want. How God answers our prayers are all opportunities to trust the One Who far exceeds all our expectations.

The gains of expectant prayers are of God Himself.

This happened in my own life when my husband and I were faced with the decision to keep our children in the Christian school in which they were raised or to homeschool them. We prayed and prayed and prayed. I knew God would answer; I expected Him to answer. I asked for a neon sign and got one … actually two. We wanted to keep our kids in their beloved school, but God showed us directly that we should homeschool. And guess what … I cried sad and happy tears; I felt alone being away from a community that I loved, but I saw where God was leading our family and ecstatically followed Him because there's no place I'd rather be than in His will. I felt God's transcendental peace.[19] A few weeks after our decision, He gave us a second unasked for neon sign: we got coveted spots in a charter school (when charter schools were shut down and defunded during Covid-19). Praying can come with tumultuous decisions; sometimes we get a sign, but most of the time we don't. There will most certainly be losses. But the gains of expectant prayers are of God Himself. Isn't that what we're after? We must never forget that we are in the presence of an ordered God. Do I hear an amen? I love what I learn through prayer as I bask in a closer

---

18   1 Samuel 2:8.
19   Philippians 4:7.

relationship with God. Prayer never moves God; rather, it moves us closer to Him and His will.

OBEDIENCE TO PRAYER

Talk about prayer moving us. Prayer certainly moved Hannah even closer to God. Her obedience to prayer was two-fold: she raised up a son in the Lord, and she fulfilled her vow to God as she gave Samuel back to Him. Our prayer can be the conduit of God's truth powerfully showing up in the next generation. I am astounded at Samuel's faith at such a young age. "And when she had weaned him, she took him up with her … and she brought him to the house of the Lord at Shiloh. And the child was young … And he worshipped the Lord there."[20] "Ancient Hebrews completed weaning at about three years. Most children in traditional societies are completely weaned between two and four years of age."[21] Hannah most likely weaned Samuel between three and four, according to her culture. Note that 1 Samuel 1:28 says, "And he worshipped the Lord there."

Our prayer can be the conduit of God's truth
powerfully showing up in the next generation.

Have you ever brought a three or four year old to church and had a "worship the Lord" experience? Never have I had a worshipful experience with a small child while in "big church." This verse gives us profound insight into the kind of woman that Hannah was and the kind of child that Samuel was. Samuel had intense spiritual maturity and a sense of the Divine at a young age. He worshipped because his parents worshipped, as seen in 1 Samuel 1:3, 19. When Hannah left Samuel with the priest and

20 1 Samuel 1:24–28.
21 "Weaning from the Breast." *Paediatrics & Child Health*, Pulsus Group Inc, Apr. 2004, www.ncbi.nlm.nih.gov/pmc/articles/PMC2720507/. Accessed May 2, 2021.

went home, "The boy (three or four years old) was ministering to the Lord in the presence of Eli the priest."[22] Wow. This is the boy of whom God says, "I will raise up for myself a faithful priest, who shall do according to what is in My heart and in My mind. And I will build him a sure house, and he shall go in and out before My anointed forever."[23] This is the boy to whom the Lord directly spoke after many years of "no frequent vision" and the word of the Lord being rare.[24] This boy did according to what was in God's heart and mind, because he was raised by a mama who did according to what was in God's heart and mind. This reality was not the result of a perfect parenting equation but of a humble, prayerful connection with the Most High God. A three year old who knows how to minister to the Lord does so, because he ministered to the Lord at home many times before he showed up at Shiloh. A three year old like this was raised by a human who was an excellent wife, a Godly mother, a faithful worshiper, and most likely a loyal friend and kind neighbor.

Are you feeling who Hannah was? Are you in awe? Wouldn't you love to have a book of the Bible full of just her prayers alone? Do you want to be like her? Hannah is a tangible example of the Proverbs 31 woman. She most likely was humble and would be appalled that we're still talking about her today. Unless … unless she knew that our talking about her made us talk more about the Lord, which it does. Thank you, Hannah. We love you.

Not only did Hannah raise Samuel humbly to show reverence to God, [25] but she gave him back to God. She didn't ever consider her son to be hers but always the Lord's child. Talk about a high view of God! The culmination of Hannah's identity comes in this moment: "I have lent him to the Lord. As long as he lives, he is lent to the Lord."[26] No matter how Godly you are, giving your own child over to the priest to raise him "as long as he (Samuel) lives" is no easy task. Let us not think this was easy for Hannah.

---

22 1 Samuel 2:11.

23 1 Samuel 2:35.

24 1 Samuel 3:1.

25 1 Samuel 1:28. *Bible Hub*, https://biblehub.com/hebrew/7812.htm. Accessed May 2, 2021.

26 1 Samuel 1:28.

Note: the text doesn't record anything but her obedience. Hannah prayed; she obeyed. That's all.

Hannah prayed; she obeyed. That's all.

I wonder if she saw her son year-to-year. I wonder if he knew his own mother. I wonder if they hugged. I wonder if she sent him care packages. I wonder if he began to teach her how to worship. Being women of prayer comes with a cost—God will ask us to do hard things. Remember that He did the hardest thing by sending His one and only Son away from Himself to die for us.[27] God set the example and so did Hannah. So can we. Obedience is no siesta. Often I feel uncomfortable with this light-bringing business. Do you? Good, then we're right where God wants us.

VOWING BY DEFAULT

Though we make no literal vow to lend our children to the Lord, our allegiance to Him is a vow by default. For those of you who have no children, this pertains to anyone in your sphere of influence. Personally, I attempt to pray and minister to the Lord in my daily life as to leave a legacy like Hannah did. Do my husband, children, and the people in my life worship the Lord and minister to Him as a result of being around me? I am humbled by this question, because I must answer no at times. But by the grace of God I can answer yes some of the time. Then there's a start. A vow is very serious, and so is our salvation and its effects on our prayer life. Every time we pray and obey, we use our pointers and show the watching world God's light. And when we fail (which we will), we point to the God Who never fails. Our failings won't ever get in His way. The light He brings works around our frail humanity, as He is all-powerful.

---

27   John 3:16.

HE REMEMBERS

I love studying what names mean in the Bible, especially when someone gets a new name. We'll look at my favorite meaning of a name-change in chapter twelve when Joseph gets his new name. The name Samuel means "heard of God." Hannah named him this, because of Who God was: *Hannah* was heard; *God* was the Hearer. So every time people said Samuel's name, they were called to the truth that God hears when we call to Him. My question for us today in our current culture is: How do we point a watching world to the fact that God is a prayer-Hearer? Is God hearing our prayers the same as God answering our prayers? Does it matter? Let's see what the Bible says about the kind of prayers that God hears. (This of course doesn't mean that God misses some prayers; He doesn't miss a thing.) He listens to certain prayers, or in Hannah's case, He *remembers*.[28]

- Proverbs 15:29—"The Lord is far from the wicked, but He hears the prayer of the righteous."
- John 9:31—"We know that God does not listen to sinners, but if anyone is a worshiper of God and does His will, God listens to him."
- 1 Peter 3:12—"For the eyes of the Lord are on the righteous, and His ears are open to their prayer. But the face of the Lord is against those who do evil."

We see the undeniable connection between God hearing our prayers and our righteousness. If our righteousness is still on the "filthy rags"[29] side of the equation, then we must stop, drop, and pray for Christ's righteousness right now and repent. "Believe in the Lord Jesus, and you will be saved."[30] And "everyone who calls on the name of the Lord will be saved."[31] It's His righteousness that gets our prayers heard, never our own. And if we're *in Him*, all of our prayers will be *of Him*. Stop praying for parking spots (unless you need one for the sake of the Gospel). How about praying

---

28   1 Samuel 1:19.
29   Isaiah 64:6.
30   Acts 16:31.
31   Romans 10:13.

for the person already parked in the parking spot and for an opportunity to strike up a conversation with him or her unto salvation. I know. I know. You think I'm crazy. I am.

Once I saw a woman weeping in her car on the side of the road. I made a U-turn, pulled over behind her, approached her window, and heard her sad story. We stopped and prayed together, right there on the side of the road. Seek the Spirit's leading in prayer; be willing to bathe others in it, even if it's uncomfortable. Jesus will walk people over to us as we immediately pray, even in the parking lot or on the street. Don't overthink it; He sees our hearts; He knows our motivations. For that, we can be secure in our prayer life.

Seek the Spirit's leading in prayer; be willing to bathe others in it, even if it's uncomfortable.

DIVINE APPOINTMENTS

Every time you come to God in prayer, you have a divine appointment. Clear your calendar. Get ready for it every time you meet with Him. The Bible is full of divine appointments—some in prayer, some in commands, some in whispers, some in silence, some in wrath. An appointment is "an arrangement to meet someone at a particular time and place."[32] Children of God, get ready for it! God's communion with us through prayer always, always, always points to His truth and His promise that "salvation belongs to the Lord." Don't drag your feet, run away, or have a pity-party like Jonah.[33] Union with God is our worshipful end-game every time we pray. Prayers, utterings, even reverential silence are the trickles, run-offs, streams, and rivers that all end in God Himself. And prayers that don't

---

32 "Dictionary," Google, www.google.com/search?q=appointment definition. Accessed May 2, 2021.
33 Jonah 2:9.

end in the Lord must be checked against Scripture and the Spirit. As we saw at the beginning of this chapter, the prayers of once unrighteous folk become a collective holy aroma to the Most High God. We must not save prayer for our endgame. We must not fall prey to the "prayer is all we have left" mindset. Prayer is all we have. It's all we've ever had. Start with it! Pray when we can see and pray when we cannot see.

The prayers of once unrighteous folk become a collective holy aroma to the Most High God.

PRAYING SILENT, PRAYING BLIND

Praying silent and *praying blind* are two personal ways I have grown in my personal prayer life. I learned to pray these ways through being a mother, though I know all of us can pray like this in whatever circumstances we find ourselves. I first learned to pray, for real, at the age of thirty-seven, as I prayed silent. I had been a Christ-follower my whole life and knew I had not even tapped into any type of prayer life to write home about. But I prayed nonetheless. Then, oh then, I learned how to pray when my daughter was born with her medical condition. Those first four days in the NICU, I sat in the presence of the Most High God ... silent. No words were said, no words were thought, and no words were felt. I just sat before God in silent reverent prayer. Just Him and I. The only thing I remember feeling was my utter brokenness and sorrow and His closeness and sovereignty. In this prayerful state, one thing stuck out to me: I was angry, but I was not angry at God.

We wordlessly talked so much, God and I, those first three days. I just waited in God's presence. And then on day four, the first real prayerful words came to me—"cover me." That was all I could get out. That was all I could utter. Those words came beseechingly exhaled out of me, over and over again, coupled with an image in my mind of God closing me and my daughter up tight in His almighty safe hands. In uttering them,

I was commanding God (not really commanding, but rather calling Him to His promises) to be all that He already is and never can not be—to be true to His character. But I needed my ears to hear my own mouth utter them. I had to hear myself say that He was already indeed covering me in my anguish; that He had never stopped covering me in my pain; and that He would always continue covering me and my daughter no matter what we faced.

Three months later, I stumbled across the verse, "And the Lord shut [Noah] in."[34] The Hebrew word for *shut in* means "to close, hands over something to cover it, tightly shut."[35] That's the word used for when God Himself shut the door of the ark. Isn't that beautiful? That was my very prayer in my personal storm, from within my hypothetical ark. Friends, God shuts us in—so tightly at times—not to crush us or keep us in the dark but to keep us safe unto Himself through the storm.[36] In that hard time, Who He was—the Coverer—became my only prayer. Friends, pray silent. God will fill in the words with His very presence and truths.

God shuts us in—so tightly at times—not to crush us or keep us in the dark but to keep us safe unto Himself through the storm.

I've also learned how to *pray blind*. It started like this: I awakened multiple nights, very much like George Muller,[37] and I knew the Spirit was prodding me to pray outside one of my children's doors. I didn't do it at first, but God's holy nudging didn't cease. I dragged my feet and then finally obeyed. I prayed, morning after morning, in the dark, hands on the door, sitting on the floor. I didn't know what to pray for, so my prayers

---

34 Genesis 7:16.

35 *Bible Hub*, www.google.com/search?q=appointment definition. Accessed May 2, 2021.

36 Psalm 91:1.

37 George Mueller was a Christian in the 1800s who preached the Gospel and started orphanages in Bristol, England. He refused to take a salary and solely relied upon the Lord to provide for him and the children under his care.

were general. Then it happened. My husband and I stumbled upon a lie, a four-month lie that this particular child was hiding. I cried so much at this discovery—not just sad tears, because of dishonesty and sin, but happy tears because God was telling me to pray blind for my child because *God knew, God saw.* This child was struggling, and I didn't know it. God was leading me into the throne room on that child's behalf so the throne room would and could confront my child's heart. Praying blind instantly took over my world that day. I started praying for people at the stoplight next to me in my car. I started praying blind at all three of my kids' doors almost daily. I started praying for my husband and his spiritual success. I had no idea for what I was praying, because, like I said, it was blind. God led; I prayed. One time, God said to pray for a friend's child, so I did. I saw that mother and told her I had prayed for her child that day. She asked me what time. The exact time I prayed for that child was the moment his hard heart was softened! Friends, pray blind. God sees what we cannot see.

Pray blind. God sees what we cannot see.

PRAYING IT FORWARD

Hannah is an example to all of us of a prayerful woman. Hannah instructs us about prayer as she consistently prays, expectantly prays, and responds in obedience to her prayers. Her prayers had massive effects on those around her and on her child. I want my prayers to have massive effects on my husband, kids, and everyone around me. I want Hannah-like prayers to flow out of me to the Lord for His glory. The neatest thing about Hannah (I saved the best for last) is the meaning of her name. *Hannah* means "beseech, show favor, be gracious, long for, inclined toward."[38] She had this name long before she was barren, long before she beseeched God, long before she longed for a child. Her parents gave her this name before her

---

38   *Bible Hub,* https://biblehub.com/hebrew/2603.htm. Accessed May 9, 2021.

life unfolded, before she chose to follow God. Her name implies that she herself may have been the product of a God-beseeching prayer by a God-inclined mother. Hannah's mother most likely prayed-it-forward. Hannah prayed-it-forward. We'll never know all of her history because Scripture doesn't say. What we do know is that Hannah prayed and God remembered her prayer. Oh, to be like her ... to stop, drop, and pray! Word-readers and light-bringers: let's be the consistent, expectant, obedient pray-ers who see God moving mountains out of our mustard-seed-size faith.[39]

---

39   Matthew 17:20.

PRAYER

Dear God,
Cover me,
cover my loved ones,
cover Your saints,
cover this world,
with all that You are (loving, knowing, hearing)
and everything You've always been (creating, saving, nourishing).

Teach me to pray as Jesus did,
acknowledging Your holy name
and looking for a kingdom and will that are Yours, and Yours alone.
You are my final expectation.
You are my only constant.
You are the point on which I want my life to hinge.

May my prayers focus on Your will,
grounded in Your power, justice, and unwavering hold over everything.
Make me like Hannah, praying in faith, praying big, and
praying respectfully
at the doorposts of every place of influence in my life,
to Your glory.
Amen.

DISCUSSION QUESTIONS

1. What does 1 Samuel 1 say over and over about Hannah? Could the same be said about you?

2. Open your Bible to Hannah's Prayer (1 Samuel 2:1–11). Underline everything the text says about God. Now pray it back to Him aloud.

3. Who do you most relate to in 1 Samuel 3: Eli, who was passed by, *or* Samuel, who was chosen? Note how the Lord uses both people, each at a different season, for Israel's salvation and God's glory. How is God calling you to serve Him right where you are in your current season?

4. Why do you think the Lord's Prayer is one of the most well-known passages of Scripture? Read Matthew 5–7 to refresh the Biblical context of the Lord's Prayer. Why might teaching the disciples (and us) how to pray be important in light of the Scriptural themes that surround it?

WHAT TO DO:
RESPONSE/WORSHIP/SELFLESSNESS

CHAPTER 10
LEVEL UP

Psalm 1; Joshua 1:1–9

"I'm a sailor. I sail!" Do you remember these lines from the movie *What About Bob?* In this scene, Bob (Bill Murray's character, who struggles with mental health and is completely lovable) is tied to a sailboat yelling, "I'm a sailor. I sail!" It's a hilarious demonstration of a heartfelt yet incorrect proclamation by Bob that just because he's on a ship that's sailing, he's automatically a sailor. It's lovable nonsense. Bob's internal compass is off in this regard. We know whether or not a person is a sailor based upon his or her time spent studying sailing, actual hours of experience sailing on a vessel, and success at sailing. Merely saying one is a sailor doesn't make one a sailor. Personally, there are many times when my internal compass is off.

"I am a fitness trainer." It's my fun day-job. It's what I've done for a living over the past two decades. Whether or not I'm exercising, I'm still a fitness trainer. This is so because of my time spent studying physical fitness and pursuing continuing education and certifications. It's also seen as I actually do the exercises I purport are good for people. I also have measurable personal success as well as the success of my clients.

"I am a Christ-follower." We say this often enough in our spoken words.[1] We know this to be true as we meet with God and behold Him. We love studying and meditating on God's Word. We do our best to make our thoughts/words/actions/choices worthy to be hung on the walls of heaven (my life motto).[2] We experience the Biblical prosperity of spreading God's fame in our lives. This is all because of God's pursuit of us and dwelling in us. Our success as Christ-followers is seen in our lives. No pressure or anything—I'm serious. I grew up in a legalistic sphere; we should never feel pressured by God, the Bible, or the church to perform. If we're in love with Jesus, we will automatically show it in our daily lives. Bearing fruit as believers starts with God's grace, is fueled by God's power, and ends with God's glory. Fruitful living is the result of God's work in us; it's the evidence of His "inside job" in our minds and souls that we discussed in chapter seven.

Bearing fruit as believers starts with God's grace,
is fueled by God's power, and ends with God's glory.

As a fitness trainer, I'm constantly thinking up the best combo of exercises to get total body strength for the long haul. As a believer, I'm often contemplating how to level-up my intimacy with God, exhibiting itself in a WWJD lifestyle.[3] As God's children, we get to give glory to God in the spiritual fitness routines called OUR LIVES. We're to be God-oriented go-getters—that is, we're to go toward God to get Him in all that we do. Personally, any hustle I put forth in any arena has first been sifted through

---

1   Romans 10:9.
2   Revelation 21:15. This is my way of saying that everything in heaven will be focused on God, not us. On a side note, there will be actual walls in heaven. For a full picture of the New Jerusalem, read Revelation 21:9–27. Heaven will center on and point to God and God alone; therefore, our lives should do the same.
3   WWJD = "What Would Jesus Do?" This is a question originally asked in the book *In His Steps* by Charles Sheldon (1886), then made popular in the 1990s with the WWJD movement with its slogan displayed on bracelets and other paraphernalia.

my overarching life filter (as mentioned before): "Can it be hung on the walls of heaven?"

1 Corinthians 6:11–15 says that the foundation of all reality is Jesus, and "each one's work will become manifest, for the Day will disclose it, because it will be revealed by fire, and the fire will test what sort of work each one has done." The only things hanging on the walls of heaven are those that point to Jesus. This side of heaven, our carnal lens blurs our mindsets and our attempts at deciphering what will or won't be inside those pearly gates. For the most part, I know when my thoughts are wandering down a path that is unworthy of the walls of heaven. By the power of the Holy Spirit, I take them captive.[4] Often, this is a full-on wrestling match. There are times when I look like Smeagol-turned-Gollum from the J. R. R. Tolkien's Middle-earth legendarium, talking back and forth with myself. So often I want to keep the hypothetical ring, to my own demise! If I discover my emotions becoming best friends, or even flirting, with jealousy, idolatry, selfishness, coveting, erratic glum, etc., the truth of Who God is levels-up in me due to my time spent reading His truth and listening to His Holy Spirit.

Sanctification, fleshing-out truth in our daily grind, is the Holy Spirit's work of leveling-up in us. We are never told that it's our task to do alone. "Level-up" is a term made popular by our culture's current obsession with virtual gaming. I have a teenager who plays video games; I know what leveling-up looks like. When one levels-up in a game, he or she advances to the next level of development. Synonyms include "elevate one's game, propel forward, rise to the next level, take it up a notch."[5] On a spiritual plane, it is truly a supernatural occurrence when the call of the Gospel advances inside us to the next level of intimacy with God and results in infinite holy living. There is no end to "taking it up a notch" in Christ. The advances Christ made over sin for us are as far as the east is from the west.[6] Christ's success in closing the gap between the sin that separates us from

---

4   2 Corinthians 10:5.
5   "Level up," *WordHippo*, www.wordhippo.com/what-is/another-word-for/level_up.html. Accessed May 2, 2021.
6   Psalm 103:12.

His love knows neither height nor depth.[7] This was the leveled-up lifestyle and advanced walk that Joshua led; it was also seen in David's life. This is our calling too. We are no different from them. We spiritually level-up by meditating on God's Word, doing what it says, and experiencing Biblical prosperity, as described by Joshua in Joshua 1 and by David in Psalm 1. Joshua 1 commissions us to *do*,[8] *meditate*,[9] and make our way *prosperous*.[10] Psalm 1 also exhorts us to *meditate*,[11] *do*,[12] and *prosper*.[13] We'll get into what each of these rungs on our sanctification agility ladder mean. This is no online workout or virtual game. THIS. IS. LIFE. And our eternal standing is displayed (not attained, but proven, as John 15:8 says)[14] in our God-fueled, leveled-up lives of meditating, doing, and succeeding.

It is truly a supernatural occurrence when the call of the Gospel advances inside us to the next level of intimacy with God and results in infinite holy living.

LET THE GOODNESS BEGIN

Be certain of this: life is no game; it's a fight to the death. Either we die or our sin dies.[15] Ironically, our sin dies as we die to self.[16] So rather than saying "let the games begin," I say "let the good begin." Let the goodness of our good good God (as both our texts purport) bless us, yield fruit in us, take

---

7   Romans 8:37–39.

8   Joshua 1:7–9.

9   Joshua 1:8.

10   Ibid.

11   Psalm 1:2.

12   Psalm 1:3.

13   Ibid.

14   "By this my Father is glorified, that you bear much fruit and so prove to be my disciples" John 15:8.

15   Romans 6:5–11.

16   Dying to self means we are now living sacrifices. Romans 12:1–2.

root in us, keep us thriving, discipline us, prosper us, keep us alive, be with us, not leave us, strengthen us, guide us, remain with us, and encourage us. "But when the goodness and loving kindness of God our Savior appeared, He saved us, not because of works done by us in righteousness, but according to His own mercy, by the washing of regeneration and renewal of the Holy Spirit."[17] Meditating, doing, and succeeding don't save us; they reveal that we are saved.

Meditating, doing, and succeeding don't save us;
they reveal that we are saved.

Let's look at our texts, Joshua 1 and Psalm 1. Take a moment and pray before you fire-hose yourselves. Let's jump in.

> After the death of Moses the servant of the Lord, the Lord said to Joshua the son of Nun, Moses' assistant, "Moses my servant is dead. Now therefore arise, go over this Jordan, you and all this people, into the land that I am giving to them, to the people of Israel. Every place that the sole of your foot will tread upon I have given to you, just as I promised to Moses. From the wilderness and this Lebanon as far as the great river, the river Euphrates, all the land of the Hittites to the Great Sea toward the going down of the sun shall be your territory. No man shall be able to stand before you all the days of your life. Just as I was with Moses, so I will be with you. I will not leave you or forsake you. Be strong and courageous, for you shall cause this people to inherit the land that I swore to their fathers to give them. Only be strong and very courageous, being careful to do according to all the law that Moses my servant commanded you. Do not turn from it

---

17   Titus 3:4–5.

to the right hand or to the left, that you may have good success wherever you go. This Book of the Law shall not depart from your mouth, but you shall meditate on it day and night, so that you may be careful to do according to all that is written in it. For then you will make your way prosperous, and then you will have good success. Have I not commanded you? Be strong and courageous. Do not be frightened, and do not be dismayed, for the Lord your God is with you wherever you go."

Joshua 1:1–9

Blessed is the man who walks not in the counsel of the wicked, nor stands in the way of sinners, nor sits in the seat of scoffers; but his delight is in the law of the Lord, And on His law he meditates day and night. He is like a tree planted by streams of water that yields its fruit in its season, and its leaf does not wither. In all he does, he prospers. The wicked are not so, but are like chaff that the wind drives away. Therefore the wicked will not stand in the judgement, nor sinners in the congregation of the righteous; for the Lord knows the way of the righteous, but the way of the wicked will perish.

Psalm 1

Like I said, it's a fight for our lives; the binary bookends of Psalm 1 highlight that as well: "blessed" or "perish." There will be times when we will need Joshua-like strength and courage because we will be afraid and dismayed, as Joshua 1:6 and 9 tell us. So how do we read these parts of the Word in order to bring the light first to our very own souls and then to those who are perishing?[18] Let's begin with meditating, something the original authors did.

---

18   1 Corinthians 1:18.

HIGHLY MEDITATED

My favorite tank top has this phrase on the front: "HIGHLY MEDITATED."
I wear it proudly, because I am highly meditated—on God's Word. Day and
night, and night and day, and day and night … we are to meditate. Inhale
Jesus. Exhale Jesus. Drink in His presence. Sit at His feet. Saturate our
souls in Scripture … over and over and over again. Then we find He meets
with us, like He does with many, like He did with Joshua, David, Hannah,
Samuel, George Muller,[19] Hudson Taylor,[20] and others. Have you had those
intimate moments where God awakens you in the night, calls you during
the day, and all of the sudden you're talking to Him, praying, communing
with the Most High God? You're not sure when it started or when it ended
because your soul has sponged up so much of God's goodness (character
and promises) from time spent (lots of time spent) in His inspired written
Word? I have. I've even dreamed Bible verses, as they're written-out all
over my slumbering soul-scape. It's as if I'm highly *medicated* … with Him.
It's because I've meditated on Him and Who He is. It is this very type of
meditation that convicts us of sin, hunts-down our personal idols, grows
holy fear, brings sanctification to completion, allows the Living God to
dwell with us, and levels-up through us.[21]

Now if we know our texts' two authors, Joshua and David, then we know
that the former was "full of the spirit of wisdom"[22] and the latter was a "man
after God's own heart."[23] Go read Joshua, 1 Samuel 16–31, and 2 Samuel in
one sitting. I know that's a lot of reading. Plan for it. If you don't come back

---

19   Preacher and orphanage director in Bristol, England in the 1800s.
20   Missionary from the UK who went to China in the 1800s.
21   "What agreement has the temple of God with idols? For we are the temple of
the living God; as God said, 'I will make My dwelling among them, and I will be
their God, and they shall be My people. Therefore go out from their midst, and
be separate from them, says the Lord, and touch no unclean thing; then I will
welcome you, and I will be a Father to you, and you shall be sons and daughters
to Me, says the Lord Almighty.' Since we have these promises, beloved, let us
cleanse ourselves from every defilement of body and spirit, bringing holiness to
completion in the fear of God" (2 Corinthians 6:16–7:1).
22   Deuteronomy 34:9.
23   1 Samuel 13:14.

to me, because you've become enthralled with God's Word, then I have done my job. These Biblical accounts of meditating, doing, and prospering are epic. Yours and my story can be epic too. After all, God is epic. But in between the battles miraculously fought and won, the deathly arrows avoided, and the BIG BOLD crimson banner of the promised Messiah,[24] we see the daily grind of two ordinary humans (and sinners) just like you and me. Let's narrow-in on one story from Joshua's life. Turn to Joshua 7:6–9.

> Then Joshua tore his clothes and fell to the earth on his face before the ark of the Lord until the evening, he and the elders of Israel. And they put dust on their heads. And Joshua said, "Alas, O Lord God, why have You brought this people over the Jordan at all, to give us into the hands of the Amorites, to destroy us? Would that we had been content to dwell beyond the Jordan!
>
> O Lord, what can I say, when Israel has turned their backs before their enemies! For the Canaanites and all the inhabitants of the land will hear of it and will surround us and cut off our name from the earth. And what will You do for Your great name?

Here we are:
- The battle was fought.
- The battle was lost.
- The hearts of the people melted as water (Joshua 7:5).
- It looked like Joshua was humbly questioning God, certainly pleading with Him.

But if we take a closer look, this man, like David, was hard-wired to trust God. He wasn't questioning God at all. His humble appeal, his primary goal, his end-game was loud and clear as he asked God: "What will You do for Your great name?"[25] The one speaking this statement had

---

24   2 Samuel 7:8–17.
25   Joshua 7:9.

fame of his own to stand upon: "So the Lord was with Joshua, and his fame was in all the land."[26] David had fame as well: "And the fame of David went out into all lands."[27] But Joshua's God-game was leveled-up so high that Joshua cared only about God's name, God's fame. Joshua knew that proclaiming and living out this fact was his saving position. Joshua appealed to God's character, and we should do the same. The "faming-God lifestyle" is what we women will pursue as Word-readers and light-bringers. The cumulative effect of the meditation, doing, and prospering is the renown of God's name. Period. So how do we meditate, do, and prosper like Joshua and David?

The "faming-God lifestyle" is what we women will pursue as Word-readers and light-bringers.

BIBLICAL MEDITATION

Meditation is such a lovely experience, concept, and command (albeit a Biblical one).[28] I meditate often; I talk about meditation; I advertise that I meditate. Some Christians give me the evil eye, as if I've deterred from the "right way" of doing "it." Laugh out loud. Really? King David … boy oh boy, did he meditate! Here are some examples from David's life of His time spent on God, with God, and in God's Spirit:

- His heart was more impressive than his appearance (1 Samuel 16:7).
- His reliance on the Lord's name (1 Samuel 17:45).
- His promotion of God at every opportunity (1 Samuel 17:46).
- His trust in God's timing to be raised up as king (1 Samuel 24, 26).

---

26 Joshua 6:27.
27 1 Chronicles 14:17.
28 Psalm 48:9, 63:6, 77:12, 119:15–16, 23, 27, 48, 78, 97, 99, 148, 143:5, 145:5; 1 Timothy 4:15.

- His go-to practice (strengthening himself in the Lord his God, 1 Samuel 30:6) when people were trying to kill him and hurt his family.
- His first instinct to inquire of the Lord for everything (1 Samuel 30:8).
- His prayer life (2 Samuel 7:18–29, 2 Samuel 22, many Psalms).
- His worship, even in hard times (2 Samuel 12:20).
- His legacy (Psalms).

David didn't contemplate his navel. He did not excessively look at himself as the center of the universe, as we all have the tendency to do (at least I do). He *hagahed*. *Hagah* is Hebrew for moaning, growling, speaking, musing, declaring, pondering, uttering, studying, *meditating*.[29] It sounds like an animal growl, doesn't it? *Hagah* is a means of communication. It says to the object of its utterance or recipient of its moaning (God), "I'm here; I acknowledge that You're here and that You are God." There's an intimate homage happening when we *hagah* to God. Let's be honest—if we *hagah* to or with anything other than the Most High God, it cannot answer, interact, or relationally meet with us, because of course it is not living. Inanimate things carry no power. And when we meditate on them, to them, with them, we are idolaters (insert sad-faced emoji). But when we meditate—*hagah*—before the living God, on His living words and on Him, like David did and like Joshua was commanded to do, we are:

- Blessed (Psalm 1:1a).
- Walking in the counsel of a good person (namely God) (Psalm 1:1a).
- Standing in the same manner and place as those who love God (Psalm 1:1b).
- Sitting in the seat of those who believe God (Psalm 1:1b).
- Delighting in God's Law (Psalm 1:2a).
- 24/7 (day and night) declarers (Psalm 1:2b).
- People whose mouths are full of and dwell on God's words and ways (Joshua 1:8a).

---

29 *Bible Hub,* https://biblehub.com/hebrew/1897.htm. Accessed May 9, 2021.

- Daily-nightly ponderers of truth (Joshua 1:8b).

All of these phrases directly describe what *hagah*ing looks like. We are to meditate; we are to ponder; we are to declare, not on the vacancy of our souls and minds, but on the living God and His residency in us. Isn't this beautiful? I have these selah-moments,[30] as the Psalmist calls them, these "pause and reflect" times with God. I meditate on God—I *hagah* to Him—and then I just have to pause and take in His presence and truth spoken from His Word and Spirit to me. Have you had this, dear friends?

We are to meditate; we are to ponder; we are to declare,
not on the vacancy of our souls and minds, but on
the living God and His residency in us.

I dare you to binge read His Word, to read a book of the Bible every day for one week. I did this the first few months of quarantine in 2020. This is totally possible for anyone who binge-watches television shows or is addicted to the phone. It's merely a trade in time. And the feeling you're currently feeling from reading this is both conviction and calling. Go get highly meditated. Be like David; be like Joshua. Then wait for it—the first outer signs that the book of the Law is indeed written on your heart.[31] You will "… *do* according to all the Law."[32] Meditating leads to doing; the Word planted in us will bear fruit.[33]

I dare you to binge read His Word, to read a book of
the Bible every day for one week.

---

30   Jason Soroski, Jason, "What Does Selah Mean in the Bible and Why Is It Important?" *Crosswalk.com*, October 10, 2018, www.crosswalk.com/faith/bible-study/what-does-selah-mean.html. Accessed May 2, 2021.
31   Joshua 1:8.
32   Ibid, emphasis added.
33   Psalm 1:3.

ROADSIDE FRUIT-STAND: THE DOING

I have lived my entire adult life in Southern California. Formally being a Midwest girl, I was unaccustomed to the roadside fruit stands that are everywhere in SoCal. I love them! My favorite grab is the strawberries. I get them in the car, and the strawberry aroma is so strong that I can almost see a red hue steaming up the car windows. The roadside fruit stands are evidence that growth is close. It's happening now. It's here. It's right around the corner. It's down that dusty road. The law-delighting fruit has arrived. The streams of living water have done their thing. Fruit is born; unwitherable leaves are unfurled. And from Joshua's faith journey, as well as ours, the "be strong and courageous" fight song blasts over the loudspeakers of Joshua's life to everyone within earshot. There's an interesting word attached to Joshua's commissioned doing … it was *careful* doing, it was intentional doing, and it was accomplished doing.

FIRST PLACE BELONGS TO GOD

Nike's "Just Do It" slogan carries so much more than just simply doing something. Any athlete in any sport has a "doing" that is carefully mapped-out, perfectly implemented, and unashamedly driving at the targeted goal. For a serious athlete to train and compete just for the fun of it is illogical. As Word-readers and light-bringers, God and His glory are our targeted goals. Our best becomes our reality only when God Himself is our end goal. Let me say that again for those of you in the back row: OUR BEST BECOMES OUR REALITY WHEN GOD HIMSELF IS OUR END GOAL. First place is for Him and Him alone. If you're still on the podium of your own heart, you are not at your best. I don't mean to be the bearer of bad news. It's actually good news when the truth hits us hard and we repent and change because of it.

Our "doing," if it's of the Lord, will be an action with an effect. As we saw before, the original word for "careful doing" is *asah*, which also means "to accomplish."[34] This is the same Hebrew word used by God of David in 2 Samuel 7:9 when He says, "I will make (do) for you a great name." I cannot emphasize enough: when it's God Who's saying, "I will do this for you," it *will* happen. The Old Testament narrates God extolling Himself to the world using His chosen people, Israel, as well as those who worshiped Him. All will see this come to fruition.[35] David had this lifestyle of living (*doing*) … that God must be glorified at all costs. Psalm 1 is full of *doing*—both what to do and what not to do. Take the wheel, David.

Our best becomes our reality
only when God Himself is our end goal.

WHICH PATH ARE YOU ON?

The contrast between the wicked and the righteous person in Psalm 1 is clear, instructive, and motivating. There's *doing* in how we walk. There's *doing* in how we stand. There's *doing* in how we sit. In the original language, "doing" can be: 1. doing good for ourselves or 2. "do[ing] evil against ourselves."[36] Where we walk, stand, and sit reveals the treadmill on which we've allowed our minds and hearts to run—the righteous one or the wicked one. In Psalm 1, David calls us to stay on God's treadmill at all costs. The Lord transplants us into His perfect space and place. We are like trees planted (*transplanted* in the original language)[37] by streams of water that yield fruit in season.[38] I have always loved that in our spiritual lives there's a season for doing and a season for not doing. I can see this reality in my peach tree in my back yard. Just like trees have a season, we must rejoice in the reality that there are seasons in all of our lives. It is unBiblical

---

34   *Bible Hub*, https://biblehub.com/hebrew/6213.htm. Accessed May 2, 2021.
35   Malachi 3:12.
36   Ibid.
37   *Bible Hub*, https://biblehub.com/hebrew/8362.htm. Accessed May 2, 2021.
38   Psalm 1:3.

to assume no growth is happening when we don't see fruit. We all have doing-seasons that are underground and unseen by all but the Lord. Trust His sanctifying process. God's processing in us turns out to be His prospering through us.

We all have doing-seasons that are underground and unseen by all but the Lord.

FAMING GOD

The concept of faming God is what Christ-followers are all about. God's glory is the greatest fruit of our careful daily doing. If that's all we've got to show for it—His glory—then we indeed are living the prosperous life about which David and Joshua penned. The Biblical prosperity Gospel looks like this:

- Faming God in all we think.
- Faming God in all we say.
- Faming God in all we do.
- Faming God where we walk.
- Faming God where we stand.
- Faming God where we sit.
- Faming God in the battle.
- Faming God when we sleep.
- Faming God when we rise.

Faming God gives strength to those around us. It's the prosperity of God-centered lives that is ours, and He most certainly does not exclude material prosperity. But that's never to what the Bible points. The problem with the world's prosperity gospel is twofold: 1. We make ourselves the center of God's plan, and 2. Salvation is so easily gained or lost, at least from an onlooker's view, based on external merit, gain, and success. As believers, we should never read the words "prosperity," "blessing," and "success" with a "what's in it for me" mindset. True prosperity is a "passing away of these former things" and a doling-out from the "spring of the water of life without payment."[39] It's joining the heavenly throng saying, "Holy, holy, holy, is the Lord God Almighty, Who was and is and is to come."[40] Our inheritance is being in God's presence forever. Living out God's glory is our prosperity and success now.

RUSH HOUR

Living in Southern California, I'd say I'm an expert in "rush hour." Rush hour is a time-period when traffic peaks. It does so because everyone is in the same location at the same time, usually going to a similar destination. To prosper in Psalm 1:3 literally means to rush, to advance, to take possession (as in land).[41] I love that! Can you imagine if the watching world saw all of God's children rushing God in every area of their lives? I mean think about it. Why can't we cause a gapers' block with people craning their necks to see Who we're running to … Jesus! Not just a Jesus rush hour, but a Jesus rush life? I'm here in my earth-suit for one purpose—to run towards Jesus in such a way that my tribe is clearly seeing the One to Whom I'm running.[42] Advancement indeed! Prosperity that eternally ends upon foundations of jasper, sapphire, agate, emerald, onyx, carnelian, chrysolite, beryl, topaz, chrysoprase, jacinth, and amethyst.[43]

The prosperity gospel of Joshua 1:8 is the same advancement. I love how just a few verses earlier, God fulfils His promise[44] and tells Joshua what his literal stomping grounds are going to be: "Every place that the sole of your foot will tread upon I have given you."[45] I think I'd be programming

---

39   Revelation 21:4–7.
40   Revelation 4:8.
41   *Bible Hub*, https://biblehub.com/hebrew/6743.htm. Accessed May 2, 2021.
42   Philippians 3:12–20.
43   Revelation 21:19–20.
44   Genesis 12:1–3, Genesis 15; Deuteronomy 28:11.
45   Joshua 1:3.

my Fitbit and filling my water bottle and going for a million steps that day. How about you? This was the very land that Joshua and Caleb[46] spied-on *and* into which they were the only ones from the Egyptian exodus able to enter.[47] Talk about rushing to see the provision the Lord had promised! And the whole way, Joshua knew that his literal gains were God's presence: "I will be with you. I will not leave you or forsake you. ... Do not be frightened, and do not be dismayed, for the Lord your God is with you wherever you go."[48] If only all of God's people would stampede toward Him because they know His prosperity promises and they want to fame His great name. This is our leveling-up. We've been Word-readers and learned that we spiritually level-up by meditating on God's Word, doing what it says, and experiencing Biblical prosperity about which Joshua 1 and Psalm 1 speak. So how do we bring the light from these pages into our days?

ASKING THE HARD QUESTIONS

The real questions are: How are we leveling-up God's reputation as we meditate on His Word, do what it says, and Biblically prosper? Are we meditating on His Word? Are we doing what He tells us to do? Are we prospering? Do we see the Spirit's work of sanctification? If not, what's holding us back? The streams are there for our rooting. The strength and courage are there for our fear. Let's not get caught being the chaff that the wind blows away.[49] Let's walk, stand, and sit as Jesus did. The congregation of the righteous is waiting for us, rooting for us, supporting us.[50] "The Lord knows the way of the righteous."[51] The Spirit of the Lord knows where He dwells. He knows if that dwelling is in us or not. And we do too. Jesus is coming soon. Are we ready? I've started asking this question to strangers, because of everything I've learned based on my reading the Word and

---

46   Joshua 14:6–14.
47   Numbers 13:1–33, 14:23, 30, 38.
48   Joshua 1:5, 9.
49   Psalm 1:4.
50   Psalm 1:5.
51   Psalm 1:6.

bringing the light (meditating-doing-prospering). God is alive and well. The question is, are we? God always brings the light. Are we?

We all know that Joshua and David's lives were no cake walks. We must immerse ourselves in their stories again, but this time circle in our Bibles *Whom* God says He is and *what* He promises He'll do. Then preach out loud all that we circled in our Bibles to our hearts, minds, circumstances, hardships, and others. If we rush after God's fame in our trials, He will show up in our lives in bigger and bigger ways. I warn you, the closer we know Him, the more we advance toward Him, the more He'll entrust to us. I find that He puts women in my life with fragile pieces—broken hearts, broken minds, broken families, broken marriages, broken churches, broken body image, broken perspectives, broken health. I never feel equipped to handle or discuss what the Lord continually asks me to navigate with others. I have my own fragile pieces, and it's hard to balance those. I'm learning to step forward in faith on His promises and the strength of His truth, and I ask hard questions to myself and to others, like:

- Do you think your problem with church is your problem with Christ?
- Do you know how to read and study the Bible? Can I help you?
- What are you afraid of?
- Are you sure that Jesus is the Lord of your life? Because what you just said goes against Him.
- You say you carry anger. How do you think God is asking you to respond? What does He promise you in this situation?
- How are you faming God through your chronic pain, through your child's health condition, through your singleness, through your marriage, through your job loss?
- Do you think your kids talk to you that way, because you talk to others that way?
- You're concerned about your daughter's immodest dress. Have you looked at your own attire and social media posts and considered the example you're setting?
- There are many more hard questions I ask women that I cannot write, because of their controversial or explicit nature. Those

questions and conversations must not be avoided; they are meant for personal one-on-one dialogue.

Know this: I sweat when I ask people questions like these. I sweat when I ask myself these questions. These types of soul-searching, idol-hunting questions, though uncomfortable, are gateways to freedom in Christ. I ask them of myself. I ask them of you. We as Spirit-seeking Christ-followers can and will ask the hard questions in Spirit-led moments, regardless of literal sweat, because we value the very souls we know God is cleansing, pursuing, raising up. It's holy ground, I tell you, holy ground. Back to … inhale Jesus … exhale Jesus. He doesn't promise a sweat-free life, just a hell-free eternity with Him. Word-readers, light-bringers: this is indeed good news. Now go tell it on the mountain.

PRAYER

Jesus,
I'm coming for You,
I'm rushing You,
all because You've come after me
and rushed towards me.
I have walked wickedly,
stood sinfully,
and sat silently avoiding Your name.
Forgive me.
I see You are doing new things.

Holy Spirit, lead me to meditate on the truths I read from Your Word;
guide me to do all You've planned for me to do;
prosper me with Your holy presence.
You are the territory on which I desire to gain ground.

Father God, may my accumulated spiritual steps
be only and always advancement towards You and Your glory.
Amen.

DISCUSSION QUESTIONS

1. Psalm 1 is a masterpiece, isn't it? In reading it, how are you person-ally convicted and how are you personally called to level-up and change *today*?

2. Compare and contrast Psalm 1 and Jeremiah 17:7–8. How are you like or not like the tree? Pray and thank God for the areas in your life that honor Him and ask Him to change the areas that are chaff.

3. How does the life of David, the author of Psalm 1, exemplify the medi-tation, doing, and prospering about which he pens? (For review, see 1 Samuel 16, 2 Samuel, 1 Kings 1–2:12).

4. Joshua 1:1–9 is well-known for good reasons. Who is God in this passage and how is He the centerpiece through what He says to Joshua? How does your personal meditation, doing, and success show-case God?

CHAPTER 11
GOD WITH US

Various Passages

Immanuel has always been my favorite name of God, ever since I can remember. Of course, I first heard it at Christmas time as I was primed by well-known holiday songs filling my childhood home and heart with musically-framed "Immanuel." As I began to comprehend what Immanuel meant to me as a growing believer, saying "God with me" became a way I worshiped. Even now, I meditate on the certainty this assuring name of God provides. When I have no words in prayer, I utter "God with me." I believe that all names of God bring power and peace; even my frailest uttering of one of them is my daily saving worship, hope, and assurance. Each name of God is its own theology of a sort. His names exhibit Who He is, as title and character are wed with the Lord. His names are the signage of how He exists and displays Himself. In this chapter, we're going to focus on Immanuel.

I'm not trying to oversimplify things, but the best Person to be with is Immanuel. As believers, knowing God is with us is our daily super power. When God steps into our linear timeline with His omnipresent stance, that's a whole different kind of presence. I'm not here to convince you of this, just to remind you of it. God's all-encompassing nearness is astounding, life-altering. It was first gifted to Adam and Eve, after which they went down the "God *not* with us" path.[1] Through original sin, they were separated from their daily connection with God. "God beside us" manifests Himself throughout all of Scripture and into the throne room of eternity.[2] He zeros-in His ever-always present state onto our human plane (talk about loving kindness and grace). He manifests Himself to those who don't know He wants to be with them. Why does He do this for humanity? That we might see Him through general revelation; that we might know Him through special revelation; that we might be His through personal salvation.[3] Selah.

Meditation on His names increases our "logos of Theos"[4] (understanding of God), which in turn affects our adoration and worship of Him. Worship fuels our saved souls in a way that feelings alone never can. Worship should never wait on feelings. I admit that at times I drag my feet into worship, waiting for the "pneuma and gnosis" (Spirit and knowledge) stars to align. Worship *of* God cultivates relationship *with* God. The "being with Israel"[5] that His name states extends to all believers.

Worship fuels our saved souls in a way that feelings alone never can. Worship should never wait on feelings. Worship of God cultivates relationship with God.

DEFINING IMMANUEL

By now, I hope you've made the observation that Immanuel simply and profoundly means "God with us." In Hebrew, *Im* means "with, along, among,

---

1   Genesis 2-3.
2   Revelation 21:2.
3   Ephesians 2:8–9.
4   *Logos* means "reasoning and understanding expressed by words." *Bible Hub,* https://biblehub.com/greek/3056.htm. Accessed May 2, 2021. *Theos* means "God." *Bible Hub*, https://biblehub.com/greek/2316.htm. Accessed May 2, 2021.
5   Isaiah 7:14.

before, beside, close, near, together."[6] This word carries similar connotation to "dwelling" that we studied in chapters five and six. *El* means "God, mighty One, power, strong."[7] In the Old Testament, voicing "Immanuel" was a declaration by the nation of Israel of trust and confidence in the one true God. Israel knew God to be a Person of His Word.

In the New Testament, Immanuel becomes a Messianic title, specifically for Jesus; it is equivalent to Savior.[8] God with us is the "guarantee of the eternal triumph of the faithful remnant of Israel,"[9] *and* to all of us "outsiders" who believe. Thank you, Jesus, that the door is held open to us who are out in the deadly Gentile rain, outside of the original promise. I could stop right here. Off we go, into our prayer closets, as we meditate on this fact: God the Mighty One, powerful and strong, is beside us, close to us, near us, saving us as He guarantees victory for those who believe, both to Israel and now to all of us grafted into the family tree.[10] This is all we're going to do in this chapter: worship God as He is near us. Deeper understanding leads to deeper worship.

IMMANUEL IN SCRIPTURE

In Scripture, Immanuel is mentioned three times. Let's look at these verses as a precursor to our worship session.

- Isaiah 7:14—"Therefore the Lord Himself will give you a sign. Behold, the virgin shall conceive and bear a Son, and shall call His name Immanuel."
  - Speaker/Author: The Lord through Isaiah.[11]

---

6   *Bible Hub*, https://biblehub.com/hebrew/5973.htm. Accessed May 2, 2021.
7   *Bible Hub*, https://biblehub.com/hebrew/410.htm. Accessed May 2, 2021.
8   Ibid.
9   See Matthew 8:10 footnote in John MacArthur, *MacArthur Study Bible*, (Nashville, TN: Thomas Nelson, 1997), 967. Isaiah 10:20–22.
10   Romans 11:11–24.
11   Isaiah 7:3.

- Recipients: King Ahaz and Israel.[12]
- Context: Response to God telling Ahaz, the evil king of Judah, to ask for a sign that his enemies will be defeated. Ahaz, an evil king, says he will not test the Lord, though his lack of faith is apparent.[13] Then God replies with this verse, promising a Messiah as a sign to Israel despite their wicked king and ways,[14] and of course later to us post-cross believers.[15]
- Isaiah 8:8, 10—"... O Immanuel ... Take counsel together, but it will come to nothing; speak a word, but it will not stand, for God is with us."
  - Speaker/Author: The Lord through Isaiah.[16]
  - Recipients: Isaiah, "reliable witness" (Uriah the priest and Zechariah the son of Jeberechiah),[17] and Israel.
  - Context: The Lord is sending the Assyrian king and army ("the waters of the River, mighty and many, the king of Assyria and all his glory," Isaiah 8:7) to destroy Israel (except those who fear Him and take sanctuary in Him),[18] because they have turned away from God ("refused the waters of Shiloah that flow gently," Isaiah 8:6).[19]
- Matthew 1:23—"Behold, the virgin shall conceive and bear a Son, and they shall call His name Immanuel."
  - Speaker/Author: Matthew, a Jewish tax collector, disciple, and eyewitness to Jesus, quoting Isaiah 7:14.
  - Audience: Jews, and anyone who happens to read this, including us.

---

12 Ibid.
13 Isaiah 7:13.
14 Isaiah 7:1–17.
15 Hosea 2:23; Romans 9:24–26.
16 Isaiah 8:1.
17 Isaiah 8:2.
18 Isaiah 8:13–14.
19 Isaiah 8:5–10.

- Context: After Matthew cites an extensive royal genealogy of Christ, Matthew beautifully scripts the story of Christ's birth quoting Isaiah's prophecy (now fulfilled).[20]

I invite us to trace the lines of Immanuel in Scripture and preach His worth to our needy souls.

YOU ARE INVITED:
SPIRIT-LED PRAYER, READING, WORSHIP, AND APPLICATION

Worship God with me, won't you? I invite you on a different journey in this chapter. It's a short chapter, but my hope is that it's a worship retreat for each of us, even if it's only for a few minutes. Like exercise, every minute with God is valuable. Let God minister to you, whoever you are, wherever you are, whenever you have need (which humbly for me is most conscious moments). The "us" in His name's meaning is not a universalist sort of promise. The *us* is Israel, in its original context. We see in Israel's story the ramifications of God's presence to God's people, which overflows to believers today. The Word never goes out void, whether it's written, spoken, or personally fleshed out by God Himself in Christ. The imminent effects of God's companionship to them/then is just as powerful a reality to us/now.

Like exercise, every minute with God is valuable.

I'm not here to instruct on various forms of personal worship. My simple goal is that we indeed worship, however that looks for each individual child of God. Pause and prepare your heart to be with God. Pray for the Holy Spirit to help you cling to the old rugged cross.[21] We mustn't

---

20   Matthew 1.
21   Taken from the famous hymn written in 1912 by George Bennard, "The Old Rugged Cross."

think for a single second that God can't be with us like He was with Israel. He was among them as He spoke to their leaders[22] and met with the high priests in the Holy of Holies.[23] Jesus was among us in the flesh as He walked this earth.[24] The Holy Spirit is now in us.[25] These Biblical experiences and accounts ignite in us adoration of God. In the Spirit's leading, let us fly in solo worship. I encourage you to read these Scriptures aloud. I picked just a few on this topic. I underline the parts directly stating God's presence. Let's trace how Scripture uses "God with us." Pause and reflect on each Scripture passage, and worship God by reading aloud the underlined phrases.

- Genesis 21:22—"At that time Abimelech and Phicol the commander of his army said to Abraham, 'God is with you in all that you do.'"
- Genesis 26:24–28 - "And the Lord appeared to [Isaac] the same night and said, 'I am the God of Abraham your father. Fear not, for I am with you and will bless you and multiply your offspring for My servant Abraham's sake.' So [Isaac] built an altar there and called upon the name of the Lord and pitched his tent there. And there Isaac's servants dug a well. When Abimelech went to him from Gerar with Ahuzzath his advisor and Phicol the commander of his army, Isaac said to them, 'Why have you come to me, seeing that you hate me and have sent me away from you?' They said, 'We see plainly that the Lord has been with you.'"
- Genesis 28:15—"'Behold, I am with you and will keep you wherever you go, and will bring you back to this land. For I will not leave until I have done what I have promised" (God to Jacob).
- Exodus 33:14–16— "Now therefore, if I have found favor in Your sight, please show me now Your ways, that I may know You in order to find favor in Your sight. Consider too that this nation is Your people.' And He said, 'My presence will go with you, and I will give you rest.' And he said to Him, 'If Your presence will not go with me,

---

22 Genesis 17:7–8 (Abraham), Genesis 26:2–5 (Isaac), Genesis 28:13–15 (Jacob), Genesis 41:25 (Joseph), Exodus 3 and Numbers 13:1–2 and Numbers 27 (Moses), Deuteronomy 31:23 and the book of Joshua (Joshua).
23 See chapter five on the tabernacle.
24 Luke 2:1–7.
25 John 14:16–17.

do not bring us up from here. For how shall it be known that I have found favor in Your sight, I and Your people? Is it not in <u>Your going with us</u>, so that we are distinct, I and Your people, from every other people on the face of the earth?'" (Dialogue between God and Moses prior to going to Egypt to free the Israelites).

- Leviticus 26:11–12—"<u>I will make My dwelling among you</u>, and My soul shall not abhor you. And <u>I will walk among you</u> and will be your God, and you shall be My people" (God to His people and Moses in the wilderness).

- Numbers 14:8–9—"'If the Lord delights in us, He will bring us into this land and give it to us, a land that flows with milk and honey. Only do not rebel against the Lord. And do not fear the people of the land, for they are bread for us. Their protection is removed from them, and <u>the Lord is with us</u>; do not fear them'" (Joshua and Caleb to doubting Israel).

- Deuteronomy 20:1–4—"When you go out to war against your enemies, and see horses and chariots and an army larger than your own, you shall not be afraid of them, for <u>the Lord your God is with you</u>, Who brought you up out of the land of Egypt. And when you draw near to the battle, the priest shall come forward and speak to the people, and shall say to them, 'Hear, O Israel, today you are drawing near for battle against your enemies: let not your heart faint. Do not fear or panic or be in dread of them, for <u>the Lord your God is He Who goes with you</u> to fight for you against your enemies, to give you the victory'" (Moses to God's people instructing them how to go into battle).

- Deuteronomy 31:6, 8—"Be strong and courageous. Do not fear or be in dread of them, for <u>it is the Lord your God Who goes with you</u>. He will not leave you or forsake you. … <u>It is the Lord Who goes before you. He will be with you; He will not leave you or forsake you.</u> Do not fear or be dismayed" (Moses, near the end of his life, to Israel and Joshua).

- Joshua 1:9—"Do not be frightened, and do not be dismayed, for <u>the Lord your God is with you wherever you go</u>" (God to Joshua after Moses' death).

- Judges 6:12–13, 15–16—"And the angel of the Lord appeared to him and said to him, 'The Lord is with you, O mighty man of valor.' And Gideon said to him, 'Please, my lord, if the Lord is with us, why then has all this happened to us? And where are all His wonderful deeds that our fathers recounted to us … Please, Lord, how can I save Israel? Behold, my clan is the weakest in Manasseh, and I am the least in my father's house.' And the Lord said to him, 'But I will be with you, and you shall strike the Midianites as one man'" (dialogue between the angel of the Lord and Gideon).
- 2 Kings 6:15–18—"When the servant of the man of God rose early in the morning and went out, behold, an army with horses and chariots was all around the city. And the servant said, 'Alas, my master! What shall we do?' He said, 'Do not be afraid, for those who are with us are more than those who are with them.' Then Elisha prayed and said, 'O Lord, please open his eyes that he may see.' So the Lord opened the eyes of the young man, and he saw, and behold, the mountain was full of horses and chariots of fire all around Elisha.'"
- 1 Chronicles 22:17–18—"David also commanded all the leaders of Israel to help Solomon his son, saying, 'Is not the Lord your God with you? And has He not given you peace on every side? For He has delivered the inhabitants of the land into my hand, and the land is subdued before the Lord and His people'" (David's charge to the leaders of God's people and Solomon to build the temple).
- Psalm 23:4—"Even though I walk through the valley of the shadow of death, I will fear no evil, for You are with me; Your rod and Your staff, they comfort me" (David to God).
- Psalm 41:12—"But You have upheld me because of my integrity, and set me in Your presence forever" (David to God).
- Isaiah 41:10—"Fear not, for I am with you; be not dismayed, for I am your God; I will strengthen you, I will help you, I will uphold you with My righteous right hand" (God to His people).
- Isaiah 43:2, 5—"When you pass through the water, I will be with you; and through the rivers, they shall not overwhelm you; when you walk through fire you shall not be burned, and the flame shall not consume you. … Fear not, for I am with you; I will bring your

offspring from the east, and from the west I will gather you" (God to His people).

- Jeremiah 46:28—"Fear not, O Jacob my servant, declares the Lord, for I am with you. I will make a full end of all the nations to which I have driven you, but of you I will not make a full end. I will discipline you in just measure, and I will by no means leave you unpunished" (God to His dispersed people).
- Zephaniah 3:15, 17—"The Lord has taken away the judgements against you; He has cleared away your enemies. The King of Israel, the Lord, is in your midst; you shall never again fear evil. ... The Lord your God is in your midst, a Mighty One Who will save; He will rejoice over you with gladness; He will quiet you by His love; He will exult over you with loud singing" (Zephaniah to God's people).
- Haggai 1:13, 2:4—"Then Haggai the prophet, the messenger of the Lord, spoke to the people with the Lord's message, 'I am with you, declares the Lord.' ... Yet now be strong, O Zerubbabel, declares the Lord. Be strong, O Joshua, son of Jehozadak, the high priest. Be strong, all you people of the land, declares the Lord. Work, for I am with you, declares the Lord of hosts."
- Zechariah 8:22–23—"Many peoples and strong nations shall come to seek the Lord of hosts in Jerusalem and to entreat the favor of the Lord. Thus says the Lord of hosts: In those days ten men from the nations of every tongue shall take hold of the robe of a Jew, saying, 'Let us go with you, for we have heard that God is with you.'"[26]
- Matthew 28:20—"And behold, I am with you always, to the end of the age" (Jesus' last recorded words to His disciples).
- John 14:16–17—"And I will ask the Father, and He will give you another Helper, to be with you forever, even the Spirit of truth, Whom the world cannot receive, because it neither sees Him nor knows Him. You know Him, for He dwells with you and will be in

---

26 See Zechariah 8:20–23, footnote for context. John MacArthur, *Macarthur Study Bible*, (Nashville, TN: Thomas Nelson, 1997), 1318.

you" (Jesus to His disciple Philip answering his request to be shown the Father).[27]

- Revelation 21:3—"And I heard a loud voice from the throne saying, 'Behold, <u>the dwelling place of God is with man. He will dwell with them</u>, and they will be His people, and <u>God Himself will be with them</u> as their God" (John's prophetic dream about the New Jerusalem).

I have this last verse hand-painted on a plaque in my bathroom; it is my endgame verse.

THE EFFECTS OF WORSHIPING IN SPIRIT AND IN TRUTH

Did one or two of the passages stick out to you more than the others? They did for me. If the woman at the well got it, so can we.[28] Do you know her story? She was an outcast for various reasons.[29] Jesus reached out to her,[30] shot straight with her about her sin as He told her private things about herself that she'd never shared with Him,[31] and held out His water of life to her.[32] Go read about her in John 4:1–29. In her famous New Testament story, worship is mentioned ten times.[33] God with us means our worship is not attached to a mountain or a city[34] but right here, right now, in Spirit-led prayer, reading, and application. Join me in a reverent holy fist pump on this one. What happened in our Scripture narratives as a result of God's partnership?

First, and most basically, "God with us" was apparent to outsiders. The "stars of the show" (Israel) were not the only ones who knew He was

---

27 John 14:8.
28 John 4:23, 29.
29 She was a woman and a Samaritan, sadly both looked down upon in her culture.
30 John 4:7.
31 John 4:16–18.
32 John 4:10, 13–14.
33 John 4:20–24.
34 John 4:20–21.

there. In the first two passages from Genesis,[35] an enemy king and his army commander state to Abraham and to his son Isaac that they know God is with these two men and their families. Talk about first-place in line to witness God Himself. Is God's presence in us so apparent that our enemies take notice? Ponder that. Generation after generation in Scripture, God shows up again and again—from Abraham to Isaac to Jacob to Moses to Israel to Job and Ruth (both Gentiles) to Joshua and Caleb to Gideon to Elisha to David to Solomon to Isaiah to Jeremiah to Zephaniah to Haggai to Zechariah to Matthew and John and the disciples, to the church, and many more. He doesn't just show up. I have a secret for you (He never left). He never leaves! We see it; our enemies see it; onlookers see it. Sure (like Israel) we forget, we complain, we sin against God (I do daily), we need reminders. But *Who He is* never ceases: being with us, coming at us from so many different divinely-appointed angles. I worship Him for this.

WHEN GOD TRENDS

Have you ever been around someone who oozes Jesus? Authentically? Not those people who "… love to stand and pray … at the street corners, that they may be seen by others" (Matthew 6:5). I have fallen into this category of hypocrite many times. I'm talking about "little Christs" (the meaning of the word "Christian") who pray in secret, who hallow God's name, who beg Him for His will to be done, who focus on needs not wants, who love big, who forgive in the deepest parts of their souls, who return good for evil, who repent and make it right when they sin.[36] What happens in their private Immanuel-ing flows out of the throne room and all over their world and ours too. God has a way of seeping into everything, even the places where He's not welcome (this is sanctification for those who are saved). Authentic relationship with and worship of the Most High God don't look perfect— just real, deep, and lasting. Authentic relationship *with* Him always points *to* Him. This is what the Old Testament lives of God's people (when they

---

35 Genesis 21:2, 26:24–28.
36 Matthew 6:9–13.

obeyed) looked like to those around them. Many nations, rulers, armies, and enemies immediately recognized that God was with Israel. This is why the New Testament believers were martyred.

In Scripture, responses to God's presence were usually twofold: people either feared and fought Israel, *or* feared and allied with them. Note the fear—God's presence was undeniable, and it made them squirm. The same is true for us. God's presence in our lives is impossible to deny. Something bigger than humanity becomes plain as God showcases Himself.[37] The Most High God should make us uncomfortable, in a holy fear kind of way. He is our best friend, but He is also God. I'm awed by how the beginning of eternity will look, as foreshadowed in Zechariah 8:22–23. We see "many peoples and strong nations ... of every tongue" asking, "let us go with you:"

> Many peoples and strong nations shall come to seek the Lord of hosts in Jerusalem and to entreat the favor of the Lord. Thus says the Lord of hosts: In those days ten men from the nations of every tongue shall take hold of the robe of a Jew, saying, "Let us go with you, for we have heard that God is with you."

How does the above sentence, "let us go with you," finish? "... For we have heard that God is with you." God is trending, and some people want to know Him because they've heard and seen He's with us. The millennial kingdom is reserved for God's children of all time. In the Old Testament, God's people were less than perfect. In the New Testament, God's people were less than perfect. Today, I am less than perfect; you are less than perfect. Newsflash: some people want what we have, because they can clearly see (despite our blaring shortcomings) that God is with us. Jesus came. He manifested physical presence in a physical body. He is (or should be) the Object of our want.[38] As believers, we get the privilege of bringing this light, here and now, before Jesus comes back. Like a broken record, we

---

37   Romans 1:19.
38   John Piper, *Desiring God*, (Sisters, OR: Multinomah Books, 1996).

must humbly remind ourselves: He is coming. Are we ready? How is the Holy Spirit using us to take as many people as we can with us to meet Jesus?

Conclusively, for believers, God's presence annihilates fear. He tells us over and over again not to fear, because He is with us. We are to recount to ourselves all of these times of divine preservation for all who call on the name of the Lord.[39] In Judges 6:12–13, 15–16, out of fear, weakness, and hardship, Gideon said:

> Where are all [God's] wonderful deeds that our fathers recounted to us …? … Please, Lord, how can I save Israel? Behold, my clan is the weakest in Manasseh, and I am the least in my father's house.' And the Lord said to him, But I will be with you, and you shall strike the Midianites as one man.

We are modern-day Rahabs[40]—filthy sinners who by the grace of God are saved by faith by the red cord of Jesus' blood.[41] Hypothetically, let's hang that cord out of our windows, especially in the context of our current time in history. From a human perspective, as a non-Jew, the odds for Rahab to believe in Israel's God were low. All are invited, pursued, encouraged into the family of God, us included! Here we are, living the saved-by-grace new covenant life (no longer under the law),[42] to the glory of God. Amen! May we be like Gideon, Rahab, and everyone in history blessed and protected by the reality that "O Come, O Come, Emmanuel" is true. Let's end our time of worship humming this famous song about Immanuel's promise to be with Israel, and personalizing it with our own names. Note all the elaborations on Emmanuel: Rod of Jesse, Dayspring, Key of David, Adonai, and Lord of Might.

---

39 Romans 10:13.
40 Joshua 2:1–21.
41 Joshua 2; Hebrews 11:31.
42 Romans 8:2.

PRAYER: "O COME, O COME, EMMANUEL" (AUTHOR UNKNOWN)

O come, O come, Emmanuel,
And ransom captive Israel [my name]
That mourns in lonely exile here (for me, any place away from God can be
considered exile),
Until the Son of God (Jesus) appear.
Rejoice! Rejoice! Emmanuel
Shall come to thee [me], O Israel [my name].

O come, Thou Rod of Jesse, free
Thine own [me] from Satan's tyranny (against them then and me now);
From depths of hell Thy people [me] save,
And give them [me] victory o'er the grave.
Rejoice! Rejoice! Emmanuel
Shall come to thee [me], O Israel [my name].

O come, Thou Dayspring, from on high,
And cheer us [me] by Thy drawing nigh (coming near me);
Disperse the gloomy clouds of night [my current trials],
And death's dark shadows [my sin and oppression] put to flight.
Rejoice! Rejoice! Emmanuel
Shall come to thee [me], O Israel [my name].

O come, Thou Key of David, come
And open wide our [my] heav'nly home;
Make safe the way (Your way to me) that leads on high,
And close the path to misery.
Rejoice! Rejoice! Emmanuel
Shall come to thee [me], O Israel [my name].

God With Us

O come, Adonai, Lord of might,
Who to Thy tribes (my Jewish brothers and sisters) on Sinai's height,
In ancient times didst give the law
In cloud (God appeared to Israel in a cloud) and majesty and awe.
Rejoice! Rejoice! Emmanuel
Shall come to thee [me], O Israel [my name].

DISCUSSION QUESTIONS

1. Of the selected Scriptures in this chapter about God being with people, which ones stood out to you the most and why? (Revelation 21:3 is my favorite).

2. Why do you think there are so many instances in Scripture where people need to be reminded that God is with them? What might this emphasize about human nature? See Psalm 103:14.

3. Have you ever studied the theme of worship in the story of the woman at the well (John 4:1–30)? Are you like this woman who, when she encounters the One Who deserves all worship, immediately goes and shares her good news? Do you do this? What holds you back from doing this?

4. Going back to the first time God was "with us," read Genesis 1:26–31, 2:15–25. What characteristics of God being Immanuel emerge from this text? How does He being with humanity from the very beginning change how you relate to Him today? Has He changed?

CHAPTER 12
THE OUT-LOVING LIFE

Genesis 37, 39–45, 50:15–21

The self-loving life is like making a homemade pie and eating the whole thing by yourself. The *out-loving* life is like making a homemade pie and sharing it with those around your table. There's solo-time that goes into making that pie: searching for the best recipe, shopping for the finest ingredients, prepping your kitchen for flavorful greatness, careful measuring, watchful baking, purposeful plating, all-inclusive summoning of the guests, and then, oh then, the delight of the scrumptious community-shared first bite. And it doesn't stop there. They'll come back for more. So back to the kitchen of life ... alone ... restocking, re-dreaming, recreating, not for self but for others. The fellowship and community that come from out-loving is addicting—the good kind of addicting, the kind of addiction that God put into each of us when He created us. Please don't ever hear me saying that we should never be alone, never refuel, never rest, never recharge, and never address the very immediate issues and brokenness that are a reality for all of us. What I *am* saying is that caring for ourselves, from the bottom of our souls all the way out to the tips of our toes, should be with the intention of benefitting our world around us, to the glory of God. Christ left the fellowship of His Father ... alone ... for us. Christ withdrew into the garden to pray ... alone ... for us. Christ went to the cross ... alone ... for us.

Caring for ourselves, from the bottom of our souls all the way out to the tips of our toes, should be with the intention of benefitting our world around us, to the glory of God. Christ left the fellowship of His Father ... alone ... for us. Christ withdrew into the garden to pray ... alone ... for us. Christ went to the cross ... alone ... for us.

What if Jesus was all about self-love? What if the Son of God chose to stay with His Father? What would that look like? He certainly would not have gone to the cross. Thank goodness He wasn't self-full but rather selfless. Self-loving dims the light. Out-loving brings the light. Self-loving stops way short of our calling. Out-loving is the way of the cross. It was also the path that Joseph chose to take in the book of Genesis. Joseph was the epitome of the out-loving life. Just like Jesus, Joseph leveled-down, not by his own choosing (whereas Jesus made that deliberate choice), and he used his alone time in slavery and prison to rise up and return good for evil. Let's not forget, he wasn't ever truly alone, was he? I AM was with him.[1] We will see in our reading about the life of Joseph that the selfless, God-centered life is the best life.

Joseph's selfless, God-centered life reveals six truths: the power of family, the power of words, the power of time, the power of God's presence, the power of trials, and the power of compassion.

The selfless, God-centered life is the best life.

---

1   Genesis 39:2, 3, 21, 23.

SNEAK PEAK

I'm going to give you a sneak peek of the finale of Joseph's story. In the end, it is from the God-laced lessons mentioned above that Joseph was able to speak these famous well-timed words to his family:

> Do not fear, for am I in the place of God? As for you, you meant evil against me, but God meant it for good, to bring it about that many people should be kept alive, as they are today. So do not fear; I will provide for you and your little ones.[2]

What if Joseph had bought into the self-loving movement? This is a movement which, by the way, isn't new. According to today's "take care of self" mantra, he had every right and justification to defend himself and live a self-preserving life. How might this famous passage above be written differently if Joseph was all about learning to love himself and have "self-care Sunday" every week? Perhaps like this:

> You should be afraid, because I am the center of my universe. I am enough. I am strong. I am worthy. You should go dig deep and find your strength, destiny, and food on your own power. You harmed me. Therefore, since you provide nothing that serves me, I walk away from you, because this relationship is toxic for me. God wants me to be happy, so I, knowing what's best for me, will pursue all the good God has planned for me, and that does not include you, since you don't make me feel happy. I'm not sure how you'll stay alive without food, but that's not my problem. I release you from my circle to be alone in your fear. Furthermore, I will not help you or your children, because you have not contributed to my self-worth.

---

2   Genesis 50:19–21.

I realize I've taken a lot of liberty here, but the point is made. Joseph's self-love would have killed a nation, literally. Thank God that this world-changer's worth was founded upon God's presence. We get to read about his story in God's Word so that we can learn to bring the light like he did. So what did God say to Joseph and his family in a story where loving others was essential for survival?

GOD USES WHAT THE WORLD THROWS AT US

You know the drill: it's time for you to put down this book and pick up The Book. Go to Genesis 37, 39–45, 50:15–21 and read these chapters aloud in one sitting. I get speechless as I read about the full circle of events that transpire here. In this story there are self-loving moments and out-loving moments and everything in between. I warn you, it gets ugly. Talk about a dysfunctional family. No one is perfect. This story has many pathetic, selfish, short-sighted, human moments. My story does too. Don't all of our stories have many moments we wish we could go back and edit? With God on our side and others on our radar, we learn from Joseph that worth comes from God and God alone; it is from this identity that selfless out-loving character emerges. Joseph started out seemingly self-loving, vulnerable, and prideful. He emerged out-loving, protected, and humble.

We learn from Joseph that worth comes from God and God alone; it is from this identity that selfless out-loving character emerges.

THE POWER OF ...

Can you see the out-loving life at work here? Let's go through this story with a sifter so that we can gain all the sweetness God has for us from the life of Joseph. Do you remember the six lessons of Joseph's selfless,

God-centered life? They are the power of family, power of words, power of time, power of God's presence, power of trials, and power of compassion. To stay true to the text, we will follow the story in order. As we go, our characters develop, and as they progress, these six aspects begin to come full circle and overlap. First, let's address family. Not only is family the centerpiece in Joseph's life but also of our lives, of every culture, and of God's eternal plan.

THE POWER OF FAMILY

Often we hear phrases like "family first," "family is what matters," "family time," "the perfect family," and other familial ideas. Just do an internet search beginning with "family" and you'll see that family is always trending. Family is at the top of every list, because God designed us that way. It's in our blood. We're supposed to stick together. We're made of the same substance. We're familially fashioned. But as we all know, family can be ... well, not so perfect. Every human on this earth can relate to this fact. That's why Joseph's story hits us to the core.

Joseph's family is messed up. No, really, it is. But doesn't this imperative inform us that our families are like Joseph's family, like everyone else's family, and, sometimes, like God's family of believers? This side of heaven, family is going to be a constant ride of ups and downs—full of irresolvable regressions as well as glory glimpses. The more God-centered and out-loving we are, the less regression and more glory we'll individually exhibit in our own families. Please don't mistake my words for a glory-guaranteed equation to the perfect family. There are plenty of times that from our human perspective there will never be a "happily-ever-after" stamped on our families. Joseph had terrible, unjust, agonizing courses in his life. In the great feast of his human years, God blessed him and his family with a delicious earthly dessert ... hypothetically speaking. They all tasted the benefit of repentance, humility, forgiveness, and restoration. They had a happily-ever-after ending, at least in that chapter of their story. This is such a testimony to God's work in dysfunctional families and relationships. God promised to preserve this very messed-up family, and He fulfilled those promises through sinless Christ, Who came out of this messed-up family! We find out about the dysfunctional home from which Joseph came in the first four verses of Genesis 37.

This side of heaven, family is going to be a constant ride of ups and downs—full of irresolvable regressions as well as glory glimpses.

FAVORITES

To start with, Joseph's father, Israel, had four wives.[3] This fact is something we don't palate well in today's culture, nor did God condone it. Imagine being one of those four wives back in that day … a recipe for an epic family fail, I'd say. Next, "Joseph brought a bad report of [his brothers] to their father" (Genesis 37:2). So here we see Joseph the tattletale. The Merriam-Webster Dictionary defines a tattletale as "a person, especially a child, who reveals secrets or informs on others; a person habitually engaged in idle or incriminating talk about others." To be honest, I've done that. I'm like Joseph. At seventeen years old, this Bible hero was not so heroic. He seems to have been the kind of teenager with whom we all tell our kids not to be friends. The Proverbs warn against such a person.[4]

It doesn't stop there. "Now Israel [Jacob] loved Joseph more than any other of his sons, because he was the son of his old age."[5] What? Now I'm no therapist, but this is wrong.[6] Even my young daughter says, "You'd think Jacob would've learned this the first time around when he grew up in a home where he was his mother's favorite child and his twin brother, Esau, was his father's favorite child!"[7] Once married, Jacob (now Israel) had a

---

3   Genesis 29:1–30:1-9.
4   Proverbs 16:28.
5   Genesis 37:3.
6   Ephesians 6:4; Colossian 3:21.
7   Genesis 25:28.

favorite wife,[8] Rachel, Joseph's mother—just yuck. Playing favorites is a lose-lose game. It's sad, but it does happen.

This favoritism isn't exclusive to Joseph's family. I'm sure you've seen favoritism in your own family or in other families, especially with the baby, or the youngest. Joseph was the eleventh of twelve sons. That doesn't make favoritism right. What we do see is this: God can work through former gossips and favorites. This is indeed good news. Jacob loved Joseph so much more than his other twelve sons that "he made him a robe of many colors."[9] Now who doesn't love a good shopping spree? Getting that brand new coat sure sounds great to me, but not this way, not at the detriment of others, especially one's own brothers. Don't you just want to ask Joseph's father, "Israel, what were you thinking?" We don't have time to unpack Israel's backstory,[10] but if you know it, that explains a lot.

THE SLIPPERY SLOPE OF HATE

This recipe for family disaster isn't done. Let's throw hatred into the mixture. This passage mentions *hate* three times in a growing, all-consuming way. Exodus 37 says, "When his brothers saw that his father loved him more than all his brothers, they hated him and could not speak peacefully to him ... they hated him even more ... they hated him even more."[11] When the Bible says the same thing three times in five verses, we know to pay attention. Their hatred was deepened by the fact that Joseph had dreams and shared his dreams with his whole family. Not the smartest choice, in my opinion, when one is dealing with people who hate him. Taking some liberty here, Joseph was either immature, self-centered, or both. He did this dream-telling not once, but twice. Get a clue, Joseph! We'll discuss Joseph's diarrhea-of-the-mouth soon.

Joseph's brothers' hatred towards him and Joseph's self-centeredness, pride, and ill-timed verbiage were the forerunners of bigger sins and

---

8 Genesis 29:14–30.
9 Genesis 37:3.
10 Genesis 27–30.
11 Genesis 37:4–5, 8.

bigger choices. But God's salvation of Israel's family came from it. Hate and pride are choices. Hate and pride do not just show up one day and surprise us. They are long-term, slow-growing sinful mindsets that are grown, groomed, and trained when the first emotions of anger, selfishness, and hurt are felt. Joseph and his family gave into emotions the wrong way. I'm not here to break down the slippery slope[12] of individual sins. If we're honest, all of us have allowed our minds and hearts to marinate in unhealthy emotions resulting from familial conflict and then sinfully acted (both in our minds and our outer choices). Even as I write this, I gave in to sinful emotions toward a family member today. Lord, forgive me. Family is so very powerful, both positively and negatively. And it appears that Israel, their father, wasn't parenting so well. He showed favoritism, and then all he did was rebuke Joseph for telling his dreams.[13] At this point, the Bible tells us "his brothers were jealous of him."[14] Who wouldn't be?

So far we've got polygamy, gossip, favoritism, hate, pride, and jealousy. When we throw all these elements into the pot of family life, the heat turns up on its own and boils over into a plot of murder. Sin begets sin. Once on the sin slope, it gets progressively more slippery. James confirms this: "But each person is tempted when he is lured and enticed by his own desire. Then desire when it has conceived gives birth to sin, and sin when it is fully grown brings forth death."[15]

Sin begets sin.

---

12 The term *slippery slope* has accurately been attributed to James 1:14–15. The slippery slope is the four stages of sin, described by James: evil desire, conception, sin, and death. It's often depicted as a curve, with each step getting steeper and more slippery. The more one progresses into these stages of sin, the more difficult it is to stop sliding into the next stage. The end result is death.
13 Genesis 37:10.
14 Genesis 37:11.
15 James 1:14–15.

The dreamer, as they called him, went to check on his brothers in the fields. "They saw him from afar, and before he came near to them they conspired against him to kill him."[16] Reuben, the oldest brother, advised not to take Joseph's life, but rather to throw him into a pit; he hoped to rescue Joseph later.[17] This chapter closes with two horrid crimes: the brothers happened to see Ishmaelite[18] slave traders passing by on their way to Egypt. Instead of murdering Joseph as planned, they sold him, their own brother, for twenty shekels of silver and then deceived Israel into believing his son had been devoured by a fierce animal. At this point in the story, I am always speechless. Who sells anyone into slavery, especially their own sibling? Who deceives their own father about a son being dead who's not dead? This brings us to the second point in Joseph's story—the power of words. Just like family carries the power to hurt or heal, we see that words carry the power to hurt or heal.

THE POWER OF WORDS

The power of words has already colored our story with dark and dismal shades. Joseph started out as a favored tattletale and prideful dream-teller. Joseph, at this point, seems immature to me. This isn't stated in the text itself, but if we look at the facts from the text, I think it's safe to say that, at the very least, Joseph had some growing up to do. The text doesn't say whether or not he struggled with self-centeredness and pride, but his confidence is evident in what he says throughout Genesis 37.

The text does show that he had a propensity to gossip and to ill-timed dream-sharing. Even in his dreams, he was the center of the universe, prophetically so. He dreamt that his brothers bowed down to him. Spoiler alert: they do end up bowing down to him at the end of the story. Little did Joseph know what difficulties these dreams would mean for him; little did

---

16 Genesis 37:18.
17 Genesis 37:21–22.
18 Scripture tells us that the Ishmaelites (descendants of Ishmael, Abraham and Hagar's son) were blood-relatives of Jacob's twelve sons. They both came from Abraham's line. In other words, they were family as well. See Genesis 16:1–16.

Joseph's brothers know what blessings these dreams would mean for them. But let's not overlook the fact that there's a time and a place to share our stories in a verbal manner that creates community rather than sends relationships up in flames. Though Joseph's words themselves were prophetic, the manner in which he shared them appears to be divisive and full of self. Joseph was already struggling with his brothers, so his words just "rubbed it in" and poured salt into their wounds. Read the text over and over again to see what the Holy Spirit shows you. One thing is for sure: in Genesis 37, Joseph had not yet mastered his tongue. Neither had his brothers. Because of their hate, they "could not speak peacefully to him." There will be an ah-ha moment with peace speaking at the end of this story. Wait for it! God had indeed given Joseph a gift with words. Joseph's maturity in this area comes. It comes from being sold into slavery and imprisonment.

We leap from an arrogant, selfish, tattle-taling seventeen year old boy to a successful, attractive, selfless young man. What happened? We've seen the negative power of words at work up until now. All of the sudden, we find Joseph overseeing an important household. The next recorded words in the text out of Joseph's mouth in response to his master's wife's sexual advances are these:

> But he refused and said to his master's wife, "Behold, because of me my master has no concern about anything in the house, and he has put everything that he has in my charge. He is not greater in this house than I am, nor has he kept back anything from me except you, because you are his wife. How then can I do this great wickedness and sin against God."
>
> Genesis 39:8–9

Wow! Talk about a mature selfless response. We don't know exactly how he changed, but he had character in him that trials and hardships birthed. We see this in the power of his now wise words. In his weakest moment, he flees from sin and is imprisoned for it. There's so much more we'll uncover in Joseph's wise words; but next let's look at the power of time—his time as a slave and his time in prison.

THE POWER OF TIME

Time heals. Sometimes this is true; sometimes it's not. But time has much greater power than healing; it matures, it refines, it releases. Time itself can be the very soil that God uses to bring out His image in us.

Time itself can be the very soil that God uses
to bring out His image in us.

This is the case for Joseph. From the time he was seventeen to the time he gets out of prison, thirteen years,[19] something wonderful brewed inside Joseph. We know the Lord was with him from the very moment he was sold into slavery. So did everyone around him. Genesis 39:2–6 says,

> The Lord was with Joseph, and he became a successful man, and he was in the house of his Egyptian master. His master saw that the Lord was with him and that the Lord caused all that he did to succeed in his hands. So Joseph found favor in his sight and attended him, and he made him overseer of his house and put him in charge of all that he had. From the time that he made him overseer in his house and over all that he had, the Lord blessed the Egyptian's house for Joseph's sake; the blessing of the Lord was on all that he had, in house and field. So he left all that he had in Joseph's charge, and because of him he had no concern about anything but the food he ate.

One can't deny the transformation that occurred in Joseph over this period. The text doesn't say how long Joseph served until his master made him the household overseer, nor does it say how many total years Joseph spent in prison after his master's wife falsely accused him. Either way, that's

---

19   Genesis 37:2, 41:1, 46.

a lot of time spent alone. Knowing the end of the story, we see that Joseph made his alone time of great value to his relationship not with himself, but with the Lord and with those around him. No self-love here anymore. Joseph saw where that train landed him and chose instead to hop on board the out-loving train. All we know is that over a thirteen year period of time (time as a slave and time in prison), God's presence in Joseph's life powerfully changed this man and those around him. God's presence indeed has power. When we are in the hypothetical pits into which life throws us, are we so powerfully living out God's presence with us that everyone around us sees this and is blessed? Let's bite into this truth.

When we are in the hypothetical pits into which life throws us, are we so powerfully living out God's presence with us that everyone around us sees this and is blessed?

THE POWER OF GOD'S PRESENCE

We already saw that the "Lord was with Joseph" and that his "master saw that the Lord was with him."[20] But then a very distasteful ingredient falls into his story—Potiphar's wife. After multiple attempts to seduce Joseph, she falsely accuses him of sexually attacking her. So he was lied about to his father and now to his boss. Being lied about is very hurtful. Has someone ever lied about you? Those who have tasted the evil of lies know the pain of the feelings and outcomes of being on the false side of a lie. Of course, Potiphar believed his wife and put Joseph into prison. At this point in Joseph's story, everyone who reads it—the Israelites back in the day all the way to us now—should be feeling sorry for Joseph. But if we marinate in all that we learned about God's presence in our study of the tabernacle—His steadfast love and His desire to meet with us—the very next verse in the text should give us God-shaped goosebumps.

---

20   Genesis 39:2–3.

But the Lord was with Joseph and showed him steadfast love and gave him favor in the sight of the keeper of the prison. And the keeper of the prison put Joseph in charge of all the prisoners who were in prison. Whatever was done there, he was the one who did it. The keeper of the prison paid no attention to anything that was in Joseph's charge, because the Lord was with him. And whatever he did, the Lord made it succeed.

Genesis 39:21–23

God's presence gave Joseph success in a power-job in Potiphar's household. God's presence gave Joseph success in being in charge in prison. The key here is God's presence. The Lord's presence is never based on externals. The power of God's presence is self-sustained—it runs on Him. It powerfully sustained Joseph. Let's not for a moment think that God's presence just showed up one day. We've got to believe, knowing of God's presence in Israel's life, that despite his epic parent fails, he taught Joseph the foundational truths of *God-with-us*.[21] They would have known it by firsthand experience, and later generations through Isaiah's prophecies.[22]

God's presence gave Joseph success in a power-job in Potiphar's household. God's presence gave Joseph success in being in charge in prison. The key here is God's presence.

A NEW NAME

God's presence wasn't only known by Joseph, but the people around him noticed it as well. Later in the story, Pharaoh says,

---

21   As seen in the previous chapter, *God with us* is the very definition of one of God the Son's names, Immanuel. *Bible Hub*, https://biblehub.com/hebrew/6005.htm. Accessed May 2, 2021.
22   Isaiah 7:14; Matthew 1:23.

> Can we find a man like this, in whom is the Spirit of God? ... Since God had shown you all this, there is none so discerning and wise as you are ... he set him over all the land of Egypt ... [he] called Joseph's name Zaphenath-paneah ... he gave him in marriage ... two sons were born to Joseph.[23]

When names are given in the Bible, we can't miss the significance and meaning. Joseph's new Egyptian name meant, "The God speaks and He lives."[24] So much happens in our own lives as well as in the lives of those around us when God is with us and we follow Him. Notice that in the very name Pharaoh gave to Joseph (coming from a polytheistic worldview as well as from culture that viewed all pharaohs as gods), Pharaoh saw that this was *the* God rather than *a* god. He also recognized that God was communicating and speaking, that He was alive and real! None of the Egyptian gods were alive or real. Don't miss this crucial moment. Even in the Old Testament, God revealed Himself to pagans. Pharaoh had a front row seat to watch *the* Most High God at work.[25]

Do we Christ-followers today live such Godly lives that the watching world sees that God speaks and lives? If I were to be given a new name from a person of influence outside my sphere, oh that he or she would give me a new name that testifies to the One I worship—the God Who communicates and is living! Even in the names that Joseph gave his two sons, we see the power of God's presence. Joseph named his firstborn Manasseh, meaning, "God has made me forget all my hardship and all my father's house."[26] Joseph named his second born Ephraim, meaning, "God has made me fruitful in the land of my affliction."[27] This is indeed a beautiful moment of a God-centered, out-loving man finding his worth in God to

---

23 Genesis 41:38–50.
24 *Bible Hub*, https://biblehub.com/hebrew/6847.htm. Accessed May 2, 2021.
25 In contrast, King Nebuchadnezzar replaced his Israelite captives' names, changing them from names with God in them to names referring to Babylonian gods. See Daniel 1:6–7.
26 Genesis 41:51.
27 Genesis 41:52.

such a deep level that his sons' names reveal that he has forgiven and moved on in gratitude and humility. I'm sure he never forgot the pain, but we see that a constant gaze upon God gave Joseph the foundation to show protection, kindness, and compassion to those who hurt him most. At this point in his story he didn't know that he would see his family again. Staying on course, we see that coupled with the power of God's presence, the power of trials had a God-centering, self-abandoning influence on Joseph.

Do we Christ-followers of today live such Godly lives that the watching world sees that God speaks and lives?

THE POWER OF TRIALS

Trials are … not fun. They are debilitating, painful, numbing, confusing, and just plain hard. They also produce steadfastness, as James 1:2–4 reminds: "Count it all joy, my brothers, when you meet trials of various kinds, for you know that the testing of your faith produces steadfastness. And let steadfastness have its full effect, that you may be perfect and complete, lacking in nothing." Do you remember our very first chapter, where the ultimate trial, Jesus' death and resurrection, saved humanity? Joseph is a type[28] of Christ. Through Joseph's trials, God saved His people. Go ahead … do a praise-the-Lord happy dance right now. That's what I'm doing as I write this. Joseph knew trials: hatred, slavery, lies, false accusation, and imprisonment. That's right, in all of his personal growth, alone time, meeting with God, honing his speech skills to help others rather than tattletale or brag, this man was forgotten for two more years. Eleven years had passed since he served in Potiphar's home and lived in prison. His God-given dream-telling had come full-circle. Rather than telling his own

---

28   A *type of Christ* is a resemblance, form, model, or shadow (in part) of the true figure to come, Christ Himself. There are many types of Christ found in the Scriptures who point to Jesus, Joseph being one of them. *Bible Hub,* https://biblehub.com/topical/t/type.htm. Accessed May 9, 2021.

dreams, Joseph used his words to help others by interpreting their dreams. Remember what a tattletale is? This tattletale dreamer came through his trials in a positive way, revealed the secret meaning of dreams, and informed other dreamers what their dreams meant. The power of words, the power of God's presence, and the power of time all start mingling together at this part of Joseph's story.

FORGOTTEN … NEVER

Joseph used his words, interpreted dreams by God's presence with him, managed his time responsibly, responded to trials patiently, and gave homage to God humbly. After all this, he was forgotten by the very man he helped. "The chief cupbearer did not remember Joseph but forgot him."[29] Have you ever been forgotten, especially in a crucial time in your life? Forgotten is a hard place to be. If we have God's presence, are we ever truly forgotten? No. Was Joseph truly forgotten? No. Joseph gave God the glory for his ability to interpret dreams when he said, "Do not interpretations belong to God?"[30] He still had to wait on God's timing. The power of God's timing ultimately is for His glory and our eternal good. Joseph's trial in prison went on for two more years. These were two more years for Joseph to trust God, to remind himself God sees, and to experience God's remembrance. Though it wasn't yet written, this fitting truth about God from the Psalms perfectly applies to Joseph's situation:

> You have kept count of my tossings; put my tears in your bottle. Are they not in Your book? Then my enemies will turn back in the day when I call. This I know, that God is for me. In God, Whose Word I praise, in the Lord, Whose Word I praise, in God I trust; I shall not be afraid. What can man do to me?[31]

---

29 Genesis 40:23.
30 Genesis 40:8.
31 Psalm 56:8–11.

This truth applies to our trials. God remembers every tear; God sees every fear; God is for me; God remembers.

Forgotten is a hard place to be. If we have God's presence, are we ever truly forgotten? No.

God caused the cupbearer to remember Joseph. The cupbearer was serving Pharaoh for two years. It was Pharaoh's troubling dreams that pricked the cupbearer's memory and conscience to remember the man in prison who'd helped him. Then he used his current position of authority to return the favor to Joseph. "Then the chief cupbearer said to Pharaoh, 'I remember my offenses today … a young Hebrew … interpreted our dreams to us.'"[32] Joseph's trials came to an end because of this remembrance. "Then Pharaoh sent and called Joseph, and they quickly brought him out of the pit … he came in before Pharaoh. And Pharaoh said to Joseph, 'I have had a dream, and there is no one who can interpret it.' … Joseph answered Pharaoh, 'It is not in me; God will give Pharaoh a favorable answer.'"[33] I love the contrast of Joseph being thrown into a pit twice, and now he's quickly brought out of the pit.[34]

God uses pits but doesn't leave us there for good. Psalm 40 attests to the pit, and though David wrote it, I think Joseph could have written it as well. God is our Deliverer; He delivers us; He delivered Joseph. Joseph, with God at his side, was "back in the kitchen" prepping flavorful greatness to give the bread of life (literally) to Pharaoh, to Egypt, and to those who caused him so much hardship—his own brothers. This is where the power of family, the power of words, the power of God's presence, the power of time, and the power of trials come out of the oven of life to culminate in the greatest relational feast of all time—returning good for evil (which

---

32   Genesis 41:9–12.
33   Genesis 41:14–16.
34   Genesis 37:24, 40:15, 41:14.

foreshadows Christ's sacrifice on the cross).[35] The cherry on top is the power of compassion.

THE POWER OF COMPASSION

Compassion means "sympathetic consciousness of others' distress together with a desire to alleviate it," says Merriam-Webster Dictionary. Synonyms for compassion are "feeling, empathy, understanding, care, tender-heartedness, gentleness, mercy, warmth, brotherly love, kind-heartedness." I'm not bringing my own word into the text. Genesis 43:30 uses the actual word *compassion*. Other ingredients of care are mentioned as well in Genesis 42, 43, and 45. Genesis 42:24 says, "Then he turned away from them and wept." Genesis 43:23 says, "Peace to you, do not be afraid." Genesis 43:30 says, "Then Joseph hurried out, for his compassion grew warm for his brother, and he sought a place to weep. And he entered his chamber and wept there." Genesis 45:1–5 says,

> Then Joseph could not control himself before all those who stood by him. He cried, "Make everyone go out from me." So no one stayed with him when Joseph made himself known to his brothers. And he wept aloud, so that the Egyptians heard it, and the household of Pharaoh heard it. And Joseph said to his brothers, "I am Joseph! Is my father still alive?" But his brothers could not answer him, for they were dismayed at his presence. So Joseph said to his brothers, "Come near to me, please." And they came near. And he said, "I am your brother, Joseph, whom you sold into Egypt. And now do not be distressed or angry with yourselves because you sold me here, for God sent me before you to preserve life."

Genesis 50:17–21 says,

---

35   John 3:16.

"Please forgive the transgression of the servants of the God of your father." Joseph wept when they spoke to him. His brothers also came and fell down before him and said, "Behold, we are your servants." But Joseph said to them, "Do not fear, for I am in the place of God? As for you, you meant evil against me, but God meant it for good, to bring it about that many people should be kept alive, as they are today. So do not fear; I will provide for you and your little ones." Thus he comforted them and spoke kindly to them."

Compassion is powerful. There is absolutely no way Joseph's compassion could have been authentic apart from God's presence and Joseph's forgiveness. Here we find a grown man, second in command over Egypt, weeping four times. I am not a crier, yet I get teared up reading this story, because of the compassion of this man to people who were horrible to him. It's hard enough for me to feel and show compassion to people who hurt me once or twice. I distrust them. But look at Joseph! He has let it all go—in the greatest sense of the phrase. We sense no bitterness, anger, or I-told-you-so coming from him. His care is legit, loving, raw, and authentic, because its source is God. Joseph lived out in Genesis 50 what Jesus commands us to live out in Matthew 5:3–12, the Sermon on the Mount. All of this weeping is completely understandable based on the total story. This is so much for all of them to process. He's got nothing to lose because he already lost it all, and in the process, he realized God's presence is truly all he needs. It's win-win for him to show his brothers all the things they didn't show him: peace, compassion, warmth, feeling, physical nearness, honesty, forgiveness, spiritual perspective, emotional assurance, humility, physical protection, comfort, and kindness. Talk about bringing the light! Talk about serving up homemade pie for everyone … even those who treat you poorly and don't deserve it. I love the contrasts throughout this story between how Joseph's brothers treated him versus how he returned good for evil.

BROTHERS VERSUS JOSEPH IN GENESIS 37-50

BROTHERS	**JOSEPH**
Could not speak peacefully to him. 37:4	Spoke kindly to them. 50:21
Hated him. 37:4, 5, 8	Cared for them. 45:4-7, 50:21
Harmed him (planned to murder, threw into a pit, sold into slavery, lied about his death to his father). 37:18-33	Protected and provided for them and their children. 45:7, 11, 20, 50:21
Did not trust God took matters into their own hands.37:18-33	Trusted God and gave Him glory. 40:8, 50:20
Caused fear. 37:24, 28	Told them not to fear. 43:23, 50:19, 21
Caused distress. 37:24, 28	Brought them peace and comfort. 43:23, 50:21
Cold-hearted. 37:18, 32	Warm-hearted. 43:30
Paid evil with evil. 37:24	Repaid evil with good. 50:20
Physically removed him as far away as they could (to another country). 37:28	Physically drew them near. 45:4, 10
Plotted to take life. 37:18	Acted on preserving life. 45:7, 50:20
Broke-up family; sold their little brother and lied about him. 37:28, 32	Brought family together; cared for his brothers and their little ones. 45:4-20, 50:21

WE GET IT FROM OUR DADDY

The power of authentic sustaining compassion is always founded and grounded upon a compassionate God.[36] Again, the Christ type found in Joseph can't be missed. When we experience first-hand a compassionate God Who forgives our own sins, restores our familial hot messes, and repays our evil with His saving good, we become the greatest out-lovers of our spheres. Joseph did this for his family, and we can do this for ours: we "bake the pie" over and over again and then share it over and over again—even with people who mistreat us, are toxic, try to destroy us, and undermine our worth. As God's people, our worth is not tied to others, their treatment of us, or their thoughts about us. Our worth is in Christ, Who exemplified returning the ultimate good for the most despicable evil. We get this divine ability to show compassion and forgiveness from our Daddy. Our location and the people we're with doesn't matter when we know that God is with us. With God, we are on location wherever we are. When we believe this fact with all of our being, it doesn't matter if we're in charge or in the pit or anywhere in between the two. When God is with us, His compassion in us is our secret ingredient to Godliness and loving others.

The power of authentic sustaining compassion is always founded and grounded upon a compassionate God.

THE OUT-LOVING LIFE FOR EVERYONE

Do you see how the out-loving life came full circle in Joseph's life? As seen in the power of family, power of words, power of time, power of God's presence, power of trials, and power of compassion, Joseph exhibited a selfless, God-centered life. Rather than kicking out of his circle those who

---

36   Psalm 103:13; Lamentations 3:22–23, 31–33; Matthew 14:14.

harmed him, Joseph used his time alone and his time with anyone currently around him to point to God's presence and power. In their greatest time of need, the very people who kicked him out of their circle were beckoned-in, called close, and drawn tight into a circle of safety and care they did not deserve. This is God's divine calling to humanity. He gives us what we don't deserve—grace.

It would have been absurd, bordering on insane, if Joseph's brothers had said, "Nah, we're good." Yet so many people around us say this to God when He's holding open the doors into His kingdom to them. Our sin kicks God and His grace out of our circle. We should be the ones begging to get in, yet in His great mercy and compassion He continues to say, like Joseph, "Come near to me, please … you shall be near me. I will provide for you."[37] This is the secure[38] life I want. This is my circle—a circle in which all are invited. We out-love because He first out-loved us.[39]

We out-love because He first out-loved us.

I exhort you to spend all the time it takes alone in your kitchen of life, quieting your soul, reading the Word, and preparing the goods. Then throw open the banquet hall doors, invite a guest or two, or even more, and bring the light of Jesus. Show those at your hypothetical table Who you serve—not yourself, but the Most High God. Focus on Him, not on yourself. You have an Audience of One. Stay humble. Pray often. The psalmist David focused on and served the Most High God and therefore knew God was for Him. Joseph focused on and served the Most High God and therefore knew God was for him. As children of God, let's focus on and serve the Most High God and know He's for us! If God is for us, who

---

37   Genesis 45:4, 10, 11.
38   Salvation includes eternal security, also called by John Calvin "perseverance of the saints." See R.C. Sproul, *What Is Reformed Theology?: Understanding the Basics*, (Grand Rapids, MI: Baker Books, 2016), 229–253. John 10:28–29.
39   1 John 4:19.

can be against us?[40] We don't need to be for ourselves when God is for us. We don't need to love ourselves when the God Who knit us together[41] loves us at all expense. The Bible says we already love ourselves ... and in the wrong way.

> For you were called to freedom, [sisters]. Only do not use your freedom as an opportunity for the flesh, but through love serve one another. For the whole law is fulfilled in one word: 'You shall love your neighbor as yourself.' But if you bite and devour one another, watch out that you are not consumed by one another.[42]

We are free in Christ, not to be consumed with ourselves, but to serve others with God's all-consuming love.[43] Galatians 5:16 goes on to say, "But I say, walk by the Spirit, and you will not gratify the desires of the flesh." In response to all the plates that life throws at us, like Joseph, let's be prepared to say, "You meant evil against me, but God meant it for good."[44] Let's be like Joseph and like Jesus and make our alone time be of great value to our personal relationships with God, to our tribes, and to the world around us. Going back to the opening words of this chapter and the kitchen of life, let's pass out slices of God's steadfast love like we're made of them.

Let's pass out slices of God's steadfast love
like we're made of them.

---

40 Romans 8:31.
41 Psalm 139:13.
42 Galatians 5:13–15.
43 Romans 8:31–39.
44 Genesis 50:20.

PRAYER

God,
I am amazed to be at Your divine table,
feasting on Your Holy Word,
taking in as much of You as I can.
Use my alone time to fill me with Your presence
and to teach me Your ways.
As I daily prep with You in my alone time,
mold me to look like You,
so that as I head out into my community,
I share how very good You are.
Prepare me for inevitable trials, injustice, and wrongdoing done to me,
just like you prepared Joseph.
Being human is hard,
And You, Jesus, know this fact all too well.
At the end of every day,
may those around me only and always see
that You are the God Who speaks and Who lives,
and that You take what is evil and turn it into good,
for Your glory.
Amen.

DISCUSSION QUESTIONS

1. When we read Scripture through the Holy Spirit's aid, it can be like the first time communing with God *every time* we do it. How does the text about Joseph reveal that God remains astounding, new, and real to Joseph through thick and thin? See Genesis 39, 40, 41, 45:1–15, 50:15–21.

2. To which aspects of Joseph's life do you most relate (good/bad): family, words, time, God's presence, trials, compassion? Why?

3. If Jesus asked you right now to get rid of all the influences of self-love the world has sold you, what thought patterns, phrases, actions, would need to go? Who is the Lord calling you to invite to your "table" right now?

4. As a child of God, what would a foreign ruler (or someone who knew nothing about God prior to meeting you) name you? For what would you want to be renamed or known?

RECOMMENDED RESOURCES FOR STUDYING THE BIBLE

www.9marks.org
www.bibleequipping.org
www.biblehub.com
www.bibleproject.com
www.bible-history.com
www.olivetree.com
www.readscripture.org
www.simeontrust.org

CPSIA information can be obtained
at www.ICGtesting.com
Printed in the USA
FSHW022249301121

9 781039 114593